Putting Medicare Consumers in Charge

AEI STUDIES ON MEDICARE REFORM
Joseph Antos and Robert B. Helms
Series Editors

What ails Medicare is what ails health care in America. Medicare spending is growing substantially faster than we can afford, with potentially disastrous consequences for the federal budget. Worse, although the program is paying for more services, it is not necessarily providing better care for the elderly and the disabled. AEI's Studies on Medicare Reform is designed to examine the program's operation, consider alternative policy options, and develop a set of realistic proposals that could form the basis for reform legislation.

THE DIAGNOSIS AND TREATMENT OF MEDICARE
Andrew J. Rettenmaier and Thomas R. Saving

MARKETS WITHOUT MAGIC:
HOW COMPETITION MIGHT SAVE MEDICARE
Mark V. Pauly

HOW TO FIX MEDICARE:
LET'S PAY PATIENTS, NOT PHYSICIANS
Roger Feldman

PUTTING MEDICARE CONSUMERS IN CHARGE:
LESSONS FROM THE FEHBP
Walton Francis

Putting Medicare
Consumers in Charge

Lessons from the FEHBP

Walton Francis

The AEI Press

Publisher for the American Enterprise Institute
WASHINGTON, D.C.

Distributed to the Trade by National Book Network, 15200 NBN Way, Blue Ridge Summit, PA 17214. To order call toll free 1-800-462-6420 or 1-717-794-3800. For all other inquiries please contact the AEI Press, 1150 Seventeenth Street, N.W., Washington, D.C. 20036 or call 1-800-862-5801.

Library of Congress Cataloging-in-Publication Data

Francis, Walton.
  Putting Medicare consumers in charge : lessons from the FEHBP / Walton Francis.
      p. ; cm.
  Includes bibliographical references and index.
  ISBN-13: 978-0-8447-4283-0
  ISBN-10: 0-8447-4283-X
  1. Federal Employees Health Benefits Program (U.S.) 2. Government employees' health insurance—United States. 3. Health care reform—United States. 4. Medicare. I. Title.
  [DNLM: 1. Federal Employees Health Benefits Program (U.S.) 2. Health Care Reform—United States. 3. Government Programs—United States. 4. Health Benefit Plans, Employee—United States. 5. Medicare. WA 540 AA1 F819p 2009]

  RA412.3.F73 2009
  368.4'2600973--dc22

                                                                2009033002
13 12 11 10 09   1 2 3 4 5 6 7

Printed in the United States of America

Contents

List of Illustrations

ix

Acknowledgments

I would like to thank for a continuing tutorial on health insurance issues the many economists and analysts expert in health insurance with or for whom I have worked, or from whom I have learned by osmosis, including Henry Aaron, Stu Altman, Joe Antos, Stuart Butler, Bryan Dowd, Alain Enthoven, Judy Feder, Roger Feldman, Jon Gruber, Bob Helms, Robert Krughoff, Jeff Lemieux, Jim Mays, Mark McClellan, Tom Miller, Bob Moffit, Mike Morrisey, Joe Newhouse, Len Nichols, Mike O'Grady, Ken Thorpe, Gail Wilensky, and Richard Zeckhauser, among others. I would also like to express my appreciation for the decades-long seminar in making sensible public policy conducted by colleagues and friends from the U.S. Department of Health and Human Services and the Office of Management and Budget, including Chris Bladen, Jerry Britten, Nancy De Lew, Beverly Dennis III, Dick Eisinger, Keith Fontenot, George Greenberg, George Grob, Herb Jasper, Renee Jasper, Dave Kleinberg, Frank Lewis, Mark Pauly, Bill Prosser, Jackie White, Ellen Wormser, and many other dedicated, able civil servants. Thanks also to Abby Block and David Lewis for their stewardship of both the FEHBP and Medicare Advantage, on behalf of the many millions who benefit from these programs, and to the many other fine workers in the Office of Personnel Management and the Centers for Medicare and Medicaid Services who have helped improve these programs over the years. Finally, thanks above all to my recently departed wife, Sarah Wilcox Francis, for the love and life we shared.

Introduction: The FEHBP as a Model for Reform

Suppose the federal government operated a major health insurance program that really worked, one that came in "under budget" and didn't threaten to raise taxes or cut benefits intolerably in future decades. Suppose that program operated side by side with Medicare, decade after decade, and provided not only equal or superior performance in cost control, in consumer satisfaction, and in every other important way, but did so as if it were on autopilot, without the endless tinkering, "rent-seeking,"[1] and political fights that attend every Medicare issue. Suppose that program put virtually all choice of plans in consumers' own hands, and left the lobbyists, bureaucrats, and lawmakers with little to manipulate. Suppose that program operated with a staff of only about 150 bureaucrats, and at minuscule administrative cost. Suppose that program seamlessly and without controversy adapted to evolution in medical care, in the health-care marketplace, and in the insurance marketplace. Suppose that program offered comprehensive benefits, tailored to meet enrollee needs, without any "one-size-fits-all" coverage or benefit decisions. Suppose that program were true health insurance because it actually provided protection against catastrophic medical expense. Suppose its benefits changed over time based on consumer purchasing decisions, not on the relative strengths of competing political forces or accidents of the political process.

These realities of the Federal Employees Health Benefits Program have fascinated many observers of the FEHBP, a program that is nearing a half-century of quiet but distinguished performance as arguably the most effective and efficient government insurance program that has ever existed. The natural questions posed by its success include the potential export of the FEHBP model not only to Medicare and other existing government programs, but also to health insurance in the private sector, and even future expansions of government programs as part of health reform.[2] Precisely

1

because of these larger implications, the FEHBP has become a lightning rod for the divergent views of those who prefer market choices in health care versus those who prefer more direct government control and intervention. In particular, because "original Medicare" is a preferred model for many of the latter, the exercise of contrasting the performance of the two programs has become charged with tensions and attracted the attention of many in both groups.[3]

> Because the way in which markets achieve results is both indirect and seldom understood, it is not surprising that more direct techniques of social intervention are usually chosen.
>
> Charles Schultze
> *The Public Use of Private Interest*

The FEHBP is certainly not a perfect program. Its design and operation are flawed in major ways described in this analysis. But in making policy and political decisions, and in real-world markets, the available options never include a perfect one. And even the negative aspects of the FEHBP offer lessons. Conversely, Medicare—particularly the competitive Medicare programs that operate alongside original Medicare—has strong and weak points that offer lessons to the FEHBP. This analysis probes these programs' strengths and weaknesses, and their often accidental and unintended causes, for lessons of value beyond the sloganeering. As we will show, while "original Medicare" remains locked into a remarkably obsolete, albeit workable, program design, "competitive Medicare" has already learned many lessons from the FEHBP, and outperforms the FEHBP in ways that will become increasingly apparent over time.

Both programs have suffered and will continue to suffer from the effects of the massive tax subsidies provided to employee health-care spending, the overinsurance of most elderly persons through Medigap and other programs (including the FEHBP itself, which offers richer wraparound coverage than any Medigap policy), and the effects of these "moral hazards" on the underlying costs of the health-care environment in which these programs operate.[4]

> I want to confess a major mistake we made. . . . We had no idea that the Medicare cost-sharing provisions—the copayments and the deductible—would be canceled out by the growth of a medigap industry. . . . The result is that neither the patient nor the physician on behalf of the patient has an incentive to think twice about the cost of a procedure.
>
> Robert M. Ball
> "Reflections on How Medicare Came About"

The saga of the FEHBP has some surprises and twists, rooted in subtle flaws in the program's design and in foolish decisions by "human resources" bureaucrats who knew nothing of markets or incentives. In the government as in the private sector, putting amateurs in charge of issues for which they have no comprehension or competence, and for which they will suffer neither penalties nor rewards for major future effects, can have completely unforeseen adverse consequences. On the other hand, a Medicare program that has always had a staff far more technically qualified and competent than that of any other public health insurance program was rescued from its statist model only after the resuscitation of a politically charged reform proposal, previously "dead on arrival," that took as its beacon the FEHBP as it had once, but no longer, existed.

The Federal Employees Health Benefits Program has fascinated students of health insurance for decades. In 1971, scarcely a decade after the program began, Odin Anderson and Joel May of the University of Chicago wrote "The Federal Employees Health Benefits Program, 1961–1968: A Model for National Health Insurance?" A decade later, Joseph Califano, then secretary of the U.S. Department of Health, Education, and Welfare, hired one of Robert McNamara's original "whiz kids," Alain Enthoven, as a consultant on national insurance. The first public product of Enthoven's work was *Health Plan: The Only Practical Solution to the Soaring Cost of Medical Care* (Enthoven 1980). This book laid out a comprehensive approach to national health insurance, applying "managed competition" driven by consumer choice, based on key features of the FEHBP model.[5] It remains influential. It was the model for reform of the California Public Employees Retirement System

(CalPERS), and in 2006 the Netherlands adopted a major reform of its health insurance that was explicitly designed using Enthoven's model (Van de Ven and Schut 2008). Enthoven has remained committed to this day to this model as the best basis for national health insurance reform (Enthoven 2008).

Dozens of health insurance proposals, sponsored by members of both political parties, have embraced key elements of the FEHBP, and have been explicitly based on features of the program. For example, Democratic representative from Missouri and subsequent House Majority Leader Richard Gephardt proposed national health insurance modeled largely on the FEHBP a quarter-century ago (Iglehart 1981). There have even been a number of proposals to use the FEHBP not just as a model, but also as an existing program that could enroll the uninsured (Dorn and Meyer 2002), with a modest literature on how this could be accomplished (Fuchs 2001, McArdle 1995).[6]

Most notably, President Bill Clinton's national health insurance proposal embraced elements of plan competition. At the same time, it was heavily criticized for its core reliance on government-designed and government-run insurance, with critics effectively using the FEHBP as a countermodel (Moffit 1992).

> Congressmen like their system so much that they often insist that they be exempted from any new health system that they would impose on other Americans. . . . What is good enough for Congress should be good enough for the American people.
>
> Robert Moffit
> *Consumer Choice in Health: Learning from the FEHBP*

Subsequently, President Clinton's National Bipartisan Commission on the Future of Medicare endorsed consumer choice among competing plans by a razor-thin but insufficient voting margin.[7] Nonetheless, Senators Breaux and Frist proposed legislation based on the commission's recommended approach. Comptroller General David Walker characterized both the commission proposal and the Breaux-Frist proposal as introducing "a competitive premium model, similar in concept to the . . . FEHBP" (U.S. Senate, Committee on Finance 2000, 10). Bill Bradley, then a U.S. Senator from New Jersey, proposed a national health plan modeled on the FEHBP before losing the 2000 Democratic presidential nomination to Al Gore. Most recently, Democratic Senator Ron Wyden of Oregon introduced in 2006 a national health insurance reform proposal, the "Healthy Americans Act," that accepts consumer choice among competing plans as a central feature.

One of these proposals, the Medicare Modernization Act (MMA), was enacted in 2003.[8] The MMA created a new consumer choice program among competing drug plans, and strengthened and expanded what is now called Medicare Advantage (MA), a consumer choice system of competing private health plans that offer alternatives to original Medicare. In defending the nascent MMA, Republican Senator Jon Kyl of Arizona emphasized that the model for this strengthening of Medicare was the Federal Employees Health Benefits Program (Kyl 2003). The Medicare Modernization Act of 2003 not only explicitly adopted competition among Medicare Advantage health plans, and between MA plans and original Medicare, but also went so far as to instruct the Centers for Medicare and Medicaid Services (CMS) to adopt design and oversight features of the FEHBP. It created premium-setting procedures for both the present and future that are, in terms of marginal incentives, superior to those of the FEHBP.[9]

A substantial body of analytical literature also focuses on the FEHBP as a model for either national insurance reform of some kind, or Medicare in particular. For example, an October 2008 search of the *Health Affairs* website for articles whose text mentions both Medicare and the FEHBP revealed 133 hits from 1981 through May 2009. This included, of course, some pieces that involve advocacy as well as analysis.

Most recently, use of the FEHBP as a model or actual component of health reform has again figured prominently in presidential politics. Notably, Tom Daschle, former Democratic Senator of South Dakota and President Barack Obama's original nominee to be secretary of the Department of Health and Human Services as well as head of the White House Office of Health Reform, has argued vigorously for adopting most elements of the FEHBP as a key component of health reform. His position is that "we should expand the Federal Employees Health Benefits Program . . . or create a group purchasing pool like it" (Daschle et al. 2008, 145).

Much of the analysis of the FEHBP as a model has been studiously neutral (Feldman et al. 2002, and Bovbjerg 2009, for example). A good deal of it, however, has an advocacy edge. Toward the liberal end of the spectrum, the AARP Public Policy Institute published *Structuring Health Care Benefits: A Comparison of Medicare and the FEHBP*, which argues that Medicare is superior because its benefits are "guaranteed" as "entitlements" and protected by a more robust appeals system (Caplan and Foley 2000). Toward the conservative end (as measured by organizational affiliation, if not by the content of their writings), staff at the Heritage Foundation have published a number of writings on this topic, including the widely read Stuart Butler and Robert Moffit piece on "The FEHBP as a Model for a New Medicare Program" (Butler and Moffit 1995). As might be expected, these two publications focus and completely disagree on the merits of Medicare's "defined benefit" structure. On the other hand, even critics of the FEHBP have been known to propose reforms using major features from the program, as in a recent universal coverage proposal with a clever scheme to enroll the uninsured in the same FEHBP plans used by members of Congress (Davis and Schoen 2003). Still other analyses, such as one by former head of the Congressional Budget Office Robert Reischauer, have been neutral but recognized the effectiveness of the FEHBP as a model for Medicare reform, provided that its design features were modified appropriately (U.S. Senate, Committee on Finance 1997).[10]

By far the most common criticism of the FEHBP is that its design fosters adverse selection.[11] In any system offering a choice of plans, and in which plan premiums are adjusted to reflect the costs of those they cover, over time adverse selection will allegedly lead to a "death spiral" as enrollees flee the most expensive plans. These assertions face the empirical problem (discussed at length later in the analysis) that such a spiral, if one has ever occurred at all in the FEHBP, did so at a glacial pace with no noticeable negative result on program stability, premiums, or availability of plan choices. After almost fifty years of stable program experience, the recurring predictions of such "death spirals" seem as bizarre as they are irrelevant.[12]

Regardless, there is no lack of affordable plans in either the FEHBP or Medicare Advantage. One national FEHBP plan is available at an annual (single-enrollee share) premium cost of $560 for 2009. Meanwhile, the Medicare Advantage program disproportionately attracts lower-income

Experience in the Federal Employees Health Benefits Program (FEHBP) has shown that competition can lead to a "death spiral" as relatively healthier enrollees flee high cost plans for lower cost plans, ultimately increasing costs in the high cost plans. [Most panel members] fear that if fee-for-service (FFS) Medicare were placed in direct price competition with private health plans . . . FFS premiums might increase to the point that FFS could become unaffordable for lower income beneficiaries.

Kathleen King and Mark Schlesinger
The Role of Private Health Plans in Medicare

Medicare beneficiaries, for the simple reason that most MA plans offer lower cost-sharing and better benefits than original fee-for-service Medicare, many with no premium above that of Part B. Moreover, the lowest-income Medicare beneficiaries qualify for government payment of premiums and for copays close to zero. It appears that fears of both death spirals and unaffordability were not just premature, but groundless.

The FEHBP, original Medicare, and competitive Medicare offer a real-world experiment in action. For almost fifty years the federal government has run two major health insurance programs side by side. One program, the Federal Employees Health Benefits Program, runs itself with only minimal stewardship. The government provides a voucher-like contribution to the premium of each plan, and the decisions of enrollees and autonomous private health plans competing for enrollees decide almost every aspect of plan design, plan service, and plan cost. The other program, original Medicare, is micromanaged by the U.S. Congress and the executive branch. For Medicare, Congress enacts almost every year a new multi-hundred-page law detailing exactly how much each kind of provider will be paid, what enrollees must pay in both premium and cost-sharing, what services are covered, and what limits will be on out-of-pocket costs by enrollees (in fact, such catastrophic expense limits have never been enacted in Medicare, thus making it a program which fails to meet the most fundamental purpose of insurance). For the FEHBP, Congress slaps the wrist of the oversight agency if it interferes too strongly with plan and enrollee decisions.

Medicare is administered through an agency that employs thousands of "the best and the brightest" civil servants to specialize in health insurance design and oversight. The FEHBP is administered by a relative handful of generalist bureaucrats, few of whom have any substantial expertise in either major program management or health insurance. This $40 billion a year program is overseen by a handful of senior executive service (SES) managers, compared to the hundreds and thousands of SES managers in each of the half-dozen cabinet departments with budgets smaller than that of this one program.

For over most of its fifty years, the FEHBP has outperformed original Medicare in every dimension of performance. It has better benefits, better service, catastrophic limits on what enrollees must pay, and far better premium cost control, despite covering a federal workforce that rapidly aged throughout this period and a retiree population that rapidly grew—both major causes of higher health-care costs. Fraud is rampant in Medicare and almost nonexistent in the FEHBP. Medicare is low-hanging fruit for "rent-seeking" private interests who leverage billions of dollars through their lobbying activities and the congressional bounty they obtain; the FEHBP has been virtually immune to such assaults.

Original Medicare is one version of the "single payer" dream: a price-controlled health insurance program run by congressional committees and experts of all kinds dedicated to the proposition that good intentions and rationality can surpass the competitive market in delivering high value at low cost, as well as resist rent-seeking by affected interests.

The FEHBP is an accidental program, based on a competitive model that was essentially forced on Congress (against the wishes of the Eisenhower administration) by the potent "grandfather principle" of politics: Do no harm to existing vested interests. Because multiple health plans were competing for federal employee enrollment when the program started, Congress, in a decision far wiser than it understood at the time, rejected the administration proposal and adopted a competitive system.

So superior has been the performance of the FEHBP to Medicare that in enacting the Medicare Modernization Act in 2003, Congress emulated, copied, and adopted major reforms to Medicare that equaled or improved upon design features of the FEHBP. Both Medicare Advantage and the Medicare prescription drug program rely on plan competition for enrollees, and, while they are still in infant stages, both appear poised to surpass the performance not only of original Medicare, but of the FEHBP as well.

Just before these major Medicare reforms were enacted, the Office of Personnel Management made a disastrous decision to place the FEHBP into the same tax-preferred "premium conversion" status as corporate health insurance. This "reform" met no discernible need and created, as an immediate effect, a multi-hundred-million dollar cost as a result of "crowd-out" incentive for spouses in the private sector to drop their plans and join the FEHBP. Far more importantly, market incentives to restrain cost growth were eviscerated at an annual cost now approaching or exceeding a billion dollars a year. Cumulatively, these cost increases far exceed the tax savings realized by employees. Today, the FEHBP limps along, achieving only a shadow of its former formidable program performance.

Reforms to restore the FEHBP and to move Medicare toward fiscal solvency are possible, desirable, and politically achievable with minimum pain. Moreover, both the weaknesses and strengths in both programs offer many lessons that can guide Congress and the Obama administration in settling the detailed design parameters that will ultimately be far more important to the success of health reform than the features that will generate newspaper headlines and color most editorial reviews. For example, choices made in setting the premium-support level, and in allocating savings for plan choices between the government and enrollees, will determine whether health insurance rewards frugality or profligacy in coming years. Likewise, the tax preference for unlimited health-care spending (FEHBP), the remaining incentives for seniors to purchase Medigap insurance that eliminates almost all out-of-pocket spending (original Medicare), and legislative restrictions that force FEHBP plans to operate as a Medigap-like wraparound to Medicare, are flawed policy choices that swamp market incentives and engender massive waste not only in these programs, but also throughout the health-care system. This analysis will also suggest that changes in health insurance design (perhaps even using the much-maligned "doughnut hole" model) to guarantee Americans of modest means protection for needed maintenance medications and routine physical examinations are not only likely to be desirable, but will also provide a perfect example of the need to avoid standardization of plans' benefit designs. (The "doughnut hole," officially called the "coverage gap," is a spending range of about $4,000 in Medicare Part D plans within which enrollees are responsible for the entire cost of all their prescription drugs, or, in some plans, of just their name brand drugs. The doughnut hole begins after plans cover most drug costs up to $2,700, thereby providing substantial protection for spending on important maintenance drugs.) Such "value-based" insurance design, payment reforms to reward cost-effective choices, and other innovations will allow private plans to compete with one another to develop the best combination of benefits, service, out-of-pocket costs, and premium costs to attract enrollees while holding down taxpayer costs.

PART I

A Tale of Two Health Insurance Programs

The Patchwork Quilt of
Federal Health Insurance Programs

During the last half-century, the United States has operated a half-dozen major health-care financing systems in parallel, each operating in its own world, and with only minimal attempts to observe and learn lessons in program A that could be useful in program B. Each program has its own story, its own stakeholders, its own particular "owner," and its own evolutionary history.

The system of federal tax subsidies for private employer-based health insurance was the creation of price controllers who, during World War II, exempted employer payment of health insurance premiums from wage and price controls. They also exempted both employer and employee shares of health insurance from the income tax, and were slapped down by Congress when they tried to correct this mistake (viewed from the perspectives of horizontal equity, minimizing tax loopholes, and keeping rates on taxable interest down) a few years later. Meanwhile, the Indian Health Service and the Veterans Administration both operated major systems of health care for their constituencies that, while not technically health insurance, provided de facto insurance for those who qualified for full benefits (for example, Indians living on reservations). The Department of Defense operated a system of military medicine that originated to serve only active-duty soldiers but evolved into a system that today provides true insurance for military dependents and retirees (but not soldiers themselves, who are provided with services, not insurance). The same Great Society initiative that proposed and obtained enactment of Medicare also proposed and obtained enactment of Medicaid, the only one of these programs to be operated by states, an oddity in itself. All but one of these programs has an annual budget in at least the tens of billions of dollars, and some are in the hundreds of billions of dollars.

All of these programs involve oddities. Why on earth should a Fortune 500 company that produces widgets be, as a practical matter, forced to become expert in health insurance to minimize the taxes its employees pay? Why should public health doctors and nurses who are uniformed personnel administer health care on Indian reservations (and nowhere else)? Why should states directly operate health insurance programs? Why should government retirees from the military services and their widows be provided with health insurance in a system not only separate from, but radically unlike, that for civilian retirees and their widows?

Two additional programs have their own oddities, and their own gigantic budgets. Medicare and the FEHBP are both models for, and exemplars of, alternative approaches to health insurance for most Americans. They were created within a few years of each other, 1965 and 1960, respectively. Of the two, the FEHBP has changed the least since its creation. Yet Medicare is widely regarded as the "dinosaur" of health insurance, with good reason. Each contains lessons for the other, and for health reform on a larger scale.

1

Medicare

Both the Federal Employees Health Benefits Program and Medicare have evolved over the last half-century, although the basic structures of both the FEHBP and original Medicare have remained virtually unchanged. In what follows, only those program features most salient to the comparison of the two programs are emphasized, and these in summary fashion.

We begin our analysis with Medicare, focusing on aspects of the program most salient to our comparative purpose. For details on the genesis and larger political context of the Medicare program, sources include, above all, Robert Ball's thoughtful reflections (Ball 1995 and 1998), Theodore Marmor's now dated political history (Marmor 2000), and Jonathan Oberlander's newer history (Oberlander 2003). None of these works presents even a beginner's guide to design and performance issues, or to the political economy of the endemic rent-seeking and pork-barrel spending in Medicare. Joseph Newhouse's technical history (Newhouse 2001) and his depressing dissection of Medicare payment policy (2002) provide a partial remedy.[1] David Hyman's interpretive history in *Medicare Meets Mephistopheles* (Hyman 2006) offers a lighter read and a different slant. Dowd and others (2005) provide a useful and analytically focused history of Medicare Advantage and its predecessors. These works provide a meta-view of the role of this vital program and of the circumstances and politics that led to its creation and evolution. Even an informed reader is unlikely to be aware of many of the twists and turns this program has taken and the forces, both purposeful and accidental, that have affected its evolution.

This chapter focuses almost entirely on Medicare, followed by a subsequent chapter on the FEHBP and later chapters comparing the two programs on many dimensions of performance. The first two chapters do, however, contain comparative comments at a number of places to alert the reader to key similarities or differences of particular interest or importance between the programs. Most of these are later analyzed in greater detail. References to the FEHBP in the Medicare chapter, and vice versa, should be considered signposts to the analysis presented later.

The Creation and Basic Design of Medicare

The Medicare program was created in 1965, at the high point of President Lyndon B. Johnson's "Great Society," after a protracted period of major political fights over whether to create such a "social insurance" program.[2] President Harry S Truman, for example, had proposed a similar program, without coming close to success. During the 1940s and 1950s, and up to the time Medicare was enacted, it was strongly opposed by many political actors, including, notably, the American Medical Association. Presaging the political fights that continue today, the issues were not only ideological, but also intensively financial.

Viewed as a social insurance program similar to those created during the New Deal in the United States over twenty years before (and even more decades later than most Western European countries), Medicare was a decided latecomer. As a Great Society program, it was arguably the greatest legislative achievement and social program accomplishment of President Johnson. The labyrinthine, ideological, bitterly fought battles over the creation of Medicare stand in sharp contrast to the smooth "good government" creation of the FEHBP several years earlier. The debates of a half-century ago have a quaint, surrealistic flavor, however, compared to the issues faced by Medicare today. Almost no one now questions the necessity and value of the program, but its impending insolvency and growing claims on the incomes of younger workers diminish all other issues.[3]

Medicare's basic design was, and remains for the most part, that of private insurance of the 1950 or 1960 vintage. It is a structural dinosaur. For example, health insurance benefits in those bygone days were usually bifurcated between hospital ("Blue Cross") and physician ("Blue Shield") policies, and to this day that distinction remains central to both the financing and benefits of original Medicare. Although its general structure has become increasingly complex in recent years, Medicare today can best be thought of as two broad kinds of programs.

"Original Medicare" consists of Part A, essentially for hospital and other inpatient expenses, and Part B, essentially for physician expenses in or out of the hospital, and all outpatient expenses other than prescription drugs. Strictly speaking, original Medicare is not insurance, since it simply involves the government's paying certain types of bills on behalf of beneficiaries, and provides no financial guarantees, as such.[4]

"Competitive Medicare" encompasses what are now called Medicare Advantage plans (covering hospital, outpatient, and, in almost all cases, prescription drug expenses), and Medicare prescription drug plans (PDPs) that provide standalone drug benefits. In sharp contrast to original Medicare, most MA plans and all PDPs do provide insurance guarantees against catastrophic levels of expense.

Original Medicare provides a set of benefits that are largely defined in law, regulation, and ensuing coverage decisions. Scope of benefits, cost-sharing limits, deductibles, and coinsurance are almost entirely set in law and regulation, as are payment rules and quality standards. This is a vast set of requirements. CMS regulations, comprising almost all of volume 42 in the Code of Federal Regulations, are set forth in approximately 2,400 pages, containing about 1.7 million mostly technical and concise words. The rest of volume 42 is 100 pages of the most dense and burdensome regulations ever written, mostly creating Inspector General rules for Medicare. The CFR regulatory text itself does not contain enough information for even experienced health-care professionals to understand without the explanatory text found in manuals, and large portions cannot be used without the coding and payment details found in downloadable databases. Hence, the CMS websites[5] hold approximately 37,000 documents and 6 million words, largely but not entirely focused on explaining Medicare requirements. As a simple example, the CMS publishes an introductory guide called *Medicare Physician Guide* with almost

---

What a charming life that was, that dear old life in the Navy! I knew all the regulations and the rest of them didn't. I had all my rights and most of theirs....

Thomas Brackett Reed, Speaker of the House
of Representatives, as quoted in 1884 from
The Life of Thomas B. Reed by Samuel W. McCall

100 pages of summary explanation of those requirements of original Medicare that apply to physicians in private practice. Once the physician enters practice, Medicare offers training courses, as well as a vast set of manuals.

The corpus of law and regulations includes a great deal of provider regulation. While Medicare defers largely to states to regulate professional qualifications for licensure, the program sets safety and other standards for institutional providers, either directly or by "deeming" its private standards as equivalent to its direct standards. Fraud and abuse laws are another major area of regulation.[6]

At the same time, original Medicare contains considerable elements of choice. Enrollees may choose freely from among some one million health-care providers, including the vast majority of each provider type in business in America (for example, approximately 95 percent of physicians and perhaps 99 percent of general hospitals). Enrollees are also free to obtain whatever services they choose (from within the extremely broad set of covered services and the relatively few coverage maximums) without any prior approval or restriction other than the provider's own determination that the service is "medically necessary." The political deals struck when Medicare was enacted included a solemn legal promise that Medicare would not interfere with the practice of medicine, and while that promise is compromised in innumerable ways as an unavoidable byproduct of fee-setting, coverage decisions, and coding decisions, original Medicare provides more freedom to both enrollees and providers in making service decisions than virtually any other health insurance in America today. For example, while FEHBP plans require prior plan approval for nonemergency hospitalization, Medicare contains no such requirement. In the world of private insurance (including the FEHBP) the practice is, overwhelmingly, to provide sharply inferior benefits (or no benefits) for using nonpreferred providers. Medicare makes distinctions between "participating" and other providers, but as a practical matter makes virtually all providers accessible on financially equal or almost equal terms. Even the pay-for-performance initiatives affect, at most, a few percent of the provider's payment.

In almost all respects except provider payment methods (which have been radically altered), the benefit structure and operations of original Medicare have remained virtually unchanged since the inception of the program. The bifurcation between inpatient and outpatient benefits remains. Enrollee cost-sharing for coinsurance remains almost unchanged after forty years (no coinsurance for most hospital stays; 20 percent coinsurance for most outpatient services and inpatient physician services). Deductible amounts have increased, but for the first three decades increases were well below the rate of inflation and now are simply adjusted approximately with inflation. A few benefits have been added, such as hospice two decades ago. Acupuncture is still missing. Strangely, but presumably reflecting the era in which it was enacted, Medicare pays for hospital delivery but not midwife services (many disabled enrollees are of childbearing age).

Until enactment of the MMA, prescription drugs were not covered by Medicare except in rare circumstances, such as injectables. Two unchanged features have not been present in private plans in many decades. First, full hospital benefits are capped at sixty days (plus thirty days of reduced benefits and a lifetime reserve). Second, original Medicare has no catastrophic limit on out-of-pocket costs. Many other features are antiquarian, including an absence of even emergency coverage abroad (except for some circumstances in Canada and Mexico). Few private insurance plans impose such a high and arguably unfair deductible for hospitalization ($1,068 in 2009). So inadequate is original Medicare as an insurance program that most enrollees who are not covered by employer "wraparound" plans (plans themselves motivated by Medicare's gaps) voluntarily purchase Medigap policies to fill in coverage gaps. In total, about nine in ten enrollees in original Medicare have supplemental insurance for hospital and medical costs.[7]

As shown in table 1-1, enrollee cost-sharing in Medicare is much higher than in the FEHBP, even after the creation of Part D:

- In the most popular FEHBP plan, Blue Cross standard option, standing alone, the "expected" average out-of-pocket cost to enrollees ages sixty-five and over was about $1,700 in 2007. This included expected medical, drug, and dental costs. Blue Cross standard is about average for national FEHBP plans in cost-sharing, and inferior to almost all HMOs in this respect.

- In comparison, age sixty-five enrollment in Medicare parts A and B and D (using an inexpensive Part D standard plan) would cost an average of over $3,100 out of pocket, close to double the cost under Blue Cross.

TABLE 1-1

COMPARING 2007 MEDICARE AND FEHBP COSTS TO THE ELDERLY

Plan	Premium cost to enrollee (no out-of-pocket cost)
Blue Cross standard with Medicare parts A and B	$2,610
Blue Cross standard with Medicare Part A only (PPO providers)	$1,490
Blue Cross standard option only (PPO providers)	$1,490
Medicare parts A, B, and D*	$1,280
Medicare parts A and B only	$1,120

SOURCE: Author's calculations using methods of Francis et al. 2008 and prior years. These calculations include expected dental costs. The average estimated cost before insurance payment is $12,950.

- Medicare parts A and B alone, without Part D, would, on average, leave the enrollee paying $4,200 out of pocket, about two and a half times as much as under the Blue Cross plan.

At high expense levels, such as $100,000 in bills, out-of-pocket levels in Medicare are double (A, B, and D) and triple (A and B only) those of the stand-alone Blue Cross standard option. Only when costs are very low—in the limiting case, when there are no medical costs and only the premium is paid—does Medicare compare favorably to this or other FEHBP plans. Of course, only the FEHBP plan has a catastrophic limit on both medical and drug costs.[8]

A similar comparison to Medicare could be made including the FEHBP's HMO plans, which would show the FEHBP benefit advantage to be even larger. Several national FEHBP plans have benefits inferior to those of Blue Cross standard, but virtually all of the national plans provide similar benefit coordination with Medicare, and none approaches the potential out-of-pocket exposure of Medicare. While most enrollees in original Medicare can purchase a Medigap plan to improve benefits to levels closely approximating those of Blue Cross, the premium costs an additional $1,000–2,000 a year, and sometimes more.

Taking into account external sources, including Medigap (a "private supplement"), insurance from former employers as well as current employers

Estimated average out-of-pocket cost to enrollee	Estimated out-of-pocket cost with expenses of $100,000	Catastrophic limit on medical and drug costs
$940	$4,160**	$4,000***
$1,650	$6,730**	$4,000***
$1,710	$6,730**	$4,000
$3,120	$13,260	Drugs only
$4,280	$20,420	None

NOTES: * The Part D plan is Humana standard, using the Washington, D.C., premium. ** Out-of-pocket cost higher than catastrophic limit because of dental costs. *** Effectively even lower than $4,000 because there are no copays for services covered by Medicare parts A and B.

(also "private supplements"), and Medicaid (a "public supplement" for poor and near-poor enrollees), original Medicare pays only about half of its enrollees' health-care costs, exclusive of premiums. Ironically, the public opinion polls discussed later in the analysis show the elderly as highly satisfied with their Medicare coverage—this is obviously in response not to Medicare alone but to Medicare plus the wraparound sources of supplementary financing that reduced out-of-pocket payments to only 15 percent of total health-care spending by the elderly even before the advent of Part D.

Medicare is financed primarily through income and payroll taxes, with current workers paying taxes to cover the costs of retired workers. This feature is unique among health "insurance" programs, with the major exception of Medicaid. It stands in sharp contrast to the FEHBP, which as part of the pay and benefits package for federal employees is viewed by economists and benefits experts as part of total compensation. For example, assuming total family health insurance premium costs of $12,000, two-thirds paid by the employing agency and one-third by the employee, an employee with nominal salary of $50,000 really receives $58,000, plus a tax subsidy of about $4,000 on both agency and employee share, for total compensation of $62,000. For federal retirees, the arithmetic is similar, but the proportion of compensation represented by insurance is higher, and there are no tax

FIGURE 1-1

TOTAL SPENDING ON HEALTH CARE SERVICES FOR NONINSTITUTIONALIZED FFS MEDICARE BENEFICIARIES BY SOURCE OF PAYMENT, 2005

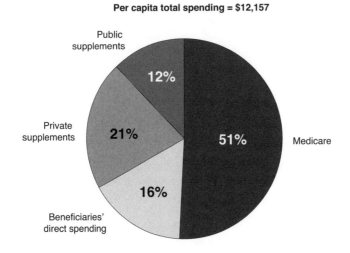

Per capita total spending = $12,157

Public supplements — 12%

Private supplements — 21%

Beneficiaries' direct spending — 16%

Medicare — 51%

SOURCE: U.S. Medicare Payment Advisory Commission. 2008a. *A Data Book: Healthcare Spending and the Medicare Program* (June 2008), 63; MedPAC analysis of Medicare Current Beneficiary Survey, Cost and Use file, 2005.

NOTES: FFS (fee-for-service). Private supplements include employer-sponsored plans and individually purchased coverage. Public supplements include Medicaid, Department of Veterans Affairs, and other public coverage. Direct spending is on Medicare cost-sharing and noncovered services but not supplemental premiums. Analysis includes only FFS beneficiaries not living in institutions such as nursing homes.

subsidies for the retiree share of premium. In the FEHBP, employees and retirees both pay about 30 percent of nominal premium cost, on average.

With Medicare, federal payroll taxes pay almost all of the cost of Part A and federal income taxes about 75 percent of the costs of parts B and D.[9] Average Medicare spending in 2007 was about $11,000 per enrollee, including prescription drugs.[10] In original Medicare, augmented by an average Part D plan, enrollees paid about $1,400 in premium costs, only about 13 percent of total premium-equivalent costs.

Part A "premium" payments are set by law at a tax rate of 2.9 percent of payroll earnings of those currently employed,[11] thereby expressly exempting retirees, without regard to actual costs of Part A. These premiums have no direct basis in either the costs of coverage or any other insurance variable, or any coherent or explicit model of intergenerational fairness or tax policy. They are decided on the basis and at the rate that the federal government sets, reflecting primarily the original financing model established when Medicare was created. As a thought experiment, consider that Part A revenues sufficient to pay benefits could just as well be set by law as an income tax, sales tax, gasoline tax, or other tax (in all of which cases, retirees as well as current employees would bear at least some of the burden), or on any other basis that generates roughly equivalent revenue. In the continuing controversy over offshore drilling for oil and gas, for example, it is somewhat surprising that the obvious option of devoting the potentially vast new federal royalty revenues from these multitrillion-dollar reserves to rescuing Medicare or Social Security are not prominently discussed. Regardless of the particular revenue source chosen, the beneficiary share of Part A costs could be set at any percentage rate, including but not limited to the current rate of zero percent.

In contrast, premium payments for parts B and D are based directly on actual program costs as projected for the next year. The "government share" is likewise levied primarily, but not exclusively, on taxpayers at large, rather than on beneficiaries. In contrast to Part A, beneficiaries finance part of the "government share" of the cost of outpatient and drug coverage, to the extent that they pay income taxes. As another thought experiment, consider that part B and D revenues sufficient to pay the government share of premiums could as well be set by law as a payroll tax like Part A, as a sales tax, as a "sin" tax on tobacco, as a tax on health care, or on any other basis that would generate roughly equivalent revenue.[12] The method actually chosen, however, of using the federal income tax has the particular effect of raising roughly half of that revenue from the top 5 percent of the income distribution, and only about 5 percent from the bottom half of the income distribution, including most elderly.

Also in contrast to Part A, part B and D beneficiaries pay about 25 percent of premiums, not zero percent.

These seemingly strange and widely differing approaches to financing and sharing in the costs of the program have no analytical or ethical rationale. They are simply derivative of the original Medicare program's financing scheme, essentially unchanged for almost fifty years except for relatively small changes in the tax rates and tax base involved.[13] While there is no coherent way to justify any one aspect of Medicare financing in larger terms, the overall effect is strikingly clear: Working Americans, not the elderly, pay the overwhelming majority of Medicare costs. Since Medicare is essentially a "pay-as-you-go" system despite the trust fund rhetoric, this is a direct and immediate intergenerational transfer. Although the precise percentage paid by workers would be quite difficult to calculate with precision, it approaches 90 percent. Although the income tax revenues are highly "progressive" (that is, disproportionately paid by upper-income persons), the payroll tax revenues are slightly regressive. As a result, lower- and middle-income workers pay a large fraction of the costs of both more and less affluent elderly and disabled persons (in sharp contrast to Medicaid, where both taxes and benefits are highly progressive). These effects are partially ameliorated by the longstanding and rapidly increasing use of means-testing in the Medicare program, which reduces the subsidy to the highest income elderly to merely about three-fourths of the total cost of parts A, B, and D.

Taking the FEHBP as representative of employer-sponsored insurance, working-age Americans who are not indigent pay directly about two-thirds or more of the cost of their own health insurance as part of their total compensation. They also pay through both payroll and income taxes close to 90 percent of the cost of insurance for the elderly and disabled. And they also pay through income taxes the great majority of the insurance and direct health-care costs of the indigent non-aged.

Though never described as such in the rhetoric of social insurance, Medicare premiums have long been "means-tested."[14] Lower-income beneficiaries, called QMBs,[15] can enroll in both Medicare and Medicaid without paying either the enrollee share of the Part B premium charge or the deductibles and coinsurance otherwise built into the program. (A similar set of premium and cost-sharing subsidies for the poor and near poor is included in Part D, termed the "low-income supplement.") The Medicare Modernization Act of 2003 created additional means-testing (euphemistically called "income-testing") by requiring higher Part B premium payments from upper-income taxpayers. Under the statute before the MMA was enacted, all beneficiaries except QMBs and other low-income enrollees paid about 25 percent of the total Part B premium ($1,157 for the year in both 2008 and 2009). Under the changes made by the MMA, higher-income taxpayers pay up to 80 percent of the total cost of Part B, or roughly $2,860 in

2008 and $3,700 in 2009 (the increase was phased in over three years start-ing in 2007). The higher premiums begin at an adjusted gross income (slightly modified to capture some tax preferences) of $85,000 for a single taxpayer and $170,000 for a couple in 2000, adjusted annually for inflation (U.S. Department of Health and Human Services, Centers for Medicare and Medicaid Services 2008c, 119).

Both presidents George W. Bush and Barack Obama have proposed adding a similar scheme to Medicare Part D. These proposals, though rela-tively small in immediate impact on financing, illustrate those likely to be considered and enacted in the future (whenever Congress decides to seri-ously consider rescuing Medicare from insolvency). The Bush administra-tion would also have expanded Part B income-testing by removing its inflation indexing. This much larger change would have had the effect of lowering the threshold by 2–3 percent a year, into perpetuity. The proposal would also have extended income-testing for upper-income taxpayers to Part D. With continued modest inflation over time, these changes would have subjected many, and ultimately most, enrollees to substantial premium increases, while greatly improving Medicare's fiscal health.[16]

In contrast, the FEHBP credits and charges all enrollees the same dollar amount, without regard to income or salary. The after-tax value of the pre-mium subsidy varies by income, however, as it does in all employer-based health insurance. Higher-income employees obtain a tax subsidy that approaches, or in some cases exceeds, 40 percent of premium cost, while lower-income employees receive a subsidy that can be as little as about 20 percent of premium cost (for truly low-wage, private-sector employees, the tax subsidy is zero). In practice, most receive a tax subsidy of about one-third (Francis et al. 2008, chapter 8, and prior years). Under the usual economists' assumption that health insurance essentially displaces wage income, the FEHBP's nominal premium financing is mildly progressive, because the gov-ernment's employer share is not proportional to income. The tax subsidy, however, is strongly regressive, and, like other employer-paid insurance throughout the economy, the net effect is that health insurance is by federal tax policy a regressive benefit. Moreover, the lower-wage employees presum-ably lose substantial economic value because they are forced to take a very substantial share of their overall compensation in the form of health insur-ance, when they might prefer to spend it on other forms of consumption, including food, clothing, and shelter.[17] The average premium cost of a family plan in the FEHBP is over $12,000 in 2009 for both employer and employee share. For a relatively low-salaried federal worker earning $36,000 in cash compensation—about $18 an hour—an average policy represents about one-fourth of both total compensation and take-home pay. The economic value or utility of such a policy is certainly far less than its nominal value for almost all workers at that earnings level—which undoubtedly explains why federal employees who decline health insurance comprise perhaps two hundred thousand or more of the uninsured.

In sum, in contrast to almost all employer-sponsored insurance, including the FEHBP, which is essentially employee compensation taken in the form of an insurance purchase rather than cash wages, Medicare is a system in which current workers, predominantly upper-income taxpayers, pay seven-eighths of the insurance costs of most beneficiaries, and all of the cost of low-income beneficiaries, almost all of whom are retired. This system is frequently characterized by terms such as "social insurance" or "intergenerational compact." However characterized, the premium-financing system viewed as a whole is a highly progressive income transfer program, financed overwhelmingly by persons who do not benefit directly and currently from it.

In original Medicare, the Part B premium is identical in dollar terms throughout the nation. There is no geographic or risk adjuster. Likewise, the Part A premium, set at zero, is nominally identical nationally. This does not mean, however, that either premium or benefits are equal nationally in "real" terms. Benefits are unequal because cost-sharing has unequal burdens and incentive effects for enrollees at different income levels, the cost of medical care varies by area, and patterns of medical practice vary widely by geographic area. The premium payment is unequal because wage and pension differences among areas make the Part B premium a different proportion of income—for example, it is more burdensome on average in the South than in other regions of the country. The FEHBP contains essentially the same nominal equality of premium and benefit, regardless of age or location.[18]

The final feature of original Medicare worthy of special attention is the reliance of its beneficiaries on supplementary insurance. This is an extraordinary program weakness when looked at with fresh eyes: an insurance program so badly flawed that about nine in ten of those covered by it feel impelled to purchase costly supplemental insurance, often subsidized by former employers, but more often entirely at their own expense. Medigap plan rates vary substantially by geographic area, age of enrollment, and plan type. Some of the most popular plans are not atypical, however. The AARP-sponsored United HealthCare Medigap plans of types C, D, E, F, G, and J, for instance, cost between $1,500 and $1,700 in 2008 premiums. These plans all reduce hospital and skilled nursing facility costs to zero, reduce Part B coinsurance to zero, cover foreign travel emergencies, and, in most cases, pay the Part B deductible. The ability to avoid these premiums while still filling the worst of Medicare's benefit gaps is probably the most important incentive driving the increase in Medicare Advantage enrollment.

From the beneficiary point of view, the most important aspect of these plans is the reduced risk of incurring high out-of-pocket expenses. From the taxpayer's point of view, their most important attribute is that they increase Medicare costs quite substantially. The literature on the effects of Medigap on Medicare spending generally agrees that excess utilization of medical care is on the order of 15–25 percent or, at today's per-capita spending levels, from $1,500 to perhaps over $2,500 a year per enrollee in costs to original Medicare, and (as a "ballpark" estimate) in the range of $45 billion to $75 billion a year in total original Medicare spending. This amount exceeds the Medigap premiums because it is Medicare, not the Medigap plan, that pays the great majority of additional costs (close to 100 percent of hospital costs and 80 percent of physician costs).[19] Just how much excess spending is involved is a matter of some dispute, but the lowest credible estimate is about 15 percent (Lemieux et al. 2008), and other estimates are considerably higher. The Congressional Budget Office (CBO) has consistently used an estimate of 25 percent (critiqued in a 2003 study by Lemieux as too high) in analyzing restrictions on Medigap cost-sharing (U.S. Congressional Budget Office 2007a, spending reduction option 570-20, page 188, and 2008a, option 82, page 155).

Of course, the near-term political feasibility of eliminating Medigap insurance by legislative fiat is in a category generally termed "dead on arrival," but there are less drastic possibilities. One is the decision codified in the MMA to pay Medicare Advantage plans more than the cost of original Medicare, and to allow private fee-for-service plans to attract current beneficiaries away from the dominant Medigap alternative. Strangely, the U.S. Medicare Payment Advisory Commission (MedPAC), the U.S. Government Accountability Office, and even the CBO have not focused on this rationale for current Medicare Advantage payment rates, nor estimated the substantial savings that it is already bringing to the federal budget, as discussed later in this analysis.

The Evolution of Medicare

Original Medicare has been essentially stable in benefit levels, cost-sharing, and methods of interaction with beneficiaries throughout its history. Periodic financing crises, occurring as program costs expanded far more rapidly than foreseen and far more rapidly than revenues, have been resolved through increases in taxes, shifts in allocation of costs between parts A and B, and minor changes in benefits (see Oberlander 2003 and Marmor 2000). Provider payment changes to control rising costs have been far more significant. Changes of particular note include the introduction of prospective payment and the diagnosis-related group (DRG) system for hospitals in 1983, the adoption of the resource-based relative value scale (RBRVS) system for physicians in 1989, and a host of other prospective payment reforms and reductions enacted in the Balanced Budget Act (BBA) of 1997.[20]

Medicare's most important reform prior to the Balanced Budget Act was evanescent. In 1986, President Ronald Reagan proposed to add catastrophic coverage to Medicare. After protracted debate, and the addition of a prescription drug benefit as well, the Medicare Catastrophic Coverage Act (MECCA) was enacted in 1988. Its costs were substantial, and financing rested on a substantial new supplemental premium that would have fallen primarily on millions of the more affluent elderly, a group largely already protected against catastrophic expense and with prescription drug coverage. Political fallout from these stakeholders was so intense that the statute was repealed in 1989 (see Hyman 2006 for a lively discussion in his chapter on "Gluttony," and Rice et al., 1990, for a detailed postmortem). In a famous incident, an elderly beneficiary threw herself onto the hood of the car of then chairman of the Ways and Means Committee Dan Rostenkowski. This protest was caught on camera and played on the evening news not only that evening but for months to come, portraying the congressman as willing to hurl the bodies of the elderly aside.[21]

Competitive Medicare brought many of the benefit improvements that were sought in MECCA, as we will now see. It did so, however, without protest.

Medicare Advantage Offers New Options for Private Plans. Medicare has for decades allowed some private plans, until recently almost all HMOs, to participate in the program and compete for enrollees. Prior to enactment of the BBA in 1997, these plans typically offered modestly improved benefits, including some prescription drug coverage, with payment of additional premiums. HMO plans were generally paid 95 percent of the "adjusted average per-capita cost" (AAPCC) of original Medicare in their local areas. These participation arrangements were greatly expanded with enactment of the BBA, and renamed "Medicare+Choice" (M+C). The BBA added features to the HMO payment formula, including a "floor" to deal with areas where original Medicare costs were at very low levels that no HMO could possibly meet, as well as a minimum rate of increase. HMO enrollment expanded greatly for several years after the BBA was enacted, but peaked in 1999 and declined as a proportion of total Medicare enrollment from almost 16 percent in 2000 to about 12 percent in 2002. Those trends reflected several factors, far and away the most important of which was the BBA's reduction in the payment levels of original Medicare, to which HMO payments were tied (Gold 2001).

Medicare+Choice enrollment then remained stable until enactment of the Medicare Modernization Act in 2003 provided additional financial incentives to plans to participate. The MMA also renamed the private plan program "Medicare Advantage" and added new kinds of options for private plans to participate. MA plans presently include not only HMO plans but also preferred provider organization (PPO) and fee-for-service (FFS) plans. There are even medical savings account plans—though with minuscule enrollment through Medicare—in sharp contrast to participation by employer-sponsored plans. Medicare Advantage plans are now breaking prior enrollment records for private plans, recently reaching almost one-fourth of total Medicare enrollment, as shown in table 1-2.

It is hard to compare these numbers directly to the FEHBP. There, national PPOs have dominated preretirement enrollment for the past two

TABLE 1-2

ENROLLMENT IN PRIVATE PLAN ALTERNATIVES TO ORIGINAL MEDICARE

Year	Total Medicare enrollment (millions)	Medicare Advantage and other private plan enrollment (millions)	Percent private plan
1985	30.62	1.27	4.1%
1990	33.75	2.02	6.0%
1995	37.18	3.47	9.3%
2000	39.26	6.86	17.5%
2001	39.67	6.17	15.6%
2002	40.01	5.54	13.8%
2003	40.74	5.30	13.0%
2004	41.48	5.38	13.0%
2005	42.23	5.79	13.7%
2006	43.08	7.29	16.9%
2007	43.94	8.67	19.7%
2008	44.85	10.00	22.3%
2009 est.	45.55	10.88	23.9%

SOURCES: U.S. Boards of Trustees 2009 and prior years.

decades, evolving from national FFS plans. Almost all of these plans continue to have both PPO (network) and FFS (out-of-network) benefits. HMOs have typically garnered a third or more of employee enrollees. At age sixty-five, retirees have special incentives to sign up for national plans that operate as PPOs for employees, but essentially as fee-for-service plans without medical cost-sharing for retirees with Medicare. Hence, these private plans operate virtually as Medigap wraparound plans.

In Medicare, the essential role played by MA plans has been to serve as an option with better benefits (such as prescription drugs and catastrophic protection) and far lower premium costs than the combination of original Medicare with a Medigap plan. In return for a financially superior benefits package, MA enrollees have accepted restrictions on provider choices. MA enrollment is still predominantly in HMOs, though growing most rapidly for private fee-for-service (PFFS) MA plans. As a result of these factors, the HMO proportion of aged enrollees is much higher in Medicare than in the FEHBP.

TABLE 1-3

MEDICARE ADVANTAGE ENROLLMENT BY PLAN TYPE (THOUSANDS)

Type of plan	August 2004	August 2005	August 2006	August 2007	August 2008
Local coordinated-care plans	4,756	5,104	5,922	6,239	7,150
HMOs	4,651	4,980	5,511	5,750	6,462
PPOs	105	124	411	489	689
Regional PPOs	0	0	89	183	293
Private fee-for-service	39	135	802	1,710	2,285
Other (e.g., cost plans)	604	612	592	732	420
Medical savings account	0	0	0	2	4
Total	5,399	5,851	7,405	8,866	10,153
(Special-needs plans)	0	0	(603)	(989)	(1,244)

SOURCES: Kaiser Family Foundation n.d. and Gold 2007.

The MMA made many changes in addition to improved premium support to attract new plans and new types of plans into the Medicare Advantage program. Hence, not only has enrollment grown dramatically, but the kinds and mix of plans have changed. One way to think about the menu of choices facing any individual beneficiary is that, as in the private sector (and the FEHBP), there is a continuum of plan types in which generosity of benefits and scope of provider access are inversely related. HMOs typically have the best benefits and the smallest networks, PPOs provide better benefits in network, and PFFS plans have benefits only modestly better than under original Medicare, with similarly unconstrained access to almost all providers.

As shown in table 1-3, the composition of MA enrollment has changed drastically as a result of the MMA. Until enactment of the MMA, PPO and PFFS plans were not a significant component of MA enrollment. Now, with enrollment under the new MA rules beginning in 2006, they have become the fastest growing components. Special-needs plans (SNPs) have also grown very substantially within most of these categories. SNPs enroll the institutionalized, those with serious chronic or disabling conditions, and dual Medicare/Medicaid eligibles. About two-thirds of SNP enrollees are dual eligibles.

The most remarkable and unexpected growth has occurred in private fee-for-service plans, which were first authorized in the Balanced Budget Act. HMOs were rarely offered in rural areas, both because of problems in assembling networks and because regional payments were typically far lower than urban payments, reflecting the pattern of utilization and spending in original Medicare. PFFS plans offered another means of providing choices to rural beneficiaries. The BBA's addition of the "floor" segment to the capitation formula made it possible for some PFFS plans to take advantage of the difference between local MA payment and local cost patterns. Because of this unique ability to exploit the foibles of the MA payment system, the average payment of PFFS plans relative to original Medicare has been higher than for other plan types—about 8 percent higher for benefits comparable to those provided by parts A and B, and about 17 percent higher taking into account additional benefits the PFFS plans provide (U.S. Senate, Committee on Finance 2008b).

PFFS plans are particularly valuable to employers as a tool to reduce retiree health costs (Brown et al. 2008). They allow employers to provide essentially a single plan nationwide to their retirees, with little administrative cost and bounded premium costs (often nothing more beyond the regular Part B premium), but with better benefits than original Medicare. Within the PFFS category, group enrollment through employer contracts has been the fastest growing component (ibid., 7).

PFFS plans also have a major advantage over PPO and HMO plans: By law, all Medicare-participating physicians and other providers must accept Medicare rates in payment when enrollees in these plans use those providers. Although PFFS plans were originally offered almost exclusively in rural and low-cost urban counties, they are now available in all areas to all Medicare beneficiaries and are by far the fastest growing Medicare Advantage plan type (Blum et al. 2007 and U.S. Senate Committee on Finance 2008b).[22]

Medicare Advantage Plans Limit Catastrophic Costs. Protection against catastrophic expense is the keystone of true health insurance. It has come to Medicare through Medicare Advantage, silently and with little fanfare, and, arguably, at a bargain rate. One way to think about the extra payments currently made to PFFS and other MA plans is as financing for catastrophic protection that enrollees would either not have or could only have at major expense, to themselves directly and to original Medicare through wasteful overutilization. Amazingly, little of the literature on MA plans addresses the prevalence of such protection in either MA plan offerings or enrollee choices. The plan comparison tool at Medicare's website, however, readily demonstrates the ubiquity of such features in PFFS and other MA plans.[23] One study found that, as of 2006, the prevalence of catastrophic stop-loss protection was 100 percent in regional PPOs (where it is required), 80 percent in PFFS plans, 54 percent in local PPOs, and 33 percent in HMOs (Pope et al. 2007). Overall, 42 percent of MA enrollees had explicit catastrophic guarantees in 2006, and the percentage has presumably grown substantially since then with the increase in PFFS and PPO plans. Most of the rest had an implicit guarantee by virtue of enrollment in HMOs with nominal copays and, hence, a practical near impossibility of facing the tens of thousands of dollars and potentially unlimited expense faced by those original Medicare enrollees who do not purchase Medigap or have other wraparound coverage. (While this is impressive, over 80 percent of FEHBP enrollees are in plans with explicit catastrophic limits.)[24]

Of particular importance, the most important benefit of Medicare Advantage FFS plans, available in the great majority of them and gained by four-fifths of enrollees, is the provision of such a catastrophic limit on out-of-pocket expenses (ibid., 68). In effect, for about 2 million beneficiaries, these plans fill the largest and most important insurance gap in original Medicare which, in rural areas not well served by other types of MA plans, can otherwise be filled only by buying Medigap plans costing thousands of dollars a year. Their second most important benefit is that they enable enrollees to fill other holes in original Medicare as well by, for example, offering lower hospital deductibles without enrollees' having to buy a Medigap plan. Furthermore, the PFFS plans are far superior in design to Medigap plans in providing incentives to avoid wasteful care. All contain significant cost-sharing requirements—for example, all have a copay for emergency room visits, and almost all have a copay for visits to primary-care physicians and a higher copay for specialist visits (ibid., 66). Thus, the PFFS plans are close cousins in design and operation to the kind of reforms proposed for original Medicare during the Reagan administration. They provide a simple alternative that meets most of the goals of that proposal for those willing to take advantage of them.

Notwithstanding catastrophic protection and other valuable benefits they offer to enrollees, and the substantial savings generated for Medicare by substituting for Medigap plans, PFFS plans have been repeatedly criticized by the U.S. Medicare Payment Advisory Commission (U.S. House of Representatives, Committee on Ways and Means 2007a and U.S. Senate Committee on Finance 2008b) as the type of MA plan with the least valuable model for controlling costs and the greatest payment differential, compared to original Medicare. MedPAC argues that PFFS plans violate the "basic axiom of Medicare payment policy" (no source for this alleged axiom is cited), to pay only the cost of "the most efficient provider," which, in MedPAC's view, is original Medicare (implicitly, original Medicare as supplemented by a Medigap plan and generating wasteful spending; U.S. Senate Committee on Finance 2008b, 9). MedPAC harps on creating a "level playing field for all plan types, with no type having an advantage over another type" in the absence of "special circumstances" (ibid.). Among the "unfair" advantages MedPAC says PFFSs have over other MA plan types are not having to use a provider network (which is the fundamental distinguishing characteristic of a fee-for-service plan), not having to report quality measures for every provider (an extreme burden on a plan that cannot impose a paperwork burden on any provider an enrollee might select), and not having to provide a catastrophic limit on enrollee out-of-pocket costs (when most of these plans do so, in contrast to the HMO plans).

Strangely, of the shortcomings in MA plans that PFFS plans are said "unfairly" to remedy, all except the ability to compel paperwork apply with equal or greater force to original Medicare, which is unmentioned in the MedPAC comparison. Regardless, the MedPAC position (and the apparent basis for pending action by the administration and Congress discussed later in this analysis) is that it is somehow unfair to allow, but not require, these and other MA plans to provide additional benefits if doing so entails any additional Medicare spending and allows escape from any Medicare red tape. (In fairness to MedPAC, it recommends that all MA plans, not just PFFS plans, be held on average to 100 percent of the costs of original Medicare.) Conspicuously lacking from this comparison—for all plan types, not just PFFS plans—is the possibility (according to CBO estimates, a certainty) that by attracting enrollees away from Medigap policies, PFFS and other MA plans are saving original Medicare a great deal of money that would otherwise be spent on "free" overuse of health-care services financed primarily by original Medicare.

CMS issues an annual "call letter" informing plans of changes it would like to see, and in some cases insists on seeing, in plan bids for the coming contract year.[25] For 2010, the CMS call letter strongly encourages all plans to establish an overall out-of-pocket maximum for services covered under parts A and B (but not Part D prescription drugs) of $3,400 or less (U.S. Department of Health and Human Services, Centers for Medicare and Medicaid Services 2009a). Clearly, whatever final decisions are made by plans in their proposals and by CMS in approving bids, the catastrophic cost protections of Medicare Advantage are likely to improve significantly through the elimination of loopholes and addition of catastrophic limits in plans that do not have them now.

Open Enrollment Season. Another major change brought by the MMA was the creation of a disciplined open season for enrolling or disenrolling in health plans. Until enactment of the MMA, a Medicare+Choice enrollee was allowed to disenroll from a plan essentially at will and return to original Medicare or join another plan. This flexibility was justified as a beneficiary protection against potentially harmful and abusive plan practices—a rationale without any substantial empirical basis in proven plan abuses, then or since. In contrast, the FEHBP has always allowed only once-a-year disenrollment, during open season, except under rare special circumstances. Despite many millions of person-years of enrollment by retired federal employees and their aged surviving spouses, there has been no documented pattern of abuse of any kind by plans in the FEHBP. (While marketing abuses do occur in Medicare Advantage, particularly in "churning" enrollees, they are reduced by allowing plan changes only once a year.)[26]

This disenrollment difference might seem unimportant, but the Medicare+ Choice system had two harmful results. First, some proportion of enrollees in the Medicare HMO plans used the ability to disenroll and join other plans as a way to maximize prescription drug benefits by "gaming" the system, changing plans upon exhausting the maximum annual benefit in one to start over in another. This adverse selection behavior in turn influenced plans to limit drug benefits more tightly than would otherwise have been the case. Equally important, it essentially eliminated the financial incentives for plans to manage care to keep costs down and enrollees healthy over a multiyear investment horizon. Hence, prior to the MMA, enrollment in HMOs was unlikely to produce significant savings to Medicare from plan management of enrollee costs over time.

Medicare's Private Plan Payment System. From the earliest days of allowing private plans to enroll beneficiaries, Medicare faced the vexing problem of how, and how much, to reimburse those plans for their costs. A natural and obvious solution was to pay plans based on their actual expenses, and another was to pay them a capitated amount for each person enrolled based on what Medicare was spending on those in original Medicare. In fact, the earliest private plans were paid on a cost basis, and some are paid so today. Medicare soon moved toward a capitated system, however.

Under capitation, a secondary decision was based on the easy and obvious assumption that medical costs varied widely from place to place, if for no other reason than that the cost of living seemed to vary from place to place—New York presumably being more expensive than any rural hamlet for rent and other expenses. The United States had then (and does not have today) a national system of cost-of-living or cost-of-doing-business adjustments.[27] But Medicare does have data on what it spends on every beneficiary, and where every beneficiary is located. So capitated payments were adjusted for geographic difference (hence, "average adjusted per-capita costs," or AAPCC).

Finally, it seemed reasonable to pay plans no more than what Medicare was spending per enrollee, and preferably less. Since these decisions were being made at a time when HMOs were the only plans considered likely candidates for private participation, and HMOs had been shown by research to spend less per enrollee than traditional fee-for-service medicine, the predecessor systems to Medicare Advantage evolved into payments of 95 percent of AAPCC, except for "cost plans." These amounts are subject to increasingly complex adjustments.[28]

These reasonable-sounding decisions rested on a seemingly sensible myth—that the cost of health-care services varies widely across geographic areas—that has led to complex problems profoundly affecting Medicare Advantage and its predecessors to this day, but with little relevance to the FEHBP.[29] In Medicare Advantage, HMOs, PPOs, and other private plans are paid based on a complicated capitation formula that gives most weight to the local costs of treating enrollees in original Medicare. These costs bear little, if any, rational relationship to the costs that would be incurred by a well-managed HMO or PPO (or, for that matter, a well-designed PFFS plan, with the kinds of utilization controls and incentives that are absent from original Medicare), and are notoriously sensitive to local practice patterns that a good deal of empirical evidence suggests are profoundly wasteful (see, for example, U.S. Congressional Budget Office 2005 and Fisher et al. 2003). Indeed, these studies of geographic variation conclude that higher spending areas are associated with lower quality of care. Moreover, other evidence shows that HMO variations in cost by geographic area are, in fact, relatively insubstantial compared to the wide variations in original Medicare's geographic cost variations.[30]

The use of original Medicare as a basis for geography-driven capitation rewards private plans in areas like Florida, where Medicare spending levels are much higher than average, and penalizes them in areas like the upper Midwest, where utilization and practice patterns are much more frugal. Indeed, so substantial is the payment imbalance that until enactment of the MMA, large areas of the United States attracted no private plan choices, and in other large areas participating plans offered limited benefits. During the period 1997–2001, on average about one-third of all Medicare beneficiaries had access to no private plan choices, and another one-tenth had access to only one plan (Gold 2001). Of the plans that did participate, only half offered drug coverage. These effects were particularly harmful to lower-income beneficiaries, whose only potential access to inexpensive coverage for prescription drugs was through private plans—a Medigap plan covering drugs would at least double, and often triple, the amount spent on insurance premiums. Thus, the private plan payment formula created major inequities among Medicare beneficiaries, penalizing many for no other reason than the accident of their locations. In contrast, every federal employee and retiree has access to at least a dozen plans, and HMOs serve all but the most remote rural areas.

As figure 1-2 shows, the huge and arguably irrational differentials in payment rates remain in Medicare Advantage to this day, albeit tempered by such features as floor payments.[31] In the Miami metropolitan area, capitation rates are almost $14,400 a year, compared to under $10,800 in the Washington, D.C., metropolitan area and just over $9,600 in such midwestern cities as

FIGURE 1-2

ILLUSTRATIVE MEDICARE ADVANTAGE BENCHMARK RATES, 2009

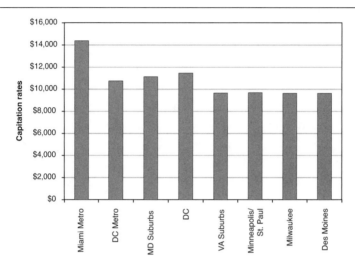

SOURCES: U.S. Department of Health and Human Services, Centers for Medicare and Medicaid Services 2009 and prior years.
NOTE: Rates shown are simple averages of data for aged in parts A and B for selected counties.

Minneapolis–St. Paul, Milwaukee, and Des Moines. Within the D.C. area, plans in the Maryland suburbs are paid almost $1,500 more per enrollee than plans in the Virginia suburbs, even though all operate within a common medical market. These differences may reflect in part some small differences in average health status among jurisdictions, but there is a separate risk adjustment in Medicare payments based on the health status of those individuals who enroll in each plan, so using the original differential for Medicare Advantage payments is inherently arbitrary within medical markets, and for the most part arbitrary across market areas, as well. I say "arbitrary," but, as discussed later, the basic cause is well known: difference in usage of health-care services for persons with comparable conditions, as decided by physicians and other health-care providers. These differences are vast among areas, and the examples above are by no means the most extreme. For example, in 2006 Medicare spent about $15,000 per enrollee in McAllen, Texas, and only $7,500 per enrollee in El Paso, cities with essentially identical disease profiles and demographics (Gawande 2009).

With essentially arbitrary differences like these as the primary factor in Medicare Advantage payments, and lacking any market basis other than the rates of other Medicare Advantage plans, problems with payment levels remain endemic in MA. In contrast, Medicare Part D relies entirely on the enrollment-weighted bids of Part D plans in setting its benchmark levels, and completely avoids large differentials (only Alaska varies consequentially from the national average). The cost differences in original Medicare undoubtedly reflect practice and, hence, utilization variations that are quite real, as well as variations in levels of fraud and abuse; but why those variations should dictate HMO, PPO, or even PFFS payment levels verges on the outlandish, especially considering that these plans are supposed to be able to eliminate unnecessary spending through cost-sharing, utilization controls, and disease management.[32]

These large payment differentials do, of course, buy something. In the case of Miami, they buy a lot. According to *The Miami Herald*, "At the new Leon Medical Center in Hialeah, Fla., a white-gloved and uniformed doorman welcomes seniors in front of bubbling waterfalls. Inside, along with marbled restrooms, seniors get free dental and vision care." At another clinic, "seniors are participating in free exercise classes, playing dominos and competing in bingo tournaments, as well as getting free coffee and breakfast pastries" (Dorschner 2007). Reports *Health Affairs*, "The difference in lifetime Medicare spending between a typical sixty-five-year-old in Miami and one in Minneapolis is more than $50,000, equivalent to a new Lexus GS 400 with all the trimmings" (Wennberg et al. 2002).

The Balanced Budget Act of 1997 created a separate problem. The BBA tightly limited provider payment rates in original Medicare. The effect was actually to reduce payments to hospitals below prior-year levels in 1998, 1999, and 2000. Average per-beneficiary costs went from about $5,600 in 1997 to about $5,550 in 1998 and about $5,500 in 1999, even though costs for medical care in this period were rising (U.S. Boards of Trustees 2006, 160). Since private plan payments were pegged largely to the level of original Medicare spending, the results for Medicare+Choice plans and enrollees were devastating. Underlying health-care costs were still rising at rates greater than inflation, on the order of 5 percent a year. While the underlying payment formula did not mirror these trends precisely and had differential effects in areas protected by a "floor," there was a significant reduction in real levels of capitation (Gold 2003). Hence, changes in payment rates for Medicare providers had the unintended consequence of wreaking havoc on the Medicare+Choice program. Quite apart from the many beneficiaries who lost access to any private plan, the number of plans with zero premiums and prescription drug coverage dropped drastically (see ibid.).

An example may convey the kind of problem this change to original Medicare payment rates created for beneficiaries enrolled in plans tied in large part to those rates. In the late 1990s, millions of beneficiaries decided to drop their expensive Medigap coverage and join zero-premium HMOs with drug coverage as good as that in any Medigap plan. In the Washington, D.C., area, there were then four participating HMO plans. Over a three-year period, this number went down to one. As a result, HMO enrollees in the D.C. area were forced to change plans each year, and finally had no choice left but the Kaiser HMO plan.[33] Kaiser is an excellent plan, but few of these enrollees would ever have voluntarily chosen such a staff HMO. Reenrollment in a Medigap plan was either impossible or far more expensive. Well over a million persons had their lives similarly disrupted, as total Medicare+Choice enrollment went from a high of 6.2 million in 1999 to a low of 4.7 million in 2002.[34]

The MMA partially corrected the unnecessarily high reliance of plan payments on geographic cost variations under original Medicare and raised premium contributions as well. At present, payment rates for MA plans are unusually generous by historical standards—by all reckoning, about 12 percent and perhaps 14 percent higher than costs under original Medicare (U.S. Medicare Payment Advisory Commission 2007 and 2009; Biles et al. 2006 and 2008; U.S. House of Representatives, Committee on Ways and Means 2007c; U.S. House of Representatives, Committee on the Budget 2007). As critics of this generosity point out, the historical practice had been to pay 95 percent of the average per-capita cost in original Medicare, in the expectation that HMOs could realize enough savings through managed care to thrive under this ceiling. Under the current payment system, enrollees get back as much and more in better benefits or reduced premiums. Plans that offer benefits at bids less than the benchmark amount paid by the government (as almost all do) are required to return the difference to enrollees in the form of increased benefits or rebates on Part B or D premiums. As a result of this requirement and the workings of competition, the majority of MA plans charge no extra premium for providing a prescription drug benefit as good as or better than the standard Part D benefit. The CMS has calculated the extra benefits of MA enrollment compared to original Medicare plus Part D as worth an average of $86 a month, or over $1,000 a year, taking into account reduced cost-sharing, reduced premiums, and additional benefits (U.S. House of Representatives, Committee on Ways and Means, 2007b). This slightly exceeds the average 12 percent higher payment to MA plans calculated for 2007 by outside bodies. Except for the consumer inertia discussed later in this analysis, MA enrollment would likely already have sky-rocketed far beyond even the recent enrollment gains.

This payment differential will be substantially reduced under current law, as four of the twelve percentage points are due to an arcane factor called "budget neutrality" that will be phased out by 2011. Plan competition can also be expected to reduce payments over time, with Medicare recouping 25 percent of savings for costs below the benchmarks. (As will be discussed later, the Obama administration has already taken early administrative steps to reduce payment levels even further for 2010. As will also be discussed later, the nominal 12–14 percent in allegedly excess payment ignores the massive savings that these plans create for original Medicare.)

The Advent of Part D. With the beginning of the Part D prescription drug benefit program in 2006, Medicare finally became an arguably modern health insurance program, more than four decades after its creation, although such anomalies as hospitalization cost-sharing that rises rather than falls with length of stay remain. While the Part D program has some unusual design features, discussed further below, it fills what was by far the largest gap in original Medicare, and even contains a catastrophic limit on what enrollees pay for drugs. The program operates by consumer choice among competing plans, and, despite bumps arising from automatic assignment of dual eligibles to prescription drug plans, some marketing abuses, and some computer glitches, it is operating quite smoothly. For a program with many complexities (such as shifting millions of persons from Medicaid to Medicare for payment of drug costs, and millions of others from Medigap plans to Medicare as well), its initial year was surprisingly smooth.[35]

Perhaps most impressive is that the level of Part D costs and premiums has been over a third below the amounts predicted in pre-enactment estimates by both the Congressional Budget Office and the Medicare actuaries.[36] Also surprisingly, Part D premiums were essentially stable during the first three years, despite continuing increases in retail prices for prescription drugs; and despite larger premium increases in 2009 (perhaps reflecting early premiums that were bid somewhat low to attract market share), the program's overall costs remain far below the original projections. As in the FEHBP, consumer choices among Part D plans during the first several open enrollment periods showed a movement toward lower-cost plans, and hence a drop in average premiums. This phenomenon is likely to accelerate in 2009 as enrollees shift away from some of the most popular plans that are undergoing substantial premium increases.

There are various ways of computing and presenting Part D premiums, depending, for example, on whether data are enrollment-weighted, are calculated using present enrollment or changed enrollment after enrollees change plans, cover only standalone Part D plans, or cover all Part D plans, including those sponsored within MA plans (commonly abbreviated as MA-PD plans). For example, according to CMS, the average monthly premium offered by all plans (including MA-PD plans) in 2006 was $32, but during the open enrollment period beneficiaries generally elected to join lower-cost plans, and the resulting average premium was $24. The projected all-plan-weighted bid for 2007 was also $24, but it wound up at $22 after enrollment choices were made. For 2008, the projected and actual averages were both $25. The 2009 projection is $28.[37]

The standalone PDP premiums are considerably higher than those for MA-PD plans, however; in 2009, there will be about an $11 difference between the two, up from $9 in 2008. This differential arises because MA plans can use part of their revenues to lower the Part D cost to enrollees. Viewed from the perspective of these data, during the first four years of the program the average premium will rise from $24 to $28, or only about 5 percent a year, from a far lower base than originally projected before the program was enacted or even than projected in its first year.

There are other ways to view the data, though. For example, many press reports followed a September 26, 2008, announcement by consulting firm Avalere that, by its calculations, the enrollment-weighted, standalone PDP premium would increase by 24 percent from 2008 to 2009 (Avalere Health 2008). Increases of this magnitude, however (31 percent on average in the ten most popular plans), likely would result in substantial migration to lower-cost plans and a much lower increase after enrollment choices were made.

Similarly, the Kaiser Family Foundation has analyzed premium increases using data from standalone PDPs only (Hoadley et al. 2008). According to this analysis, the 2008 monthly premium would have risen by 17 percent from 2007 if all enrollees stayed in the same plans, but after enrollment shifts, it rose only by 9 percent, from $27 to $30. For 2009, premiums were projected to rise by 25 percent to $37, similar to the Avalere projection. Again, assuming substantial enrollee shifting in open season, the likely increase will be much less.

Under Part D virtually all enrollees have a choice of about fifty plans. Some argue that this presents enrollees with overwhelming complexity. Most FEHBP enrollees, who are younger and better educated than those in Medicare, on average, have "only" about two dozen plans from which to choose. Of course, for a substantial fraction of enrollees, any number larger than one creates confusion.[38] The "confusion" issue is one of the bugaboos discussed later in this analysis.

Regardless, numerous decision aids and tools are available to Part D enrollees, plus counseling help from family, friends, and trained professionals in state and local agencies funded by the CMS and the Administration on Aging (another agency of the U.S. Department of Health and Human Services). All Medicare beneficiaries receive a carefully organized and written handbook, *Medicare & You*. Service representatives at the 1-800-MEDICARE number have detailed scripts to assist with almost any situation. These representatives are able to enroll beneficiaries over the telephone in plans that meet their stated needs. CMS sponsors an excellent website for beneficiaries at www.medicare.gov, and one of its many useful online services, Plan Finder, provides ratings of Part D plans based on which ones least expensively meet an enrollee's current drug usage needs and pharmacy preferences. Taken as a whole, the current scope and depth of support services far exceed those available under the FEHBP, leaving aside the federal agencies that subscribe to *CHECKBOOK's Guide to Health Plans for Federal Employees* (Francis et al. 2008 and prior years) to provide online access for all agency employees.

The prospect for Part D's actually functioning as planned when it was enacted was highly uncertain. The MMA provided for a "fallback plan" to be run by the government in case no plan submitted bids in a particular region. Measured against either the original uncertainties or the performance of other large programs in their start-up phase, the program is, arguably, a dramatic success. Of note, about a million veterans who receive free drugs from the Veterans Administration have joined a Part D plan, paying the same premium as other enrollees, presumably because of the superior convenience and far broader formularies in Part D plans.

Summary

Original Medicare has remained unchanged in its essentials since its inception, with the extremely important exception that the methods of paying providers have changed radically from cost reimbursement for hospitals and payment of usual and customary fees to physicians to a set of so-called prospective payment systems that are, in essence, nothing more nor less than fee schedules set by the government.

From a beneficiary perspective, no change this dramatic has occurred. The hospital deductible and coinsurance and physician coinsurance remain largely unchanged in real terms. The physician deductible, however, has been substantially reduced because for many years it was not adjusted for inflation. Although that oversight has been remedied, the original 1965 deductible of $40 would be many times higher today, however measured. For example, in 1965 the deductible was $40, more than the Part B premium of $36 a year, and equal to about one-fourth of average annual spending on physician and related outpatient services. Were the same relationship to obtain today, the Part B deductible would be approximately $1,300 rather than $135 a year. Some other benefits have gotten more generous (such as the addition of hospice coverage), but by and large the program remains insurance vintage 1960—separate hospital and physician systems, no out-of-pocket limit on potential costs, and, until very recently, virtually no prescription drug coverage.

The enactment of the Medicare Modernization Act in 2003 was explicitly intended to bring about a major Medicare reform, not by fixing original Medicare but by creating alternative programs using competitive market mechanisms. The MA and PDP programs are a radical departure from the

past in that private health plans make the great majority of specific decisions, and especially decisions as to benefit design and delivery, in sharp
contrast to the detailed and prescriptive government rules and government
administration of original Medicare.

Because Medicare has been largely coterminous in duration with the
FEHBP, and subject to all of the same external forces and circumstances,
most notably the vast increases in cost and substantial increases in effectiveness of medical care over the past half-century, it provides a comparative basis for evaluation of the effectiveness and efficiency of both programs.

2

The FEHBP

No contemporary works remotely comparable in depth to the sources on Medicare are available on the FEHBP. A dated but in-depth study (U.S. Congressional Research Service 1989) is available, however. Robert Moffit (1992) and Harry Cain (1999) have richly described the overall features of the program, and Mark Merlis (1999) describes the program's workings in considerable detail and compares it to Medicare+Choice, the predecessor of Medicare Advantage. The annual *CHECKBOOK's Guide to Health Plans for Federal Employees* contains a great deal of information on the structure, functions, and design of the program (Francis et al. 2008 and prior years). Also, a detailed description and evaluation of performance in the first three decades of the program was presented in an essay in Robert Helm's *Health Policy Reform: Competition and Controls* (Francis 1993).

In sharp contrast to the political history of Medicare, however, that of the FEHBP has been relatively uneventful. Its political history would put readers to sleep, were it not so short. Nothing in the history of the FEHBP has been remotely as controversial as the Medicare Catastrophic Coverage Act. The major reform of the FEHBP—making the employee share of premiums tax-preferred—received only the most minimal news coverage and to this day is scarcely known to or understood by even federal employees.

This chapter will offer background on the FEHBP to provide a foundation for our subsequent discussion and evaluation. Although the program has not received substantial legislative change in a half-century (with the major exception of increases in the government share of premium costs), it has evolved substantially through the decisions made by plans and enrollees in a changing marketplace for both health care and health insurance. As in the previous chapter on Medicare, we will occasionally compare the two

46

programs on key features, presaging the more detailed evaluative comparisons in succeeding chapters.

The Creation and Basic Design of the FEHBP

The FEHBP is the largest employer-sponsored health plan in the United States, covering about eight million lives, or almost 3 percent of the American population (Francis et al. 2008 and prior years). The FEHBP was established in 1959, six years before Medicare. Until then, the federal government had no fringe benefit for health insurance, lagging behind major private corporations by over a decade. Instead, federal employees voluntarily purchased health insurance as individual subscribers or, most commonly, through a handful of union and employee association plans and HMOs in cities with substantial federal employment. The FEHBP was designed as a multiplan competitive system through a political accident, resulting from pressures brought to bear by these existing union and employee association plans (see Francis 1993 and Anderson and May 1971). The U.S. Civil Service Commission (predecessor to what is now the U.S. Office of Personnel Management, or OPM, which oversees government-wide issues affecting the civilian federal workforce) had proposed what was essentially a single-plan system, but the "grandfather rights" so important in the American political system operated to prevent such a simple, bureaucratically tidy program.

The FEHBP once included plans, long forgotten today, such as the Professional Air Traffic Controllers Organization Plan (eliminated with the demise of the PATCO union after its famous strike early in the Ronald Reagan administration), the Alliance Plan, the Government Employees Benefit Association Plan, and others of ancient vintage. In more recent years, plans leaving the system have included the Postmasters Benefit Plan, the Postal Supervisors Plan, the National Treasury Employees Union Plan, and the American Federation of Government Employees Plan. The Secret Service Plan, for many years one of the lowest cost plans, but like many of those above too small to be viable, recently merged into the FBI's Special Agents Mutual Benefit Association (SAMBA) Plan, which soon allowed all law enforcement employees to join and most recently made itself available to all federal employees.[1]

TABLE 2-1
NUMBERS AND TYPES OF FEHBP PLANS

| Year | National total | | | Total |
	National PPO	Local	Consumer-driven	
1961	15	13	0	28
1970	18	21	0	39
1975	26	33	0	59
1980	24	86	0	110
1985	28	200	0	228
1990	26	378	0	404
1995	17	360	0	377
2000	16	260	0	277
2005	19	227	(40)	246
2006	19	262	(50)	281
2007	18	266	(52)	284
2008	17	269	(55)	286
2009	17	255	(46)	272

SOURCE: Francis et al. 2008 and prior years.
NOTES: Each offering with a different premium or a different benefit package is counted as a separate plan; for example, Blue Cross standard and Blue Cross basic count as two plans because they differ significantly in benefits and premium costs. Consumer-driven plans are offered both nationally and locally and are included within those totals, respectively

Plan Choices. Until the emergence of competitive Medicare, the FEHBP was a unique government health insurance program in that, from its inception, instead of giving employees and annuitants one "take-it-or-leave-it" choice, the government has allowed and encouraged privately run health plans to compete for consumer enrollment.[2] Every fall, during the annual "open season," enrollees have been able to decide among a number of competing plans offering a range of attributes that include coverage, cost-sharing, network, and service. In practice, relatively few enrollees have changed plans. During the 1990s, for example, the average annual disenrollment rate (not counting discontinued plans) was about 9 percent for HMOs, 1.2 percent for the Blue Cross plans, and 3.6 percent for other national plans—an average of about 5 percent across all plans weighted for enrollment.[3] These figures correlate strongly with the age distribution of enrollees in these plans,

| Washington, D.C., metro area | | | |
National PPO	Local	Consumer-driven	Total
13	2	0	15
16	2	0	18
24	4	0	28
22	6	0	28
26	10	0	36
24	20	0	44
15	19	0	34
14	8	0	22
17	10	(6)	27
17	11	(6)	28
16	12	(7)	28
16	12	(7)	28
16	12	(7)	28

suggesting not only that consumers tend to "settle" into health plans and display brand loyalty to them, but also that they do so increasingly with age.

While the vast majority of enrollees remain with their current plan each year, the ones who move have an effect. It is possible to compare the total cost of the program as if no one changed plans with its total cost after open-season changes. Over the past decade and half, the resultant program-wide average of all premiums paid has decreased approximately .87 percent on average.[4] That is, open season choices reduced program costs by almost 1 percent compared to the *status quo ante*. This measurement does not, of course, include the most important effect of plan competition, which is the dynamic effect over time of plans adjusting their offerings to do better in the next open season. In earlier decades the annual decreases were larger, because enrollees obtained a higher proportion of savings from frugal plan choices (as discussed in later chapters).

While insurance plan choices were fewer at the inception of the program, in recent decades every enrollee has been able to choose from a dozen or more options. Today most can choose from twenty or more. Among them are national plans, including Blue Cross/Blue Shield, and plans sponsored by unions and employee associations, such as the American Postal Workers Union (APWU) and the Government Employees Hospital Association (GEHA). The national plans all use a PPO model, and all but one provide fee-for-service benefits out of network, with higher cost-sharing by enrollees. Choices in most areas also include Aetna, Humana, Kaiser, and many other HMO plans, and both national and local "consumer-driven" and high-deductible plans. Nationally, almost three hundred plan options are currently offered, as shown in table 2-1.

Although the total number of choices among national plans may seem scarcely diminished over time, in reality competition among these plans has been severely limited. Chapter 89 of Title 5 of the United States Code, the statute that authorizes the FEHBP, does not allow free entry of any plans besides HMOs and other local plans that the OPM deems "comprehensive." Throughout the history of the program many, if not most, of the national plans have been fringe contenders, sponsored by unions or other employee organizations with little or no aptitude for designing or administering health plans. In recent years the remaining sponsors have, with OPM encouragement, increasingly offered two or three plan options. But the number of contending sponsors has greatly fallen. During the 1980s, Congress allowed a special one-time period for additional union plans to enter the program, but all of those entrants have since left, unable to compete with the major, professionally administered plans with large enrollments. Unions or employee organizations such as the Mail Handlers, American Postal Workers Union, Government Employees Hospital Association, and National Association of Letter Carriers sponsor all of the remaining national plans, except for those offered by Blue Cross. Aetna offers two consumer-driven plans in virtually every state, however, which are effectively national even if labeled local, a reflection of OPM's creativity in dealing with a constraining statute.

Premiums. The FEHBP program is financed by premiums paid by current federal employees and retirees, as deductions from their salary or retirement checks or by direct payment by the government as an employer or pension payer on their behalf. The government pays most of the premium cost—up to 75 percent for annuitants and most employees, and even more for postal employees—for whatever health plan the employees or retirees choose. On average, this comes to about 70 percent of nominal premiums. Taking into account tax advantages, the government pays between 80 and 90 percent of premium costs for most employees, and about 70 percent for retirees.[5] While the program must certainly confront the prospect that several more decades of growth in per-capita health-care spending will raise the employer portion of health benefits from its current share of about one-tenth of total federal employee compensation on average, it faces no long-run insolvency issue remotely comparable to Medicare's.

Although premiums paid by different categories of enrollees differ based on employment status and whether or not payments are tax-preferred, the total self-only and family premiums paid to each plan are identical for all enrollees, young or old, and regardless of Medicare status. In contrast to Medicare, there is no geographic or risk adjustment.

The most notable feature of FEHBP premiums as faced by enrollees is that they vary widely among plans. In 2009, the range in the Washington, D.C., area for the enrollee share of a self-only enrollment, after tax savings, is from $420 to $1,700. On average, premiums are somewhat higher for the PPO plans than for others. For example, the most popular plan, the Blue Cross standard option, has a premium about $500 more than most HMOs. As shown in table 2-2, the median premium for an HMO plan in the D.C. area is about $700. Consumer-driven, high-deductible plans, a new feature in the program, are about the same. Taking into consideration the savings account they all provide, however, most have negative costs—that is, the premium is less than the savings account, and an enrollee who has low health-care costs can end the year with no net cost for insurance. The major difference between HMO and PPO plans that would justify paying a higher premium is that the national PPO and FFS plans offer far larger preferred provider panels, as well as out-of-network benefits that essentially allow unlimited choice of providers in return for significantly higher cost-sharing. In the FEHBP, enrollees have proved over the years to be consistently willing to pay more for broader provider choices.

Importantly, the premium contribution formula contains a maximum "cap," so that enrollees pay the full marginal cost (except for the roughly one-third discount provided by pretax status) of plans that cost close to average. This cap is 72 percent of the average cost of all plans for retirees and most employees.[6] For most employees and annuitants, the government pays

continued on page 54

TABLE 2-2

PLAN TYPES AND COSTS TO ENROLLEES
FOR WASHINGTON, D.C., EMPLOYEES, 2008

Plan code	Plan name	Plan type	Average cost, including premium and out-of-pocket cost
Local plans in the Washington, D.C., area			
221	Aetna HealthFund CDHP	CD/HD	$460
224	Aetna HealthFund HDHP	CD/HD	$1,090
E34	Kaiser–standard	HMO	$1,100
GZ1	Coventry HDHP	CD/HD	$1,250
E91	United HealthCare HDHP	CD/HD	$1,260
1G1	Coventry–high	HMO	$1,370
JN4	Aetna Open Access–basic	HMO	$1,410
E31	Kaiser–high	HMO	$1,440
1G4	Coventry–standard	HMO	$1,480
JP1	M.D. IPA	HMO	$1,500
2G1	CareFirst BlueChoice	HMO	$1,690
JN1	Aetna Open Access–high	HMO	$2,150
National plans when using preferred providers			
474	APWU CDHP	CD/HD	$650
481	Mail Handlers HDHP	CD/HD	$1,250
341	GEHA HDHP	CD/HD	$1,320
111	Blue Cross–basic	PPO only	$1,460
401	Foreign Service	PPO/FFS	$1,630
314	GEHA–standard	PPO/FFS	$1,670
414	Mail Handlers–value	PPO/FFS	$1,730
444	SAMBA–standard	PPO/FFS	$1,750
471	APWU–high	PPO/FFS	$1,790
421	Association	PPO/FFS	$1,830
104	Blue Cross–standard	PPO/FFS	$1,910
321	NALC	PPO/FFS	$1,950
454	Mail Handlers–standard	PPO/FFS	$2,010
381	Rural Carrier	PPO/FFS	$2,100
311	GEHA–high	PPO/FFS	$2,570
441	SAMBA–high	PPO/FFS	$2,840

SOURCES: Francis et al. 2008 and prior years (data shown here are from 2007 edition), and U.S. Office of Personnel Management 2008b and prior years.

Published premium	Premium after tax savings, less savings account	Average out-of-pocket cost
$980	($590)	$1,050
$800	($210)	$1,300
$730	$480	$620
$790	$30	$1,220
$1,070	($280)	$1,540
$1,180	$1,180	$190
$1,020	$680	$730
$1,540	$1,030	$410
$930	$620	$860
$1,410	$940	$560
$1,600	$1,070	$620
$2,300	$1,530	$620
$1,010	($490)	$1,140
$880	($220)	$1,470
$1,140	$40	$1,280
$1,020	$680	$780
$1,260	$840	$790
$870	$580	$1,090
$530	$400	$1,330
$1,190	$800	$950
$1,250	$870	$920
$1,510	$1,010	$820
$1,620	$1,080	$830
$1,530	$1,060	$890
$1,360	$950	$1,060
$2,390	$1,600	$500
$2,380	$1,590	$980
$2,820	$1,880	$960

NOTES: Entries are for self-only enrollments for nonpostal employees under age fifty-five. Plans are listed by average cost within two broad groups. Because money is fungible, premium cost after tax savings is also shown after any HRA or HSA contribution by the plan. This is net employee cost with no medical expenses because savings account carries over to next year.

continued from page 51

75 percent of the overall cost of each plan, up to that maximum amount. In 2009, the maximum government contribution toward plan premiums for almost all nonpostal employees and annuitants is about $4,000 for self-only enrollment and $9,000 for families. This compares to an average total premium cost for self-only of about $5,600 and for families of about $12,800 (enrollment-weighted average from OPM data on premium and enrollment for each plan). Employees pay the difference.

Hence, in 2009, enrollees are paying on average about $1,600 for self-only enrollment, and $3,800 for family enrollment. What is important, however, is not the average, but the fact that each retiree pays the full marginal cost of the amount by which his plan's premium exceeds the fixed dollar contribution, and each employee pays about two-thirds of the marginal cost, taking into account tax savings. Unlike many private employer benefits, where the employer may pay (for example) 75 percent of the cost of either an HMO or PPO plan enrollment, no matter how high the premium, the choice of a more expensive plan is subsidized far less under the FEHBP.

Each year, the maximum government contribution is recalculated based on a weighted estimate of the all-plan average premium cost. Thus, assuming that plan benefits do not change significantly (and, in general, they do not), and that costs are forecast accurately, the government's cost over time is dictated by the dynamic interplay between, on the one hand, plans' successes at controlling costs and providing better service and benefits, and, on the other, enrollees' decisions as to which plans to join. Of course, the participating plans exist in a national marketplace of both insurance firms and health care providers, and over time premiums rise roughly in step with underlying health care trends—but only "roughly," as discussed below.

Hence, the program is generally characterized as "premium-support," in contrast to the standard characterization of original Medicare as "defined-benefit." Note, however, that the version of premium support used in the FEHBP is one in which the government does not set absolute dollar caps or artificial limits on overall contribution. The government will not pay more than 72 percent of the all-plan average premium toward the premium of any one plan, but if average plan costs and premiums rise by 5 percent from one year to the next, the government contribution will, to a first approximation, rise equally. Because average health costs rise dramatically with age, average premium costs per self-only enrollment are less than one-half of those for Medicare, where per-enrollee costs are about $11,600 in 2009 for the average cost of enrollment in parts A, B, and D, including government spending and enrollee premium payments (U.S. Boards of Trustees 2009, 173). That figure corresponds essentially to the average self-only premium in the FEHBP of about $5,600.

There are about 4 million enrollments in the FEHBP, of which 1.9 million are self-only and 2.1 million are families, with almost 8 million covered lives. Total premium costs for the program (both government and enrollee share) in 2009 are about $38 billion (calculated from OPM premium and enrollment data). This is about one-fifth the number of enrollees as Medicare, but less than one-tenth the total cost.

Open Season. A prominent feature of the FEHBP is its "open season." Each fall, some 4 million eligible employees and annuitants can enroll in whatever plan they choose, or not enroll at all. Enrollees have approximately a month to choose (in the fall of 2008, from November 10 through December 8).[7] Enrollment changes take effect at the beginning of January (for retirees January 1; for others at the beginning of the first biweekly pay period in January). Plans cannot exclude coverage for any preexisting conditions or illnesses. Enrollees may switch to gain the best coverage for their conditions, and use the new plan without penalty. In prior decades, about 5 percent of enrollees switched plans in open season, and although data are unavailable for more recent years, there is no reason to believe that percentage has increased.

Open season (along with capped premium contribution and benefit design flexibility) is one of the three most important attributes of a system of plan choice. Without an annual open season, plans would have no opportunity to compete in benefits, premium cost, network of providers, and other service features. As a corollary of annual choice, however, adverse selection is a necessary result. For example, a couple planning to have a baby might switch from a high-deductible plan to one that provides first-dollar obstetrical coverage, and many do make changes like this. Other common reasons for switching among plans are to lower premium costs, to lower total costs including both premium and out-of-pocket expenses, or to obtain a desired preferred provider. Very importantly, it is common for aspects of service quality such as convenience in getting an appointment, ease of getting formulary exceptions, and other forms of red tape to influence whether enrollees "vote with their feet" to join other plans in open season.

As previously described, competitive Medicare uses this same approach, as specified in the MMA, in deliberate emulation of the FEHBP. Some important details differ among the FEHBP and the two Medicare systems, reflecting programmatic and administrative differences, but the basic model is identical: annual open season, benefit design flexibility, and capped premium contribution.

Benefit and Other Design Decisions. The U.S. Office of Personnel Management sets minimum financial, administrative, and benefit terms and conditions for every plan participating in the FEHBP. Benefit details are not, however, set in regulations and are proposed by plans, subject only to broad oversight by the OPM in a bargaining context focusing on cost to the program, value to enrollees, and prevention of deliberate risk discrimination. Insurance companies and the OPM agree each year on contracts setting forth both benefits and costs. When the OPM reviews plan bids and benefit proposals, it negotiates changes in each if they deviate substantially from reasonable expectations and general insurance industry practices or have major implications for the cost of the FEHBP.

Certain details are left almost entirely to plans. For example, in total contrast to original Medicare, but exactly as in competitive Medicare, the OPM does not establish payment rates for providers.[8] That job is left to plans. Nor does the OPM attempt to establish provider qualifications, accepting plan decisions (which rest, in turn, on state licensure requirements), although the OPM does insist on a general showing of network adequacy. And, although the OPM preempts states' decisions in the regulation of benefits for all national plans, in order to provide for uniform national benefits and make national plans possible, it does not preempt state mandates that apply to local plans.

As a result of the immense leeway provided for variations, plans, not surprisingly, differ in many ways on benefit details large and small. These variations are not greater than those found generally in the private insurance market, but are far more noticeable when plans compete head to head for enrollees.[9] Consequently, a substantial amount of consumer information becomes necessary to provide not only for informed choice, but to offer certainty to enrollees as to the benefits a particular plan choice provides. To meet this need, the OPM runs a comprehensive and informative website for FEHBP enrollees at www.opm.gov/insure, and provides both paper and electronic pamphlets and brochures to inform them about the premium cost, benefits, premium and benefit changes, and other details for each plan.

The weakest link in otherwise excellent consumer information services is that the OPM does not mail retirees an insurance guide remotely comparable in scope, quality, or information content to *Medicare & You*. While its online guide is very thorough, enrollees without Internet access are unlikely to see a copy. A strong point in comparison to Medicare, however, is that the OPM establishes standards for, and requires plans to publish in paper and online, insurance brochures that comprehensively describe all benefits in a common format and in reasonably plain English. Unlike with Medicare Advantage, it is not only possible but also reasonably easy to determine just what loopholes (if any) or conditions are present in any benefit category, whether as narrow as prosthetic devices or durable medical equipment, or as broad and important as the catastrophic limit.

Premiums for national plans in the FEHBP are primarily based on their expected—that is, "experience-rated"—costs. While the premiums for most HMO plans are based on their "community" rates, some are experience-rated. Interestingly, the OPM has long used a clever price-setting mechanism in which plans are required to give it essentially the lowest rates they offer any other plan sponsor. This is colloquially called the "most favored nation" bidding standard. Since HMOs virtually always offer comprehensive benefits, and premium rate-setting is well understood and the results subject to audit, negotiations are, by government standards, exceptionally simple. The OPM uses only a few dozen staff members to negotiate over almost three hundred plan options offered by almost a hundred different companies.

In sharp contrast to original Medicare, each plan is free to structure its benefit package within very broad negotiating limits that are not defined in law or regulation.[10] Copays, coinsurance, deductibles, covered services, limits on particular services, and catastrophic coverage are decided by each plan. The result is a wide diversity of benefit details, although all plans provide close to 90 percent coverage of average expected medical expenses.

continued on page 60

TABLE 2-3

COST-SHARING IN NATIONAL AND WASHINGTON, D.C., AREA PLANS, 2008

Plan code	Plan name (listed in alphabetical order within group)	Savings account for self/ family	Per person/ per family	Deductibles ($) Extra for hospital stay	Extra for drugs
Local plans in D.C. area when using preferred providers					
221-2	Aetna HealthFund CDHP	$1,250/$2,500	$750/$1,500	None	None
224-5	Aetna HealthFund HDHP	$750/$1,500	$1,500/$3,000	None	None
JN1-2	Aetna Open Access–high	NA	None	$300*	None
JN4-5	Aetna Open Access–basic	NA	None	None	None
2G1-2	CareFirst BlueChoice	NA	None	$100	None
IG1-2	Coventry–high	NA	None	None	None
IG4-5	Coventry–standard	NA	$250/$500	$400*	None
GZ1-2	Coventry HDHP	$500/$1,000	$1,500/$3,000	None	None
E31-2	Kaiser–high	NA	None	$100	None
E34-5	Kaiser–standard	NA	None	$500*	None
JP1-2	M.D. IPA	NA	None	$300*	None
E91-2	United Healthcare HDHP	$1,000/$2,000	$2,000/$4,000	None	None
National plans when using preferred providers					
471-2	APWU–high	NA	$275/$550	None	None
474-5	APWU CDHP	$1,200/$2,400	$600/$1,200	None	None
421-2	Association	NA	$300/$600	$100	None
104-5	Blue Cross–standard	NA	$300/$600	$100	None
111-2	Blue Cross–basic	NA	None	$250*	None
401-2	Foreign Service	NA	$300/$600	None	None
311-2	GEHA–high	NA	$350/$700	$100	None
314-5	GEHA–standard	NA	$350/$700	None	None
341-2	GEHA HDHP	$720/$1,440	$1,500/$3,000	None	None
454-5	Mail Handlers–standard	NA	$350/$700	$200	None
414-5	Mail Handlers–value	NA	$500/$1,000	None	None
481-2	Mail Handlers HDHP	$845/$1,690	$2,000/$4,000	$300*	None
321-2	NALC	NA	$250/$500	None	None
381-2	Rural Carrier	NA	$350/$700	$100	$200
441-2	SAMBA–high	NA	$250/$500	$200	None
444-5	SAMBA–standard	NA	$250/$500	$200	None

SOURCES: Francis et al. 2008 and prior years. Data in this table are from the 2007 edition.

Hospital room and board (%)	Other hospital inpatient (%)	Visit to primary care ($ or %)	Visit to specialist ($ or %)	Generic local pharmacy	Name brand local pharmacy	Generic mail order 90 day	Name brand mail order 90 day
10%	10%	10%	10%	$10	$25	$20	$80
10%	10%	10%	10%	$10	$25	$20	$80
None	None	$15	$25	$5	$25	$10	$50
10%	10%	$20	$30	$10	$25	$20	$50
None	None	$20	$30	$10	$25	$20	$50
None	None	$10	$20	$10	$20	$20	$40
None	None	$10	$20	$10	$20	$20	$40
None	None	None	None	None	$25	None	$50
None	None	$10	$20	$7	$25	$10	$46
None	None	$20	$30	$12	$30	$20	$56
None	None	$15	$30	$7	$25	$21	$75
10%	10%	10%	10%	$10	$30	$25	$75
10%	10%	$18*	$18*	$8	25%	$15	25%
15%	15%	15%	15%	$10	25%	$15	25%
None	None	10%	10%	$5	$25	$10	$50
None	None	$15	$15	25%	25%	$10	$35
None	None	$20	$30	$10	$30	NA	NA
None	None	10%	10%	$10	25%*	$20	$40
None	10%	$20	$20	$5	25%	$15	25%
15%	15%	$10	$25	$5	50%	$15	50%
5%	5%	5%	5%	25%	25%	25%	25%
None	15%	$10–$20	$10–$20	$10	$40	$15	$65
20%	20%	20%	20%	$10	50%	$30	50%
None	None	$15	$15	$10	$25	$20	$50
None	10%	$20	$20	25%	25%	$12	$35
None	None	$20	$30	30%	30%	$15	$28
None	10%	$20	$20	$10	$25	$10	$45
None	15%	$20	$20	$10	$30	$20	25%

Enrollee pays after deductibles and after using savings account: ————Prescription drugs ($ or %)————

NOTE: * Approximation, due to complicated reimbursement structure of this plan.

continued from page 57

Table 2-3 summarizes the coverages and copays of the twenty-eight plans offered in the Washington, D.C., metropolitan area in 2008. All but one of the national plans and several local plans also offered out-of-network benefits that are not shown. Notice that although details varied widely, all plans had robust coverage. Also not shown in this table, catastrophic cost protection was provided in all plans. For example, all of the "consumer-driven" and high deductible plans (CDHP and HDHP in the table) offered loophole-free catastrophic cost limits set between $3,000 and $5,000 for self-only enrollments.

Very importantly, these differences reflect plan decisions as influenced by consumer choices and broad stewardship from the OPM. Congress sets not one of these benefit details. Indeed, when interest groups approach Congress to ask for earmarked benefits, it is easy to avoid a congressional decision because the answers always are that "some plans provide your benefit and if it is as valuable to enrollees as you say, it will grow over time through enrollee decisions" and "in this program those decisions are made by plans, not the government." In total contrast, every one of these kinds of benefit details (and there are hundreds more) is prescribed in detailed statutory provisions in original Medicare, and if the statute is not specific enough, the Centers for Medicare and Medicaid Services issues a regulation setting it in stone.

In a system operated entirely under private auspices, benefit and coverage flexibility might not loom so importantly. It will do so, however, in any context in which a legislative body can set benefit design based on, first, the idiosyncratic views of a handful of powerful committee members and, second, the rent-seeking influence of a myriad of special interest groups with millions or hundreds of millions of dollars at stake. The thousands of "benefit mandates" established by state legislatures, and in original Medicare by Congress, demonstrate that such results are inherent in American-style political systems. In the FEHBP, any benefit mandate would necessarily be an assault on the very structure of the program, and Congress has been both constrained and restrained as a result. Hence, the hegemony of plan decisions in benefit design is an essential feature of competitive plan systems for political as well as for consumer sovereignty reasons.

Variation in Plan Premiums. As a result of these design features, most notably the cap on the government contribution to plan premiums, the enrollee share of the annual premium varies widely among plans. In 2008, it ranged from about $500 to over $2,800 for individuals, and from about $1,300 to almost $7,000 for families. These substantial premium differences are due to a number of factors:

- *Plans vary in the kinds of enrollees they attract.* Some plans have a disproportionate share of older, and hence higher-cost, enrollees who joined when premiums were lower and do not realize that their plan is no longer a good buy, or who are simply "set in their ways," or who find good nonmonetary value in their plans. These plans face higher costs that have to be made up by higher premiums. Premiums in some plans considerably exceed the actuarial value of their benefits. Because there is no risk adjustment of government premium contributions based on even the simplest measures (for example, age and Medicare status of enrollees), these differences are not attenuated.

- *Plans vary in the generosity of their benefits.* Although all plans have at least good benefits, some have superb benefits. Since the better benefits generally cost more, sometimes a good deal more, and the government contribution is fixed, the enrollee share of premium varies directly with the cost of benefit generosity.

- *Plans vary in how well they manage costs.* Well-run HMOs commonly use case management to reduce hospital costs by 25 percent or more compared to traditional insurance. At present, the national plans, once pure fee-for-service plans and now predominantly preferred provider organization plans, all review utilization and use panels of preferred providers. In contrast to original Medicare, which, as a practical matter, almost all providers are forced to join through economic necessity, wasteful providers can be dropped from preferred status without costing them their livelihoods.

- *Plans vary widely in unmeasured aspects of service quality.* Some plans offer better service—such as less red tape, more courteous 800-number operators, and more responsive providers—than others. One of the few efforts to evaluate service quality estimated that roughly half the differences among plans in open season "quit rate" disenrollment were due to variation in service quality, not to such factors as costs or premiums (Francis 1986).

The FEHBP has operated essentially unchanged throughout its almost fifty-year life span, except for periodic increases in the government's share of premiums. Again differing sharply from original Medicare, the program's main parameters have always been a broad and diverse array of plan types and plan choices, competition among these plans through consumer choices, free entry of local (but not national) plans, payment (until recently) by consumers of the full marginal cost of costly plan choices, benefit and customer-service decisions as well as cost decisions made by consumers through their plan selections, administrative simplicity, and the near-total absence of political domination of all of these processes and decisions.

The Evolution of the FEHBP

FEHBP structural changes have been relatively few and modest, particularly compared to Medicare. While Congress at least tinkers (and often does much more) almost every year with Medicare benefit details and payment rules, plans in the FEHBP make their own payment decisions. For the first thirty-five years of the program there were no statutory changes of any consequence other than a half-dozen increases in the "government share" of premiums. These increases cumulatively raised the government share from less than half to about 70 percent, on average. This increase was even larger than it appears on the surface, because until "premium conversion" gave tax-preferred status to the enrollee share of the premium (a development discussed extensively in later chapters), only the government share was exempted from income taxation. As a result, the after-tax income of enrollees went up about a third more than the nominal size of any increase in government contribution.

The evolution of benefits and cost-sharing and the interaction between plans and enrollees have, however, been largely determined by market decisions since the program's inception, with little government-forced change.

From the beginning of the program there was an annual open season, with a one-year commitment to a plan chosen from a broad array of plan types, a design model that did not arrive in comparable form in Medicare until the enactment of the MMA in 2003 and the operational implementation of Medicare Advantage and the new Medicare prescription drug plans in 2006. FEHBP plans came and went, benefits steadily improved, the number and market share of HMO plans hugely increased, and PPO/FFS hybrids largely replaced pure fee-for-service plans; but the basic program design continued unchanged (other than for adjustments related to the creation and growth of Medicare and Medicare's effects on retirees, discussed later in this analysis) until premium conversion radically altered the marginal-cost calculus in 2001.

Throughout the 1980s the participation of HMOs in the FEHBP grew rapidly, mirroring their growth in the private insurance market. When the HMO market was shaken over heavy-handed "managed-care" practices, and the industry for that and other reasons shed dozens of companies and merged dozens of others, the number of HMO plans participating in the FEHBP decreased radically. Some HMOs also left the program, however, because they were unable to attract sufficient numbers of enrollees to make worthwhile the time and trouble of complying with the minimal (by government standards) red tape of the FEHBP. This was often the result of simple demographics, since government employees in most smaller cities are scarce. Many HMOs were unable to compete effectively in the larger cities, where they faced many competitors.

One of the peculiarities and major flaws of the FEHBP program is that it does not allow free entry of national plans. Although the founding statute "grandfathered" the national fee-for-service plans participating in the program in 1959, it only allowed free entry subsequently for local plans—originally all HMOs, and, in recent years, consumer-driven, high-deductible plans as well. A quarter-century ago Congress allowed a one-time, one-year opportunity for additional union-sponsored plans to join, but the resulting increase in hastily created plans targeted at particular union members led to only a temporary blip in the number of FFS/PPO plans. The OPM has been creative in allowing national plans to modify and expand their offerings of different options, and one plan currently offers three. In recent years, the most significant changes in national plans have come from new consumer-driven, high-deductible offerings encouraged by the OPM. These plans have attracted only small numbers of enrollees, despite being better buys than most traditional plans and rated as such in the widely used *CHECKBOOK's Guide* (Francis et al. 2008 and prior years).[11]

The original FEHBP statute actually set premiums at specified dollar amounts. In 1966 it was changed so as to set the overall government contribution at 40 percent of premium, with a 50 percent maximum contribution toward any plan. In 1971, while retaining the 50 percent maximum, the statute was changed to a "big six" plans formula. Invented at a time when the vast majority of federal employees were enrolled in a relative handful of plans, this formula pegged FEHBP premiums to the simple average premium of two "government-wide" national plans, the two largest national union plans, and the two largest HMOs. In 1975 the overall contribution was set at 60 percent of the average premium of the "big six" plans, with a maximum contribution of 75 percent.

Unforeseen by the drafters, the "big six" over time enrolled a disproportionate number of higher-cost retirees, and the average premium contribution therefore drifted upward to about 72 percent of the all-plan average.[12] By 1995, when Congress decided to modernize the formula by using an enrollee-weighted, all-plan average premium, anything below a 72 percent government contribution would have meant a benefit reduction, and that accidental percentage was ratified in the new legislation. As a result, a program which had originally paid only about 40 percent of premium, and allowed employees to retain half of all savings from enrolling in less expensive plans, was over the years radically changed to one in which enrollee exposure to marginal premium costs or savings was greatly reduced. All these changes were made in the name of improved fringe benefits; none was debated or decided or "scored" in terms of potential consequences for future growth in FEHBP costs.

In 1983, Congress mandated Medicare Part A coverage for all federal employees, regardless of years of Social Security coverage. While some federal retirees had previously earned Part A coverage based on pre– or post–federal employment, most were not covered by Part A or Part B. Retirees simply stayed in the same plans at age sixty-five that had served them at age sixty-four; the plans did not change, and the coverage remained good regardless of age. Medicare had already begun to inspire major changes in both plan and retiree behavior, however. Since Medicare was "primary," and since retirees were in the same rating pool as employees of all ages, plans could greatly reduce both their costs and, in most cases, the enrollee share of premiums, dollar for dollar, by enlisting older retirees to enroll in Medicare parts A and B.

Hence, most national plans in the 1970s, and virtually all by the 1980s, added special inducements for retirees to join Medicare. These inducements were straightforward. If a retiree participated in Medicare Part A, all hospital cost-sharing would be waived, without limit. If a retiree participated in Medicare Part B, all outpatient cost-sharing would be waived, without limit. These incentives had predictable effects on enrollment in Medicare, as explained below. They also had undesirable effects on both programs, by encouraging unnecessary utilization.

In 1984, in a change little noticed at the time, and whose precise motives are lost in the fog of history (but were likely rooted in the budgetary scoring rules of Congress), Congress enacted a Medicare statutory provision crafted in the House Ways and Means Committee (which does not have FEHBP jurisdiction) that prohibited FEHBP plans from subsidizing Part B premiums. The congressional budget process has, in most years, assigned ceilings to spending on programs based on committee jurisdiction. A reasonable speculation as to the origins of this prohibition is that if Ways and Means and the Senate Finance Committee could move some budgetary obligations to the committees with jurisdiction over the FEHBP, using legislation under their unilateral control, they could enhance their ability to spend on other programs under their jurisdiction, at no apparent cost to their "own" programs. While in theory the committees with jurisdiction over the FEHBP could have objected, it is doubtful they had any more insight than the committees with Medicare jurisdiction as to the tens of billions of dollars this seemingly trivial change would ultimately cost both programs.

This provision had two effects. First, it saved the Medicare program's budget some amount of money (as it turned out, a negligible amount) by attempting to discourage dual enrollment in the two programs. Since Medicare was the primary insurer, this benefited the Medicare trust funds on a one-for-one basis at the expense of the FEHBP trust funds—to a first approximation a complete budgetary wash, though not a wash in terms of scoring by committee jurisdiction. It did not, however, prevent plans from using benefit improvements to create inducements to enroll in both programs. In fact, it strongly encouraged plans to take this step, and they did, to ensure first-dollar payment by Medicare and reduce their FEHBP cost. As a result, it had the unplanned effect of significantly expanding utilization and costs for most federal retirees, who now had the ability—costless to them— of obtaining unlimited medical care. As the primary insurance program, Medicare assumed the great majority of this cost. Hence, the FEHBP was able to reduce its costs because Medicare was paying over two-thirds of the cost of retirees ages sixty-five and over.[13] A happy paper result was achieved in the short term for the committees in charge of Medicare, but both enrollees and taxpayers were the losers as utilization and costs increased.

The next major event in the history of the program was abortive. After an extensive internal and external set of reviews (see U.S. Congressional Research Service 1989), the then director of OPM proposed to abolish the FEHBP as it then existed and adopt what was essentially the Medicare model. The proposed reform would have allowed HMOs to continue to participate (as they already did in Medicare), but it would have eliminated consumer-driven competition and relied instead on the federal procurement system to control costs in administering a single fee-for-service plan whose benefit details would be determined in law and regulation.[14] Luckily, the proposal had few political pluses and many negatives (violating the "do no harm to vested interests" principle) and was never considered seriously by Congress.

A major adverse "reform" befell the FEHBP during the Bill Clinton administration: The OPM director convinced the administration—with Congress acquiescing—that to attract good talent, a "modern" civil service should have the same tax advantages as those offered to Fortune 500 employees. Hence, federal employees obtained flexible spending accounts (FSAs) that would provide a tax preference through the use of "pretax" dollars for out-of-pocket spending. FSAs, however, only cover predictable out-of-pocket expenses. The big-ticket tax preference is for what the OPM calls "premium conversion," which provides the same tax preference to pay the "employee share" of health insurance premiums. Premium conversion was glowingly described by the then OPM director as "another tool in our strategic toolbox . . . [that] keeps us competitive in the war for talent" (Lachance 2000).[15] This new benefit produced a direct one-third reduction in the cost to employees of the enrollee share of health insurance premiums.

Long a tax loophole for private-sector and state and local government employees, premium conversion had been denied to federal employees because it would merely move costs from one federal government pocket to another rather than impose them on a third party. Retirees were not eligible for it in either the public or private sector, however, which has provided a mobilizing cause for federal retiree lobbyists ever since. Employees who used to pay on average about 30 percent of the cost of health insurance now paid on average only about 20 percent.[16]

For corporations, premium conversion makes some selfish sense, since it increases the taxpayer-financed subsidy of employee wages. The corporation bears no cost; instead, the taxpayer at large foots even more of the bill for health insurance offered to its employees. In the case of the federal government, however, premium conversion makes no sense as a cost-shifting strategy since, in this case, the employer has to foot the cost of the change. For employees the change in cost is real but unperceived, because it reduces tax payments; but employee compensation could have been increased in the same dollar amount in any one year's government-wide salary increase—at a cost of about one-half of 1 percent added to the usual 2 or 3 percent. This would have prevented two bad effects for employees: the earmarking of higher compensation for health insurance costs instead of whatever other goods and services they might have preferred (such as retirement savings or college tuition), and the reduction of the competitive pressures that had kept FEHBP health insurance costs in check, thereby increasing future-year premium increases.

Premium conversion reduces the competitive advantage of plans in keeping costs and premiums low, because employees no longer pay the full marginal cost of premiums that are higher than average. Their already small share of savings from choosing lower-cost plans is likewise reduced by about a third (the average marginal tax bracket for federal employees, including all federal and state taxes; Francis et al. 2008, 116). The relatively poor performance of the FEHBP in cost containment over the past decade compared to earlier years (discussed below) is due in large part to premium conversion. Of course, the prohibition on plan payment of Medicare premiums, and the consequent inducement to eliminate most cost-sharing for retirees, has further contributed to this result. Increases in prescription drug costs have also played a role.

Two final examples of system change in the FEHBP are worthy of note. First, since 2005, a number of participating insurance companies have, at OPM urging, been introducing consumer-driven, high-deductible plans.[17] These plans offer a potentially important way to reduce unnecessary health-care utilization and insurance costs over time, and appear to be doing so successfully and without adverse effects of any kind in the private sector (American Academy of Actuaries 2009). To date, however, they have had negligible effect in the FEHBP, attracting only about 39,000 enrollees (1 percent of total FEHBP enrollment) in 2008. Second, since 2007, dental and vision plans have been offered to federal employees and annuitants. These plans are entirely separate from the health plans, though many of those continue to offer modest dental benefits. Their premiums are paid fully by enrollees, but are tax-advantaged and hence discounted by about a third for employees. As of 2008, about 1 million employees and retirees (one-fourth of total FEHBP enrollment) had joined a dental plan. The availability of these plans reduces the value of these benefits in FEHBP plans, and over time will reduce dental benefits and, hence, dental costs and plan premium in FEGBP plans. Dental benefits, however, are a small part of overall premium costs, so this effect will be small.

Medicare and the FEHBP Joined at the Hip

Because the FEHBP includes retirees in the same pool as active employees, and because Medicare is primary for retired workers covered under both plans, Medicare has played a role in FEHBP finances and practices from its inception. That role was minor at first, because most federal retirees did not have the required forty quarters of Social Security coverage to become eligible for Medicare Part A, and usually chose not to sign up for Part B.[18] Since 1983, however, with Medicare Part A eligibility automatic for all present and future federal employees, enrollment in both parts A and B has become by far the most usual decision of federal retirees ages sixty-five and over.

As shown in table 2-4, a significant but slowly dwindling number of annuitants are without Medicare Part A. These pre-1983 retirees, whose numbers have been diminishing as a natural result of time passing, constituted in 2006 about 14 percent of annuitants ages sixty-five and over. Another

11 percent, slightly increasing in recent years, decline to join Part B. This group will become much larger in the future as a result of two factors. First, Medicare Part B is providing less value over time. The annual cost of the Part B premium was $650 for calendar year 2002. For 2009 it is $1,160, an increase of $510. In the Blue Cross standard option, by far the most popular plan with retirees, the effect of Part B enrollment is to eliminate the need to pay a $300 deductible and $20 physician visit copay. Neither the deductible nor the copay amount has increased in real terms over the last decade. (Although both were raised in the last two years, this merely halted the erosion of this cost-sharing.) The two dozen physician visits that used to justify paying the Part B premium cost no longer do so. This substantial reduction in the value of Part B affects all those ages sixty-five and over who are enrolled in Part B, regardless of plan. Second, with premiums now subject to income-testing, higher-income retirees will likely drop Part B as they find it prohibitively expensive in relation to its benefits (in 2009, some high-income elderly are paying a Part B premium of $3,700).

The data in this table demonstrate that Medicare plays a large role in the finances of the FEHBP. Annuitants over age sixty-five with Medicare Part A or both parts A and B constitute some 1.16 million of total FEHBP enrollments of 4.0 million. Enrollment data alone, however, understate the magnitude of this role. Medical Expenditure Panel Survey (MEPS) data from the Agency for Healthcare Research and Quality show that in 2006 the average cost for medical, drug, and dental expenses for a person under age thirty-five was about $1,900, for a person age thirty-five to forty-four about $3,500, for a person age forty-five to fifty-four about $5,400, and for a person age fifty-five to sixty-four about $7,200. The average for those ages sixty-five and over was about $10,100—about five times as high as the youngest group and about double the average for employees.[19] Persons ages sixty-five and over represent about one-third of total FEHBP enrollment, but, as a result of these cost differences, they account for about half of total FEHBP spending. Medicare pays about two-thirds the combined medical, drug, and dental cost for those with both parts A and B, and about one-third the cost of those with just Part A, so it finances almost half of the cost of retirees ages sixty-five and over and almost one-fourth of total FEHBP costs.

While Medicare finances a large fraction of the cost of the FEHBP, the opposite is not true. Medicare is almost always primary, and, in any event,

TABLE 2-4

MEDICARE ENROLLMENT BY FEDERAL RETIREES AGES 65 AND OVER

Year	—Without Medicare A—		—With Medicare A only—	
	Number (K)	Percentage of retirees ages 65 and over	Number (K)	Percentage of retirees ages 65 and over
1995	267	21%	107	8%
1996	270	20%	112	8%
1997	292	22%	114	8%
1998	252	19%	125	9%
1999	230	17%	127	9%
2000	212	15%	128	9%
2001	222	16%	137	10%
2002	207	15%	139	10%
2003	204	15%	138	10%
2004	194	14%	139	10%
2005	NA	NA	NA	NA
2006	193	14%	141	11%
2007	197	15%	149	11%
2008	192	14%	163	12%

SOURCE: Unpublished data from the U.S. Office of Personnel Management, Office of Actuaries.

the relative sizes of the programs make FEHBP influences small in context. Indeed, the FEHBP actually contributes to Medicare costs, rather than saving Medicare money. About 90 percent of Medicare enrollees have some form of Medicare augmentation, most commonly plans (such as the FEHBP) from former employers, Medigap plans, and Medicaid. These persons also experience diminished cost-sharing, and the resulting increased utilization is undoubtedly a major cause of the substantial wasteful spending in Medicare. Rettenmaier and Saving (2007), Feldman (2008), and many other students of Medicare recommend prohibiting the purchase of Medigap plans. One million federal retirees with Medicare would cost the program about $12 billion a year without supplemental coverage; with supplementation, at least an additional 20 percent is spent unnecessarily (see the analysis below). Accordingly, the FEHBP wastes about $2.5 billion a year in Medicare

| ———With Medicare A and B——— | | With Medicare A, |
Number (K)	Percentage of retirees ages 65 and over	or A and B, as as percentage of total FEHBP enrollment
927	71%	27%
945	71%	27%
941	70%	27%
982	72%	28%
1,010	74%	29%
1,032	75%	30%
1,062	75%	29%
1,049	75%	29%
1,031	75%	29%
1,024	75%	29%
NA	NA	NA
1,006	75%	29%
998	74%	29%
1,005	74%	29%

NOTE: There are also relatively small numbers of FEHBP enrollees below age sixty-five with Medicare, or with Part B only.

funds in return for the roughly $10 billion a year that Medicare contributes to the financing of the program.

This calculation follows from one of the most robust findings of health economics, arising originally from the RAND health insurance experiment of the 1970s and buttressed by a good deal of additional research: Cost-sharing matters a great deal.[20] When cost-sharing is low, utilization and spending both grow—a lot—compared to when levels of cost-sharing are higher. Two recent studies summarize the evidence. Michael Morrisey finds moderate price sensitivity in the use of health services, varying by service, but overall on the order of a price elasticity of demand of about .2 (Morrisey 2005). Jonathan Gruber focuses on both price sensitivity and health outcomes and finds that "the lessons from the HIE are very clear: higher co-insurance rates, with an out-of-pocket limit, can significantly reduce health

TABLE 2-5

HMO AND FFS/PPO ENROLLMENT BY RETIREMENT STATUS IN THE FEHBP

(Enrollees in thousands)

Year	————Employees————			————Annuitants————		
	FFS/PPO	HMO	HMO percentage of total	FFS/PPO	HMO	HMO percentage of total
1985	1,842	462	20%	1,299	119	8%
1990	1,560	886	36%	1,407	176	11%
1995	1,174	937	44%	1,733	262	13%
2000	1,342	877	40%	1,557	307	16%
2005	1,458	722	33%	1,539	300	16%
2006	1,466	693	32%	1,539	305	17%
2007	1,509	646	30%	1,543	305	17%
2008	1,565	594	28%	1,566	301	16%

SOURCE: Unpublished data from the U.S. Office of Personnel Management, Office of Actuaries.

care use without sacrificing health outcomes," albeit with risks to one sub-group: those with high medical risks and low income (Gruber 2006, 8). The converse is also true: "Free" health care increases health-care utilization and cost significantly, as much as half again for outpatient care, according to the RAND results.

Recall that FEHBP plans can attract Medicare enrollees, or persuade their enrollees to join Medicare, only by offering better benefits. FEHBP benefits are good to begin with, and the decision reached by almost all national plans (but relatively few HMOs) is to waive all deductibles and other cost-sharing for services covered by parts A and B and the plan. Hospital and physician care become free, and network restrictions are eliminated. As a predictable result, shown in table 2-5, retirees disproportionately and overwhelmingly congregate in FFS/PPO plans.

The majority of the retired enrollees are in the Blue Cross standard option, with 1,041,000 out of 1,867,000 annuitants in 2008. That plan's premium is somewhat above average, and quite expensive when coupled with Medicare's. A retired couple with Medicare parts A and B will pay over $6,500 in 2009 for two Medicare Part B premiums and the Blue Cross family premium. For that payment they obtain 100 percent coverage of virtually all inpatient and outpatient costs, and a good prescription drug benefit. That same couple could reduce its premium costs to about $4,300 by switching to the Government Employees Hospital Association standard option, saving over $2,000 (the comparable savings in 2007 was $1,500). Under GEHA, they would also obtain 100 percent medical coverage, but would have an inferior prescription drug benefit. If their drug costs were low, this would be irrelevant. If their drug costs were high, they could join an inexpensive Part D drug plan, with the combined drug coverage about as good as under Blue Cross. This would, however, generate increased paperwork, as they would have to file drug claims with two plans.

Another option would be to switch to a low-premium HMO, and use Medicare as the equivalent of an opt-out "point-of-service" benefit when and if they want an out-of-network provider. A fourth option would be to drop Medicare Part B and enjoy at age sixty-five that same Blue Cross plan they found satisfactory at age sixty-four, spending one-third less in total premium costs. A final option would be to join a Medicare Advantage plan and suspend their FEHBP enrollment, thereby reducing their premium costs by two-thirds but also reducing their benefits. (For a fuller description of these choices, see Francis et al. 2008 and prior years.) A factor overriding these mere dollar considerations is that the extra benefit of joining Part B enables those retirees in Blue Cross standard (but not Blue Cross basic), GEHA, and other national plans to escape entirely PPO network limitations. Cost-sharing is zero, whether or not preferred providers are used. As these examples suggest, consumer choice among health plans can involve issues rather more complex than simply comparing the costs and benefits of competing plans.

Overriding all other factors to many enrollees, joint enrollment in both the FEHBP and Medicare provides prudent "political insurance" against future legislation or other government actions to cut back or increase premiums or otherwise damage one program or the other.

The Dominance of Blue Cross

The Blue Cross plans have long dominated the FEHBP. As shown later in table 3-1, from 1984 to 2002 the Blue Cross plans share of total enrollment rose from 39 percent to 51 percent. In 2009 it reached 62 percent of all enrollees. (In Medicare Advantage, concentration is far lower, with the largest firm, UnitedHealth, enrolling fewer than one-fifth of enrollees.)

This may appear an alarming trend, but is arguably not. First, Blue Cross is not a single dominant firm, but an association of sixty-four individual companies that share that 62 percent. Nor is the FEHBP experience substantially out of line with the overall private market, where Blue Cross plans average a 50 percent market share. Second, Blue Cross operates two competing plans in the FEHBP. The basic option was created in 2002 and has grown from 88 thousand enrollees to 550 thousand enrollees in 2009. Meanwhile, the standard option had 1,977 thousand enrollees in 2002 and 1,932 thousand enrollees in 2009, decreasing slightly from 49 to 48 percent of total enrollment. As shown previously in table 2-2, the basic option is a substantially less costly plan. It is also a network-only plan, and like most HMOs, has no coverage outside the network. Hence, the recent history of Blue Cross is that it has introduced a successful new model that is substantially outperforming HMOs, other national plans, and its own sibling plan in attracting enrollees. Third, among employees, the standard option has only about a 42 percent market share in 2009, and the basic option a share of 22 percent. The standard option dominates enrollment only among retirees with a 55 percent share, a market segment where basic option only attracts a 4 percent share.

As discussed previously in this chapter, Blue Cross and other national plans have substantially different offerings for retirees with Medicare, covering all hospital and medical costs for retirees with Parts A and B, without network limitations. But there are several other popular national plans, such as NALC and GEHA standard option, which offer this feature at far lower premium costs. Over time, Blue Cross standard option is highly likely to lose share in that market as well if other plans continue to have superior offerings.

PART II

Dimensions of FEHBP and Medicare Performance

The Natural Experiment:
The FEHBP versus Medicare

The parallel evolution of Medicare and the Federal Employees Health Benefits Program over the same period of time in the same economy and health-care environment provides a natural experiment between two competing models of insurance design. Nothing could be more dramatically different than the statist, government-administered, single-payer original Medicare program and the "hands-off," consumer-driven FEHBP.

There are five potential "threats to validity" for this comparison, however, as well as a number of comparisons that are largely irrelevant, which we will review briefly here by way of introduction to the much more germane comparisons on which this study will focus.

Threats to Validity

Five factors pose threats to the validity of a comparison of Medicare and the FEHBP, and we must take them into consideration before moving on to the analysis that comprises part 2 of this book.

First, as analyzed in the previous chapter, these two programs do not operate completely independently of one another. The impact of Medicare on the benefit design and overall costs of FEHBP plans is particularly substantial and has grown over time.

Second, these programs have changed since their inception. During the 1960s and 1970s, they performed in prototypical fashion as competing models. Original Medicare was virtually the entire Medicare program, and FEHBP enrollees originally faced the full marginal costs of their plan choices. Since then, however, Medicare has added an increasingly robust private plan component that is, in some respects, better designed to be competitive than the FEHBP. Meanwhile, the FEHBP's design has changed incrementally in ways that, cumulatively, greatly diminish its likely competitive performance. The most important of these changes lie in the increasing government subsidy of premiums and the decreasing enrollee share of marginal premium costs that has resulted, in the last decade, in enrollees' retaining only about one-eighth of the savings from joining plans whose costs were below average. These changes, which have not occurred in orderly timelines, make sorting out causality very difficult.

The third problem is that Medicare has likely influenced the healthcare market in ways that not only have raised the costs of both programs, but also may have disadvantaged the FEHBP. Amy Finkelstein argues that Medicare itself has caused a large part of the per-capita increase in healthcare spending in the last four decades, and that the growth in health insurance generally over that period may explain 40 percent or more of that increase (Finkelstein 2005). Assuming this estimate is roughly correct, it may be that the overall impact on both programs in their roles as payers was neutral. But Medicare is no longer the passive payer that it was in its first two decades. It is now an active price controller, and may be paying some providers below their cost of providing service. In particular, the possibility or probability of cost-shifting could mean that the more successful Medicare is in reducing its payments below cost, the more payments from FEHBP plans and other private payers must rise. There seems to be little agreement among researchers as to whether, and if so to what extent, cost-shifting is real. Michael Morrisey argues that cost-shifting by hospitals is all but impossible under standard economic theory, whether or not they have market power (Morrisey 1994 and 2003). Allen Dobson argues the contrary (Dobson et al. 2006), as have others (Ginsburg 2003; Lee et al. 2003). A recent study of California hospitals estimates that the effects are real and substantial, though they comprise only about one-third of the private payer revenue-to-cost ratio as conventionally measured (Kessler 2007).

What is undisputed is that there are large observed payment differentials between Medicare and Medicaid as compared to private payers, that hospitals are essentially obliged by law and implicit but coercive community pressure to take elderly patients at virtually any rate Medicare pays by fiat, and that they can do so profitably in an otherwise competitive market so long as the Medicare payment exceeds marginal cost. "Joint costs" can be charged to private plans, and they are. Regardless of the extent of cost-shifting, the FEHBP plans undoubtedly suffer from it to the same unknown degree as they do in their overall insurance business, and as do other insurers.

The fourth problem is that the effects of the tax preferences for employer-sponsored health insurance, and those for both Medicare payments and former employer payments on behalf of retirees,[1] have also very substantially and adversely influenced the growth and level of health-care spending in the United States over the past half-century (Helms 1999 and 2008). While these effects have undoubtedly hampered both programs' ability to control costs, they may have affected one program more than the other. For example, original Medicare is often slower than the private sector to adopt expensive new technologies or procedures, but has fewer tools to prevent unnecessary utilization.

The fifth and, arguably, by far the most important problem is that both programs are rife with moral hazard.[2] Roughly 90 percent of Medicare enrollees have supplementary insurance through Medicaid, Medigap, or employer plans (including the FEHBP and TRICARE for Life, the military retiree program). These people are not enrolled in programs with the nominal cost-sharing found in the official Medicare benefits. They typically pay nothing, or almost nothing, for inpatient, outpatient, and, often, prescription drug services. The excess utilization enabled by this "free" health care falls largely on Medicare, since for retirees ages sixty-five and over Medicare is the primary payer. The excess utilization fostered by "free" care is not merely a matter of differences in physician patterns of practice. A *New York Times* article with the headline, "Patients in Florida Lining Up for All that Medicare Covers," documents a culture of eager use of medical care (Kolata 2003). "Doctor visits have become a social activity in this place of palm trees and gated retirement communities," the *Times* reports. Patients "know what they want; they choose specialists for every body part. And every visit, every procedure is covered by Medicare." It is not a coincidence that researchers at the Dartmouth Center for Health Policy Research show the highest levels of waste in the areas where original Medicare pays the highest average amounts per enrollee (Fisher et al. 2003).

The FEHBP also suffers from moral hazard. As previously discussed, the dual FEHBP/Medicare enrollees enjoy unlimited "free" care for inpatient and outpatient services. But even the remaining FEHBP enrollees now pay, under most plans, only nominal copayments for these services, such as $15 or $20 for a physician visit. (In past decades, as discussed below, cost-sharing was far higher.) Hence, Medicare seeks to control costs with two hands behind its back, and the FEHBP with a hand and a half. Not only do enrollees have little incentive to be frugal consumers of health care, but providers can also profit at will simply by increasing the volume of services provided in the name of medical caution (see Cutler and Zeckhauser 2000, 576, for a full description of this problem's manifestations). Regardless of the precise relative effects of moral hazard in the two programs, whatever we observe is not the unfettered performance of each as nominally designed, but of each with all its excess wraparound coverage and attendant overutilization.

The purpose of comparing performance is to compare not the lovely ideal to the messy reality, but one messy reality to another. While some of these threats to validity are in some sense "luck of the draw" factors that may compromise comparison, most are a consequence of program design. We are not comparing an ideal version of Medicare, whatever that might be, to an ideal version of the FEHBP. We are comparing two real-world programs to each other, warts and all. Moreover, some of these factors result in large part from flaws in the programs themselves. Medicare is so poorly designed from the point of view of consumers seeking protection that it invites Medigap supplements for all and compels them for many. Likewise, if the FEHBP had retained more of its ability to reward frugal consumers for selecting less expensive health plans, plan cost-sharing would be higher and overall utilization and costs lower.

Irrelevant Comparisons

Medicare and the FEHBP can be compared based on any number of criteria. The chapters that follow focus on risk selection, cost control, benefits, provider access and choice, adaptability over time, governance, and fraud control. Some largely irrelevant comparisons also warrant passing attention, however, simply because, despite being straw men, they are commonly used by defenders of original Medicare, critics of the FEHBP, and opponents of plan choice as if they were telling criticisms.

First, defenders of original Medicare often claim that the program is superior to the FEHBP or any premium-support alternative because its benefits are guaranteed in law, "entitlements" that are protected from the vagaries of private decisions (see, for example, Caplan and Foley 2000). The response to this claim is threefold. First, laws that set parameters for the FEHBP and Medicare can be, and sometimes are, changed. While the massive volume of Medicare law appears quite solid, it is amended far more frequently and to greater effect than the FEHBP statute. Means-testing by whatever name is now firmly ensconced in the Medicare program, and the once seemingly sacrosanct Part B deductible is now indexed to inflation. Can anyone doubt that Medicare's "guarantees" will be breached as insolvency approaches ever more closely? Second, the FEHBP is every bit as much an "entitlement" as Medicare. It is so categorized in the budget process, and its existence and features are as legally binding. Third, the existential reality is that over fifty years, the FEHBP's benefits have improved and now far surpass those of original Medicare, which have remained largely static.

A second criticism argues that the nature of the statutory guarantee is different. The FEHBP is characterized as a "premium-support" program and original Medicare as a "defined-benefit" program, with a premium-support program charged with being somehow a stealthy approach to cutting benefits, and a defined benefit the only means of preventing a steady erosion of benefits over time. But a premium-support program could as well increase benefits faster than the rising cost of health-care services, as it could increase them more slowly than that cost (indeed, a faster increase is exactly what has happened in the FEHBP). Furthermore, this concern arises from the impending insolvency of Medicare and the need to reduce drastically the rate of growth in Medicare spending, reduce benefits, raise premiums, or take some other step to reduce Medicare fiscal imbalance. But moving Medicare toward a premium-support model has been proposed not as a pretext for benefit reduction or premium increases, but as a market-oriented alternative to putting those wrenching decisions to prevent insolvency into the political process under the ponderous defined-benefit model and, more importantly, to reduce the need for massive cutbacks as insolvency approaches. Nothing in a premium-support model is incompatible with retaining the highly progressive skew in Medicare financing to protect the neediest enrollees. Indeed, the premium-support Medicare Part D drug benefit does precisely this, being far more progressive in its financing design than Medicare Part A.

The premium-support model does, indeed, have political and economic ramifications. Gail Wilensky and Joe Newhouse stated these quite clearly in their 1999 appraisal of potential Medicare reforms. A premium-support model as a structural matter makes it relatively easy to execute certain kinds of reforms, such as increasing the income-tested component of premiums or the Medicare eligibility age. Premium support allows for a much finer calibration of policy than cruder all-or-nothing eligibility or benefit parameter models. But premium support as an approach also facilitates myriad adjustments to reduce costs. Most Part D plans have benefits that are better, not worse, than the "standard" plan used as a benchmark for adjustments. Costs are far lower, as well. Why would anyone prefer the "standard" plan?

Yet another criticism of the FEHBP is based on the notion that original Medicare is somehow more protective of enrollees. The government, it is said, will prevent the unfair treatment of those in government plans that befalls those in private plans. Benefits defined in law are easier to protect in appeals procedures. Of course, in either model private practitioners provide medical treatment to enrollees. By and large, the very same providers treat patients under most or all insurance programs. The many protections against bad treatment include professional ethics, peer pressure, complaint processes, malpractice claims, and patient choices, among others. Interestingly, it is government programs like original Medicare, and more particularly Medicaid, that are most likely to subject patients to poor performers. Despite the emerging "pay-for-performance" initiatives in Medicare, which are designed to reward good providers, Medicare generally pays the same whether the physician is the best in town or the worst, and whether he cures or kills the patient, so long as he retains his license.[3]

As to health-plan performance on denial of benefits, no comparative data are extant. To an observer the main difference between the two programs appears to lie in the extreme complexity and formality of Medicare appeals procedures compared to the simpler, speedier, and more straightforward FEHBP process.[4] But we can tell that the FEHBP has a good record simply by considering a few key numbers. The FEHBP uses a "disputed claims" process in which an enrollee can bring any dispute over coverage or payment—no matter how small—to the Office of Personnel Management if internal appeal procedures do not resolve the matter.[5] The number of such claims annually is on the order of one per thousand enrollees, varying by plan (Francis et al. 2008 and prior years). The national total for four million enrollees and eight million lives is about four thousand a year. After OPM review, the plans prevail in about nine in ten cases. If we assume that OPM rules fairly, that means that only about four hundred of eight million consumers were aggrieved sufficiently to complain and win reversal of their health plans' decisions—a minute fraction. Of course, there may be many more cases of aggravation or problems that enrollees simply give up on. In those cases, they have recourse to open season. Plans that provide poor service lose business. On its face, there appears to be nothing to criticize about the FEHBP process.

As the case of Medicare's anemic anti-fraud efforts painfully illustrates, less management and lower administrative costs do not necessarily mean the program is really less costly. Fraud losses are just categorized as additional spending rather than as administrative expense.

Kerry N. Weems and Benjamin E. Sasse
"Is Government Health Insurance Cheap?"

What is worse, the higher the actual fraud level, the "better" the Medicare administrative cost appears as a percentage of total spending. So the purported administrative savings are entirely illusory when both numerator and denominator are appropriately adjusted.

Walton J. Francis
Why a New Public Plan Will Not Improve American Health Care

It is commonly asserted that FEHBP administrative costs are far higher than those of original Medicare, that the ratio of administrative costs to total costs is a measure of wasteful spending, and that Medicare's lower administrative costs are a major plus in any comparison (Merlis 2003;

Davis et al. 2003, quoting Merlis). Some dispute the accuracy of such calculations, particularly by including more complete estimates of Medicare costs and adjusting to the arguably more reasonable basis of cost per enrollee rather than cost per dollar of claims paid (Book 2009). Regardless, the usual calculations leave out major portions of Medicare's administrative costs (Francis 2009, Weems and Sasse 2009, and Book 2009) and even categorize case management as wasteful administration.[6]

Even accepting the more usual calculations as if they were accurate, using any insurance program's administrative costs as a measure of performance is conceptually and factually erroneous. It is a persistent and common error. For example, the U.S. General Accounting Office (now the Government Accountability Office [GAD]) once performed a study estimating that the national fee-for-service plans in the FEHBP spent, at the time, $8.56 per $100 of benefits paid to administer claims—almost double the GAO estimate for what is now called TRICARE, and almost double that of large, self-insured private programs (U.S. General Accounting Office 1992). Incredibly, the GAO then recommended that the competitive FEHBP be reformed (abolished) to establish uniform benefits among plans and to use competitive bidding for separate claims-processing contracts (similar to those in Medicare, although no explicit parallel was drawn) to control administrative costs (10–11). The GAO calculated that abolishing competition could save $200 million in administrative costs, or just over 1 percent of total premiums, in a program that was then spending $15 billion a year in premium costs and whose total costs were growing at a rate far slower than those of Medicare or TRICARE. The then OPM director concurred and stated in her comments on a draft of the report that the program was in need of "fundamental reform" to correct the problem that, in a competitive market, "the real 'purchaser' in the Program is not the OPM contracting office, but the individual FEHB enrollee who elects a specific plan," which makes "worthwhile initiatives [such as the GAO proposal to reduce administrative costs and hence increasing total costs] virtually impossible" (75–76). Indeed. A better example of government bureaucrats' proposing to waste billions of dollars (in discounted present value) is, one hopes, scarce. One can barely imagine what either agency would have said if asked to comment on the readily available evidence (Francis 1993) that overall costs in the FEHBP were growing so much slower than Medicare costs that savings from the competitive model could be calculated in the billions of dollars.

Of course, administrative costs as a percentage of claims paid is an absurd measure focused on inputs when the proper questions should focus on outputs: whether claims are properly paid, whether unnecessary medical costs are controlled, whether fraud is controlled, whether service is good, whether care is well managed, and, above all, whether total spending is restrained. The GAO, an agency whose primary function is to spend administrative dollars to control waste, appears not to have considered even worth mentioning the possibility that spending an extra administrative dollar on control of waste or fraud or on managing care to improve health outcomes and minimize unnecessary utilization might save the government more than a dollar in unnecessary spending. The GAO did not change its conclusions even after the Blue Cross program pointed out in its comments on a draft of the report that "the total cost of our program is lower, and the satisfaction of our subscribers is higher, than one would find in a 'more efficient' centralized program" like that endorsed by the GAO and the OPM (ibid., 78).[7]

The administrative cost measure used in such comparisons is so fallacious that the better a plan is at controlling wasteful benefit costs, the worse is its ratio of administrative costs to benefits paid. According to the Dartmouth analysis, roughly one-third of Medicare spending is wasted on unnecessary procedures that, on balance, harm rather than benefit enrollees (Fisher et al. 2003). Another recent study found that roughly one-sixth of all hospital spending in original Medicare was for unnecessary readmissions of patients who had already been hospitalized (Jencks et al. 2009). Insufficient Medicare administrative spending is doubtless a major factor in this waste, as well as in fraud and abuse. If administrative costs are even relevant to the issue of which approach is best, the evidence is reasonably conclusive that the original Medicare model of low administrative costs and high waste is distinctly inferior—that is, the lower administrative costs of original Medicare are a measure of wasteful total spending, not of program savings. If authoritative data were available, a proper comparison might appear as shown in the illustrative table on the following page. This table uses a hypothetical $100 in medically effective care as its starting point for judgmental "guesstimates," and generously assumes that Medicare spends as much on effective care as do FEHBP plans, despite its failure to provide or pay for case management. It also uses hypothetical, and conservative, estimates of losses due to wasteful care and fraud.

ILLUSTRATIVE ADMINISTRATIVE COST ARITHMETIC

	FEHBP	Original Medicare
Medically effective care	$100	$100
Wasteful care	$20	$40
Fraud	$5	$10
Administrative cost	$15	$5
Total spending	$140	$155
Administrative cost percentage	11%	3%
Net savings from higher administration	$10	NA

Clearly, any analysis that does not acknowledge the likelihood that the lower administrative costs of original Medicare demonstrate insufficient spending to control waste is conceptually fatally flawed, and almost certainly factually wrong. Certainly no one can reasonably claim cost superiority for Medicare without addressing fraud and waste not prevented. (Later in this book we address both overall cost containment and fraud. To preview those findings, the evidence clearly shows the inferiority of original Medicare.) As argued cogently and eloquently in an open letter by Stuart Butler and a host of cosignatory luminaries, the administrative budget of the CMS (then HCFA) is enormously underfunded relative to its mandated responsibilities (Butler et al. 1999). The "Crisis Facing HCFA" has since grown demonstrably worse as the agency gropes with the added responsibilities of the MMA and the pay-for-performance initiatives.

By taking the fraud and abuse problem seriously this administration might be able to save 10% or even 20% from Medicare and Medicaid budgets. . . . But to do that one would have to spend 1% or maybe 2% (as opposed to the prevailing .1%) in order to check that the other 98% or 99% of the funds were well spent.

Malcolm Sparrow
Testimony before the U.S. Senate Committee on the Judiciary 2009

Another common complaint about the FEHBP is that its many plans are confusing—an argument whose logic applies forcefully against any number of plans greater than one. The same complaint has been rendered incessantly against Medicare Part D, buttressed by the claim that a very large fraction of the elderly will likely be unable to understand or compare plan literature.[8] Similar complaints have been registered against what are now Medicare Advantage plans, focusing on the vulnerability of the elderly to alleged marketing abuse, and on the absence at the time of CMS tools to assist them in choosing (Jones and Lewin 1996).

Several salient responses can be made to such criticisms. First, enrollment in health plans with good benefits and well-defined contractual rights and appeal procedures, run by reputable companies seeking to remain in business and whose services are provided by medical-care personnel bound by moral and other sanctions to promote health, is among the least risky forms of consumer participation in the economy at large. When every plan is a good plan, confusion has little cost. Second, like all of us, the elderly buy food and automobiles and electronic equipment and make many other choices among a profusion of competing products. Complexity of choice is an issue facing every American, and we all rely on similar strategies to varying degrees, such as asking friends, family, and trusted professionals for advice, reading evaluative literature, or simply taking the view that a more or less random choice among broadly accepted service providers that are succeeding in the market is a perfectly sensible strategy. We all rely on the "public good" (in the economists' sense) provided by prudent shoppers other than ourselves. Third, while open season locks enrollees in for a year, they can vote with their feet the next year if they don't like the service or benefits. Finally, both Medicare and the FEHBP offer considerable resources to assist consumers in making choices among plans, with Medicare's efforts arguably exemplary.[9] Taking all these points into consideration, it is hardly surprising that the market for private health insurance, when available through a system of managed competition, serves consumers very well indeed, as we shall see.

The broader point is that consumer confusion is a red herring. Of course, consumers are confused. They are confused about any number of car, television set, computer, physician, and plumber choices greater than one in any such category. A market economy not only generates many choices, but far more information than any of us can obtain or mentally process in the time we have available. It also fails to generate enough useful information (the systematic tendency to underinvest in "public goods") and, in many cases, produces misleading information as well. Furthermore, when every producer of widgets says his brand is best, confusion is increased even further. Is this an argument, then, for the government to decide on the best brand of peanut butter, the best brand of car, the best fast food chain, the best life insurance, the best bank, the best telephone company, and so on, and to allow us to buy only that brand? Does anyone seriously believe that the government has the competence to make such choices, or that any consumer market would be improved by such restrictions? Why, then, single out health insurance for restriction of consumer choices when the consumer confusion issues it poses aren't really any different in kind or number from those found anywhere in any market economy?

A final example of irrelevant comparisons is the citation of data by some critics to the effect that Medicare beneficiaries are highly satisfied with their situation, and significantly more satisfied than enrollees below age sixty-five in private plans (Davis et al. 2002). This is correct. But the wrong inference is drawn. Survey data are known to produce plan ratings from the elderly that are much higher than ratings from those of working age in the same plans. But the elderly disproportionately enroll in different plans from younger workers, so plan comparisons that do not control for age are misleading (Francis et al. 2008, 114).[10]

The FEHBP provides something of a natural experiment in this regard. As discussed previously, retirees congregate most heavily in PPO plans, and especially in the Blue Cross standard option, with more than half of all annuitant enrollees in 2008. Younger workers congregate more heavily in HMO plans. All these plans are required by the OPM to use the same survey instrument and techniques, administered through the National Committee for Quality Assurance (NCQA), to obtain data on enrollee satisfaction with their services. On average, 38 percent of enrollees in PPO plans in the FEHBP get the highest rating for "overall quality."[11] Among these plans, the Blue Cross standard option gets the highest rating from 45 percent of enrollees. In contrast, the average HMO plan gets a top rating from only 19 percent of its enrollees. Also in contrast, the Blue Cross basic option PPO, which uses the same administering entities and procedures, provides highly similar benefits, uses the same preferred providers as the Blue Cross standard option, attracts few retirees, and obtains the top rating from only 18 percent of its enrollees.[12] Hence, it is apparent that the primary cause of the huge twenty-five-point difference between the ratings of the two Blue Cross plans is primarily the age or Medicare status, or both, of the two enrollee groups. The same enrollment difference undoubtedly accounts for much of the poorer showing of HMOs, though here the inference is weaker because the delivery models are so different. In the Davis study, 32 percent of Medicare elderly gave the top rating to their plans, in contrast to only 20 percent of younger (ages nineteen to sixty-four) enrollees in private insurance (Davis et al. 2002, W315). It is hard to believe that this difference is not due to the same difference in enrollee groups and the same age-related difference in response rates. Of course, survey instruments and methods were not identical, but the results are strikingly parallel.

In summary, an endless series of small criticisms can be leveled against the FEHBP model, some having no merit, some irrelevant, and some reasonable points but either correctable or of minuscule importance in making larger policy decisions. Having reviewed them in brief, we now proceed to an in-depth look at far larger issues.

3

Risk Selection

Adverse selection is the tendency for people with higher-risk . . . to obtain insurance coverage to a greater extent than persons with lesser-risk . . . [Based on the evidence] I don't lie awake nights, worrying about adverse selection for the bulk of the population. I do worry about those low-income high-risk people.

Mark V. Pauly
"The Truth about Moral Hazard and Adverse Selection"

Risk selection is a problem whose adverse effects are far more feared than real. However, it is so frequently claimed as a fatal flaw in the FEHBP, and by extension in any program allowing people to choose among insurance plans, that it requires careful attention. It has even become a pejorative term, with the simple assertion that adverse selection will occur apparently sufficient in some circles to end discussion. Adverse selection is also a topic of great interest to economists, since it is a major example of asymmetries in information between buyer and seller, and hence of potential market failure. George Akerlof won a Nobel Prize in part because of his famous (among economists) article, "The Market for Lemons: Quality Uncertainty and the Market Mechanism" (Akerlof 1970). Information asymmetries are ubiquitous in the world of insurance and perhaps nowhere more evident than in health insurance. While few of us can predict the odds of dreaded health events such as cancer or heart attack in the next year, most of us can predict some health events, large or small, such as childbirth or allergies. The FEHBP allows enrollees to use their known information in selecting a plan in the annual open season, as does Medicare Advantage.

Risk Selection and Consumer Choice

The FEHBP design deliberately encourages consumer choice among different health plans with different cost-sharing and different benefits, exercised every year during open season. The stated purposes of open season include allowing enrollees to choose health plans that meet their known personal needs for the next year without any information in the hands of the insurance plans or any discretion on the part of the plans as to whether to accept them. This is the essence of adverse selection.[1] Competitive Medicare offers a similar market, as does every employer who offers multiple plans.

These systems of choice all deliberately foster risk selection. It is inherent in their design. It is inexorable even if benefits are standardized (a bad idea discussed later in this analysis) because such standardization cannot reasonably control for many plan variables, such as size of network and availability of specialists, which would still allow adverse selection.[2]

Hence, attacks on the grounds of risk selection—commonly characterized somewhat pejoratively as adverse selection—are attacks on the very idea of consumer choice of health insurance plans, and presumably apply with equal force to all other insurance markets where consumers may purchase plans of their choice. They implicitly argue that the costs of risk selection, however trivial, outweigh the benefits not only of meeting consumer needs, but also of using competitive pressures to keep program costs to all enrollees, including high-risk enrollees, lower than they otherwise would be.

Risk selection is certainly not irrelevant to appraisals of FEHBP performance. There are several levels of issue here, including not only the kinds and levels of risk selection, but their consequences and the importance they should be accorded. There are at least four types of alleged bad aspects or effects of risk selection, only the first three of which pertain to plan choice. First, risk selection is blamed for the infamous "death spiral," in which a plan is priced out of existence as lower-cost and lower-risk persons flee it in droves. Second, risk selection is blamed for unscrupulous actions by bad-actor plans that seek to attract good risks and profit by leaving the bad risks in other plans (such as original Medicare). Third, risk selection creates the alleged market imperfection and inequity of sicker people paying more for insurance than others in the pool who should be sharing risk equally while, at the same time, healthier people cannot get the higher-benefit insurance they would prefer if they didn't have to pay higher premiums for being pooled with the costlier enrollees.

A fourth type of risk selection is created when states mandate "community rates" (that is, placing all persons of all ages and health statuses into one unsubsidized pool) and then require "guaranteed issue" for individual health insurance, regardless of preexisting conditions. This practice has massive adverse effects on the price and availability of individual insurance to younger and healthier persons in states such as New York. It also fosters "gaming the system" (moral hazard) because healthy persons can avoid enrolling and paying any premiums until or unless they face substantial medical bills. This effect occurs on a small scale in the FEHBP and on a massive scale in Medicaid and the State Children's Health Insurance Program (SCHIP). According to one recent estimate, approximately eleven million of forty-four million uninsured Americans are eligible for free Medicaid insurance but disdain or postpone enrollment (Dubay et al. 2006).[3] If they become ill, they can be enrolled retroactively. Why waste one's time at the welfare office when the hospital will arrange retroactive enrollment in Medicaid after admission?

This latter type of risk selection plagues employer-sponsored health insurance to a likely substantial but unknown degree. Most employers allow their employees to decline insurance, but give them a chance to sign up in each annual open season. Large numbers of low-wage employees decline insurance unless and until illness occurs, and then use the open season to gain coverage. Although there are no precise estimates, some estimate that perhaps one in twenty federal employees similarly goes "bare" (Bovbjerg 2009, footnote 28, and American Federation of Government Employees 2009). This phenomenon is, however, mitigated in competitive multiplan systems if lower-premium plans are offered that make insurance more affordable, as in the FEHBP. Therefore, for federal employees this form of risk selection is reduced by the availability of competing plans. (Competitive Medicare, by combining an open season with a severe penalty for failure to enroll in Part B or Part D, does an even better job.)

There is no question that risk selection is common in health insurance situations of various kinds. In "The Anatomy of Health Insurance," Cutler and Zeckhauser (2000) assembled almost three dozen empirical studies; virtually all found some degree of adverse risk selection. The study synopses, however, indicate that the great majority of these dealt with situations involving at most a handful of plan choices and ones involving a clearly systematic preference among older and sicker enrollees for plans with broader provider panels. Importantly, they apparently failed to measure or control for the willingness of enrollees to pay more to keep trusted physicians who are network providers in one plan but not in another. Nor did these studies seem to demonstrate or estimate any quantitatively important effects on enrollees, such as higher premiums paid or higher health costs incurred, that would generalize to a large multiple plan system like the FEHBP and Medicare. Probably most important, the flawed insurance contribution formulas used by most employers, and presumably the employers in these studies, encourage rather than discourage adverse selection. (For a discussion of this failure and its remedy, see Pauly 2007 and U.S. Senate, Joint Economic Committee 2004.)

Aside from the prevalence of risk selection is the question of how harmful it really is. Much of the literature on plan choices just assumes or asserts that any level of risk selection is bad. For example, one analyst correctly identifies modest levels of risk selection in the FEHBP, and says that, to the degree it occurs, "people joining higher-cost plans pay a surcharge. . . . The effect may be to penalize people who join plans with older or sicker retirees" (Merlis 2003, 15). This is true. Two unanswered questions are, "How much?" and "Does it matter?" Indeed, why is it a bad thing and not a good thing—why should younger enrollees pay the same premiums as older enrollees instead of getting an actuarially fair rate, as they do for life insurance?

One critical analysis of the potential effects of moving Medicare to a premium-support system devotes many pages to scattered examples of doubtful relevance and a simulation model of a two-plan system's movements toward a death spiral (Rice and Desmond 2002). Nowhere in the analysis is any attention devoted to whether or not it would matter or why, if such a hypothetical event were to occur. The breathless finding from the two-plan simulation is that "it does not appear that risk-adjustment under the current state of the art would be able to avert a death spiral in the very long run" (28). Some might judge that "very long run" to be a very encouraging finding, even if they abhorred death spirals. Others might ask how, and in what way, a two-plan system is even relevant to the dozens of plan options offered to enrollees in the FEHBP and competitive Medicare. Still others might ask why the program manager does not terminate that plan before its natural end arrives, or otherwise change the terms of premium cost-sharing to alter that result. As is so often emphasized by Alain Enthoven, the very term "managed competition" implies that sensible decision-makers pay attention to emerging trends and make appropriate adjustments. The handwringing over death spirals implicitly assumes that sensible management is absent.

Moving from the commonsense empirical finding that enrollees in better health are more likely to join HMOs than are enrollees in poor health and, hence, will pay lower premiums, the Rice analysis announces that "major issues" will arise if risk adjustment is imperfect; but it fails to list these issues, and states that "adverse selection presents a formidable problem . . . even if a death spiral can be avoided" (23), without naming the actual problem. Only one issue is specifically identified: the possibility that plans will use aggressive marketing practices, such as health club memberships, to attract healthier enrollees. No evidence is presented that such practices have been common, or that they work even if they exist. Most fundamentally, nothing is presented that even suggests that adverse selection is undesirable, or why. The assertion that problems will exist ends the analysis instead of beginning it.

Some of the literature on the dangers of risk selection is silly as well as shrill. A study of marketing practices of Medicare HMOs found that virtually all of the advertising material made favorable claims for these HMOs, such as, "More Coverage than Medicare. For Less Money" (Neuman et al. 1998, 134). Senior citizens shown in plan advertisements were usually physically active and engaging in hobbies and family activities. According to this study, evil intent could be inferred because three California HMOs held seminars in a restaurant that was not wheelchair-accessible. One might note, however, that virtually all health-care and health insurance advertisements in every context show happy and healthy users of the advertised product. Those advertisements are seeking to persuade the sick to use their product! Claims boasting about better coverage benefits are hardly designed to discourage those who need those benefits the most. And as for holding a seminar in a single, "inaccessible" restaurant at which the rare wheelchair user who would even plan to attend might be unable to do so, any health plan managers counting on such a scheme to reduce the number of high risks joining would be utterly incompetent.

Even as aggressive an investigator as the Office of the Inspector General at the U.S. Department of Health and Human Services did not find a single risk-related or cream-skimming abuse in its investigation of South Florida marketing practices of HMOs during the height of the gold rush to make money from Medicare's excessively high payment rates in the state (U.S. Department of Health and Human Services, Office of the Inspector General 1991).[4]

As sophisticated a source as the Congressional Budget Office, in a thorough analysis of current and possible future Medicare Advantage bidding and premium-setting rules, fails to deal with the issue in any depth (U.S. Congressional Budget Office 2006b). In *Designing a Premium Support System for Medicare*, the CBO uses the term "risk" 149 times in its fifty-six pages. Yet virtually the only assessment of why risk adjustment matters is found in a single sentence saying that if risk adjustment were imperfect, "premiums for enrollees in plans that attract higher-cost beneficiaries [could] rise substantially over time," followed by a footnote referring to the irrelevant Rice simulation model (27).

In considering risk selection, the questions, "How much does it take to matter?" and "Why should we care?" loom large. Consider the following example. Two health plans offer identical benefits, except that one pays for dental costs. That plan attracts those with dental problems, and its annual premiums are several hundred dollars higher. In effect, the enrollee population sorts itself out based on benefit preference, and those who want better dental coverage pay for it. Those who don't want it don't pay for it, by staying out of that plan. The sicker—that is, those with bad teeth—pay more—hundreds of dollars more. Should we care, and why? Why isn't the operative principle that consumers should bear the costs of their own consumption decisions? Why should I pay for my neighbor's tooth care or car repair, and isn't the latter likely to be as or more vital to his well-being? Why isn't the principle of "pay for one's own consumption" particularly important in an era when health plans really sell prepaid health care for routine expenses rather than true health insurance?

One might argue that this is unfair to those who lost in the genetic lottery for resistance to tooth and gum disease, but why is that any more unfair than the difference in incomes between those who won or lost in the genetic or childrearing lottery for IQ, or for skills valuable in professional athletics, for ability to attract a better-looking spouse, or for any of a myriad of variables?

The food stamp program gives benefits to the large and fat equal to those it gives to the small and thin, to the considerable disadvantage of the former. Is that fair?

Consider another example, in which the dental plan is entirely separate. The people with bad teeth join it and the rest stay out of it. Plan actuaries in anticipation of this risk selection establish a premium likely to cover the costs of enrollees with bad teeth. The plan makes money. The enrollees get value in at least three ways: network benefits at substantial discounts, budgeting for a predictable premium expense rather than the lottery as to when the crown needs replacement, and insurance value in case their teeth create problems even worse than expected. This is exactly the kind of plan offered by many large employers (including the federal government, starting in 2007) to tens of millions of Americans. Why is it any less reasonable to find risk selection for dental problems among health plans, than to have a system in which consumers purchase separate dental plans? Or are both examples of unfair adverse selection? What makes them unfair?

All insurance involves risk selection to greater or lesser degree, if for no other reason than asymmetry of information. Some 10 percent of Medicare beneficiaries have no prescription drug coverage and did not sign up for the new Part D program. Most of these presumably made a deliberate decision to forgo drug insurance based on their current and anticipated low drug use. As a result, the "sicker" enrollees who did sign up for Part D are paying higher premiums than would otherwise have been the case. This is risk selection. It was anticipated and unavoidable. It would have occurred had there been only one government-run plan and is not an artifact of plan choice. But risk selection also exists in Part D plan choices, as consumers make decisions among plans with varying levels of benefits. It is hard to understand why that is of any ethical concern. For example, Humana offered a plan in the first year of the program that completely filled the Part D doughnut hole.[5] In the second year that plan option was eliminated. Undoubtedly, Humana anticipated and got considerable selection of higher-cost risks into that plan, and ultimately decided it was not a good business decision to offer it. What is unclear is just what the risk selection doom-sayers believe is bad in this situation: that Humana offered the plan in the first place, or that Humana dropped the plan? Suppose Humana kept the plan (full of higher-risk enrollees) and charged a high premium. Would that risk segmentation have been an unfair outcome? Under each of these scenarios, what was the harm, and to whom? And what was the magnitude of that harm averaged across total Part D enrollment? Despite the existence of a lively academic literature on risk selection and decades of theorizing by economists, to this day no one can even answer the question of whether "Risk Segmentation [is a] Goal or Problem" (Feldman and Dowd 2000).

Risk Selection: The Actual Experience

The more interesting issue, masked by the theorizing, is what works in the real world, and what meets elementary notions of fairness (not Rawlsian notions of perfect equality of outcome). By these standards, as we will see in this section, risk selection does not appear to loom large as a real-world issue in the operation of large, multiple-plan health insurance programs. One of the important reasons for this is that consumers have substantial inertia in their choices. All enrollees do not switch every year to the plan that offers the best financial outcome. In fact, most enrollees obviously pay little or no attention to open season and simply stay in their existing plans without bothering to consider whether there are lower-cost alternatives. Stability is the dominant feature of the FEHBP. It is also a dominant feature in other managed competition programs, such as that of the University of California, where older enrollees have proved to be less price-sensitive than younger ones and have manifested a stronger preference for unfettered provider choice (Buchmueller 2000).

The FEHBP is rife with small-scale risk selection and resulting risk segmentation, as is Medicare Part D, because plans vary significantly in benefit details. But original Medicare involves risk selection, as well. A low-income but astute elderly person would be foolish to pay for Part B, knowing that he or she will be eligible for free care under Medicaid when and if illness strikes. Consider also the case of retirees eligible for both programs, or for Medicare and any other employer-sponsored retirement supplement. The Medicare statute does not allow penalty-free delay in joining Part B after retirement.[6] The penalty is a 10 percent increase in premium per year of failure to join. It is surely the case that those retirees most likely to join at retirement are the sickest, fearing the worst and seeking maximum protection. In particular, those who expect substantial medical bills are most likely to value freedom of provider choice, and enrollment in both programs enables them to escape network limitations entirely. Hence, the existing Part B penalty provision, for those who have insurance as good as or better than Medicare and can keep it after retirement, costs rather than saves money for Medicare.[7]

Of greater practical importance for risk selection in original Medicare, by far, is the role played by its gaps and the cost of filling them through Medigap plans. These plans, by wrapping around the many gaps in original Medicare's benefits (most importantly, the catastrophic expenses to which the sickest enrollees are exposed), impose an expensive "tax" on the sickest elderly by forcing them to pay thousands of dollars a year in extra premiums.

In both programs, the sickest pay more. But they get at least two things of value: increased benefit coverage, and peace of mind.

An obvious systemic example of potential risk selection in the FEHBP is found in the substantial average cost differential between HMO plans and PPO plans, with HMOs superior on average in both benefits and premium cost. But the PPO enrollees get much better networks plus out-of-network benefits, both desirable to higher-risk persons. One might expect the overall HMO cost advantage to outweigh the network size advantage, but enrollees overwhelmingly prefer PPO plans. Is this unfair? In what way? To whom?

The Dreaded Death Spiral

As described in a preceding section, one of the most common arguments against consumer choice among health plans is that this will result in a "death spiral" as adverse selection overwhelms those plans that attract the most expensive enrollees who flock to them for their better benefits. This section compares that rhetoric to FEHBP and Medicare reality.

Over the years a great many plans have exited the FEHBP, for a wide range of reasons. From a high of over 400 plans in 1990, plan participation shrank to about 250 in 2005, rising slightly to about 270 today. Because many plans have entered the program, the exit rate is actually much higher than these figures suggest. By far, the greatest number of plan exits has come from HMO mergers and deaths, particularly during the "HMO back-lash" of the 1990s, and as a result of other business decisions. A few of these

HMOs had disproportionately large costs compared to the all-plan average, presumably reflecting their inability to control costs successfully in their local markets. (The FEHBP is a minor factor in almost all markets, so the failures were not due to the FEHBP, but rather reflected the overall experience of these plans.) A few cases, such as the exit of the Group Health Plan in Washington, D.C., undoubtedly involved adverse risk selection, among other factors. This plan, one of the first HMOs created in the nation, had a membership that was disproportionately very old retirees without Medicare who had joined the plan as young federal employees and had never left. It also had major managerial and cost control problems. The overwhelming reason that HMOs surviving in other markets chose to exit the FEHBP, however, was their inability to attract enough enrollees in the competitive FEHBP market to succeed in it. Many good plans that have left the program—for example, the Oxford plans, the Tufts plan, and the Harvard Pilgrim plan—continue today in their other markets.

Another systemic FEHBP phenomenon is a number of smaller PPO plans whose enrollment slowly dwindles each year as a few enrollees exit through death, and even fewer join. These plans "benefit" from their loyal cadre of increasingly older and more costly union or association members, and from the inertia of most enrollees in exploring options and using open season to change plans. Of course, there are corresponding benefits to those who remain enrolled, including avoiding the cost in time and anxiety of exercising choice, avoiding the cost of learning how to deal with a new plan's red tape, and retaining the (usual) stability of the network providers used by the enrollee. The observable differences in plan actuarial value in some cases seem implausibly large to be offset by these benefits, and therein lies the most arguably undesirable risk segmentation in the FEHBP program. This particular form of segmentation could be substantially offset by risk adjustment techniques of several kinds, as analyzed in later chapters.

Of much greater apparent relevance than HMO exit has been the exit of national FFS plans. Starting with fifteen plan options in 1961, the number of national plans peaked at twenty-eight in 1985 and has since decreased to seventeen. Moreover, the number of plan sponsors involved has dropped even more, from nineteen in 1985 to ten today. Why? The air traffic controllers' PATCO plan left after its union sponsored an illegal strike. The Postmasters and Postal Supervisors plans made the perhaps fatal error of attracting primarily their loyal union members—older employees and retirees; that might be fairly termed risk selection. (Of course, those enrollees got a psychic reward not measured by actuarial value.) The small Government Employees Benefit Association plan, already struggling, suffered a million-dollar premature-birth cost without having purchased reinsurance. The small Secret Service plan recently exited the program, despite having below-average costs, by merging with SAMBA, another law enforcement plan. And so on.

The reality is that most FEHBP national plans were sponsored by membership organizations, mostly unions, with little or no expertise in or appetite for either administering health insurance or competing in consumer-driven markets. While many of these organizations' plans were more costly than average, and enrollment often dwindled over the years, they also suffered from networks that were often inferior, provider payment rates that were higher, customer service problems, and other managerial or marketing problems. They failed as businesses, not as the victims of death spirals. After Congress opened up the FEHBP in the early 1980s to unions that had not previously sponsored health plans, a half-dozen new entrants all failed within a decade.

The largest example of allegedly bad risk selection in the FEHBP lies in the experience of the lately deceased Blue Cross high option plan. For decades this was the most popular plan in the program. But over time, for various reasons, it attracted a sicker and more expensive group of enrollees than most other plans, including its sibling, Blue Cross standard option. A seemingly genuine "death spiral" began (Cain 1999). High option had better benefits than standard option, and one benefit in particular was better than in virtually all other plans: outpatient mental health care.[8] There was no question that high option was the plan to join if the enrollee needed a weekly visit to the psychiatrist. What happened to this plan? Table 3-1 tells the story.

Despite an increasing divergence between Blue Cross high option premiums and those of standard option and many other plans, starting a decade before this table begins, high option was still the largest plan in the FEHBP in 1984 and remained one of the largest throughout its existence. During this period and even after the "death" of high option, Blue Cross maintained and increased its share of total FEHBP enrollment, counting all

TABLE 3-1

THE LAST TWO DECADES OF THE ALMOST NEVER-ENDING
BLUE CROSS AND BLUE SHIELD HIGH OPTION "DEATH SPIRAL"

Year	Total FEHBP	Blue Cross high option	Blue Cross standard option	Blue Cross basic option	Blue Cross total
1984	3,667	741	674	0	1,415
1985	3,721	631	758	0	1,389
1986	3,825	561	831	0	1,392
1987	3,888	493	899	0	1,392
1988	3,955	363	1,010	0	1,373
1989	4,035	241	1,182	0	1,423
1990	4,029	181	1,387	0	1,568
1991	4,072	149	1,464	0	1,613
1992	4,096	137	1,503	0	1,640
1993	4,086	125	1,555	0	1,680
1994	4,097	115	1,609	0	1,724
1995	4,106	106	1,648	0	1,754
1996	4,159	100	1,664	0	1,764
1997	4,126	95	1,689	0	1,784
1998	4,119	92	1,758	0	1,850
1999	4,124	91	1,814	0	1,905
2000	4,083	91	1,871	0	1,962
2001	4,081	98	1,896	0	1,994
2002	4,046	0	1,977	88	2,065

Enrollment in thousands

SOURCES: Unpublished "Head Count" enrollment data from the U.S. Office of Personnel Management, and Francis et al. 2008 and prior years.

plan offerings. For a period of years in the 1990s, high option was actually the most costly plan in the FEHBP, but in its later years it steadily decreased its costs in relation to other plans. The cost differential between the two Blue Cross plans also decreased steadily over this period, and in its last decade high option enrollment was essentially stable. For 2002 the plan sponsor made a business decision, in consultation with the Office of Personnel Management, to "pull the plug" on the high option and create a new

Blue Cross percentage of FEHBP total	——Enrollee share of self-only premium——		
	High option	Standard option	Standard option percentage of high option
39%	$780	$190	24%
37%	$810	$200	25%
36%	$800	$170	21%
36%	$880	$220	25%
35%	$1,320	$360	27%
35%	$2,200	$390	18%
39%	$2,250	$440	20%
40%	$2,490	$440	18%
40%	$2,120	$490	23%
41%	$2,040	$540	26%
42%	$1,920	$540	28%
43%	$1,790	$530	30%
42%	$1,790	$560	31%
43%	$1,760	$540	31%
45%	$1,680	$600	36%
46%	$1,650	$720	44%
48%	$1,720	$780	45%
49%	$1,820	$890	49%
51%	NA	$1,070	NA

NOTE: Not shown is that starting in 2001, premiums became tax-preferred, which lowered the cost of all premiums by about one-third for most enrollees.

basic option. Total Blue Cross enrollment rose that year and steadily thereafter, reflecting the business wisdom of that decision.

Nothing in this scenario shows an out-of-control "death spiral." What it shows is that a large number of people wanted to remain in this plan despite having available to them an attractive alternative operated by the same company which, in the later years when Blue Cross created a PPO benefit, offered the same panel of preferred providers under both options.

People in the high option plan included heavy users of mental health benefits, heavy users of home health services (another benefit better than in most plans), and those who didn't care enough about extra premium cost to take the trouble to use the open season to compare options and change plans. Some simply wanted the "Cadillac plan," at whatever extra cost. Others, doubtless, remained out of ignorance and fear, or to honor a promise to a deceased spouse to "Never lose your Blue Cross benefit."

It is hard to believe that these choices indicate a market or ethical pathology so severe that such "risk selection" by the voluntary choices of enrollees should be condemned or cited as a failure of the FEHBP model. Even if it were deemed a failure, remedies were available, such as the forced exit of plans whose actuarial experience departed widely from the actuarial value of their benefits, or the use of risk adjustment tools to vary the government premium contribution so as to reflect enrollee characteristics (as is done in competitive Medicare). Apparently, neither the OPM nor Congress shared the view that such a reform was needed.

Some program critics cite the 1990 departure of the Aetna plans from the FEHBP as a death spiral example (King and Schlesinger 2003). Aetna was dropping all of its fee-for-service insurance products at that time, however, and doubtless found its marginal FEHBP position a convenient excuse to leave the program. It could have remained. In fact, in 1989, the Aetna standard option added a PPO feature, reduced its premium, and was apparently on the road to recovery before the company reversed course.

Consider also the FEHBP union-sponsored plans that dwindled away to almost no enrollees—leaving mainly the most loyal union members and, hence, those older and sicker than average employees—due to their inability to present desirable benefit features or control their costs, or simply because they fell victim to risk selection. Isn't that what happens in the private sector to some fraction of car dealers, restaurants, and a host of other service providers? Why shouldn't it happen to health plans? Does accepting attrition as a form of risk selection mean there is a fatal flaw in systems that depend on competition among multiple plans? Actually, no. As plans exit, other plans can be admitted, or sponsor premiums can be risk-adjusted to ameliorate selection factors. The solution is as simple as the problem. Whether or not one were to characterize such a plan's experience as a "death spiral," the appropriate policy response from the program manager could be simple—let it die, or even hasten its death. It is clear that the FEHBP system viewed as a system is viable, whatever the fate of individual plans.

As these examples suggest, risk selection is not, per se, undesirable, or even necessarily of concern, regardless of whether or not it provokes the dreaded "death spiral." What would matter would be systemic upheaval threatening the viability of the program (which, the FEHBP experience suggests, is unlikely even in the total absence of risk management) through death spirals, deliberate decisions by plans to deny particular benefits that only the most expensive cases utilized, egregious marketing practices that succeeded in denying enrollment to high risks, and other pathologies. None of these pathologies has occurred, or would have been allowed to occur, in either the FEHBP or Medicare Advantage and its predecessors.

Risk selection is in the eye of the beholder. Health plans, like other consumer products, have many attributes. Reputation, service timeliness and accuracy, convenience, and "hassle" factors of all kinds are aspects of plan performance. Some plans have better networks than others. Still other plans have inferior networks that nonetheless include an "essential" family doctor. The million veterans who signed up for Medicare Part D despite being entitled to free drugs from the VA didn't do so just for the better Part D formularies, but also for convenience. Access at the corner drugstore means a lot.[9]

A number of studies[10] have addressed FEHBP risk selection by analyzing the relationship of premiums and out-of-pocket costs, starting with the classic study by Jim Price (Price and Mays 1985). In 1999, Mark Merlis focused on the FEHBP as a possible model for Medicare and found extensive risk segmentation, as measured by comparing premiums to actuarial value. Merlis suggested several methods by which risk adjusters could have lowered observed risk segmentation and correctly pointed out that the FEHBP uses no risk adjustment methods whatsoever, which results in at least some of the observed differences in actuarial fairness (Merlis 1999). Gray and Selden (2002) analyzed the capped-premium subsidy used by the FEHBP, using cross-sectional data on plan choices and comparing lower- and higher-cost cities. They found that the FEHBP premium design effectively reduced risk selection among employee enrollees, perhaps effectively enough that a similar premium design might obviate the need for risk adjusters based on enrollee health status in other programs. Another recent study found no evidence of systemic risk selection in the FEHBP among employee enrollees. Authors Florence and Thorpe (2003) determined that when premium contributions are high, as they are in the FEHBP, risk segmentation by age and age-related cost is minimal. Importantly, Florence and Thorpe emphasized the key point that there is a tradeoff between controlling costs and reducing risk segmentation.[11]

Later work by these same authors provides the best available evidence as to the potential importance of plan choices in holding down premium costs (Florence et al. 2006). In this study, the authors examined the plan choices of both active federal employees and retirees nearing Medicare eligibility. They found substantial price elasticities of demand with respect to premium increases (on the order of a –2.5 percent change in plan market share for a 1 percent increase in premiums for employees) that, while declining with age, were strong at all ages in the various subgroups studied. They also found very strong preferences for open networks, with younger workers willing to pay about $500 more for a PPO over an HMO, and older workers about $700 more. Ancillary benefits such as chiropractic services—the kinds that vary most in the FEHBP—were also preferred, as were open formularies.

I would conclude from these studies that in the real world of competitive health insurance, the handwringing concerns over gross inequities, systemic failures, and death spirals are of limited relevance, and certainly not of relevance in systems like Medicare Advantage and the FEHBP, where premium subsidies are generous. What matters most is what best controls overall plan costs, a category of outcome that benefits all enrollees. This does not mean, of course, that there is no case for risk adjustment in the FEHBP. To the contrary, it has long been known that the FEHBP's cost control performance could be significantly improved by simple forms of risk adjustment, particularly to deal with age and Medicare status, that bring plans' nominal differences in costs and benefits closer to their actuarial differences (Francis 1988, Enthoven 1989, and Jones 1989). In my conclusions to this analysis (and in earlier writings) I strongly recommend that some simple risk adjustment mechanisms be added to the FEHBP.

But the policy analysis and economist literature on risk selection need to get a grip on reality. There are huge differences among fatal flaws, inevitable and unimportant flaws, and important flaws that warrant correction. The FEHBP has plenty in the latter two categories, but with no credit to prescience has avoided fatal flaws.

What to Do Next?

There is a straightforward answer to the problems that risk selection might create. Suppose that the worst fears of defenders of original Medicare were to be realized, and that two decades from now a competitive "premium-support," private-plan system for Medicare finally were to leave the sickest and most vulnerable beneficiaries in an original Medicare plan whose premiums were rising rapidly and unacceptably compared to those of Medicare Advantage plans. Suppose further that no administrative risk adjustment measures could adequately control the problem. The death spiral will have begun. What could be done? For starters, the Congress of the United States, which has proved itself periodically capable of wrenching changes in Medicare under dire circumstances, could quite simply change the premium contribution formula to compensate, or even overcompensate, for the problem. Just as Medicare deliberately overpays MA plans today, it could deliberately overpay original Medicare tomorrow. This reform, if needed, would not even require political courage. Arguing against reform of any program—not just Medicare—on the grounds that midcourse corrections or calibration might be required to deal with some unforeseen problem or unlikely adverse event is an absurd position to take.

There are no guarantees of perfection in this imperfect world, but to hold competitive markets in health insurance (or any other field) hostage either to imagined nightmares or to anticipated minor uncorrectable effects, or to effects that are correctable if they arise, is to preclude reform. Three decades ago Senator Edward Kennedy and his staffer (now Supreme Court Justice) Stephen Breyer played a key role in replacing an air travel market micromanaged by an agency called the Civil Aeronautics Board in ways that prevented price competition among airlines, despite handwringing fears as to all kinds of imagined adverse effects. Today's air travel market is hardly perfect, but it is far superior in cost and convenience for Americans than the one it replaced. It has saved many thousands of lives and massively reduced air pollution and energy use by replacing the automobile for a large fraction of intercity travel, while saving consumers tens of billions of dollars a year through reduced airfares.[12] Perfect equality and perfect fairness are found only in death, not in the world in which we live. The only death spiral that is on the horizon is that of original Medicare itself, which cannot survive in its present form because of the costs and taxation levels its present design will entail. The latest report from the Boards of Trustees of the Federal Hospital Insurance and Federal Supplementary Insurance Trust Funds (2009, 29) puts the date of Medicare Part A insolvency at 2017, with income covering only 81 percent of spending in that year. That doomsday is less than a decade away.

> There is always inequity in life. . . . Life is unfair.
>
> John F. Kennedy, press conference of March 21, 1962

The FEHBP does have risk selection problems that should not be ignored. The FEHBP pays the same government contribution toward each plan enrollee regardless of age or Medicare status—two huge and easily measurable cost variables. As a matter of simple algebra, premium contributions could be varied on these two dimensions while leaving the overall government cost and the face of the program to enrollees virtually unchanged. This would substantially improve the extent to which plan choices reflected the performance of each plan rather than the risk pool from which it drew enrollees. This is not a new idea (see Francis 1988, Enthoven 1989, and Jones 1989). The FEHBP could even borrow the improving but always imperfect Medicare methods for measuring risk and adjusting payments to plans in terms of health characteristics of enrollees, though in practice this would be quite difficult because there is no unified database of enrollee medical records. It could relatively easily reallocate premium dollars based on the occurrence of very high-cost cases in each plan.[13] Surely, the failure of any administration to propose, or any Congress to consider, some form of risk adjustment for the FEHBP verges on the irresponsible. The simple lesson, however, is that even a system without any risk adjustment mechanism whatsoever can be dynamically stable and avoid risk selection effects of such magnitude as to render the system ethically suspect.

The biggest cost of the government's failure to make any adjustments for differential risk among different groups of enrollees lies in undercutting the competitive mechanism that drives FEHBP performance. To the extent that the marginal premium cost of joining a plan does not properly measure its real costs or reward frugal plan choices by enrollees, the competitive model loses much of its effectiveness.[14] The failure to adjust for major risk differences among different types of enrollees by age and Medicare status, at the very least, is a major error in program design, with malign effects on program performance.[15] But despite this serious design defect, the program has nonetheless avoided the calamities that have been repeatedly predicted, or alleged to have occurred, but are noticeably absent in its real-world experience.

In sum, the FEHBP has a genuine risk segmentation problem. But it is not the problem most cited by its critics—the dreaded death spiral. The ensuing bad result most decried by the critics—that the sickest enrollees will be forced to pay a great deal more to protect themselves against financial risk—turns out to be a ubiquitous phenomenon in original Medicare supplemented by Medigap. In the FEHBP, in contrast, nobody pays nearly as much in extra premiums for the best protection as is commonplace in original Medicare.[16]

The competitive Medicare programs have minor risk selection problems, but these are generally even smaller than those of the FEHBP and presumably of little concern. Most obviously, about 10 percent of eligibles did not enroll in the Part D prescription drug program (and had no alternative coverage). Presumably these persons were, on average, low risks who did not use prescription drugs or see any likelihood of needing any. As a result, program premiums for those who enrolled (the high risks) are somewhat higher than would otherwise be the case. Furthermore, those low risks can always enroll by paying a 12 percent a year premium penalty. Hence, those who face very substantial drug costs in the future (say, cancer treatment costing $5,000 a month) can enroll in the next open enrollment period and save a great deal of money in excess of premium costs and the doughnut hole through the catastrophic cost guarantee of the program.

Medicare Advantage faces a different problem—the potential effects of favorable (rather than adverse) risk selection. Suppose, for example, that low-risk enrollees were to congregate in low-cost PPO plans, obtaining rich benefits for services not covered by original Medicare (such as dental and vision care). Then these enrollees would cumulatively increase average costs in original Medicare, thereby increasing the Part B premium, increasing the subsidy to their plans, and having their additional benefits financed by other enrollees. This phenomenon is largely prevented in Medicare Advantage through a risk adjustment system that varies the premium subsidy to the MA plan based on the risk status of each enrollee. Enrollees without preexisting conditions bring a considerably lower premium subsidy than do, for example, diabetics and persons with congestive heart failure. In any event, the CMS has found only a few percentage points' difference in average cost between those enrolling in original Medicare and those enrolling in Medicare Advantage plans, so that the necessary premium adjustments are small on average. The residual problem, if any, is dwarfed by the premium subsidy differentials created by basing premiums largely on widely varying original Medicare costs in local areas.

As to extreme risk segmentation, plans have exited both Medicare Advantage and the prescription drug plan for many reasons, doubtless including adverse selection, that made plans unattractive as business offerings (recall the Humana Plan that filled the doughnut hole in the first year of the PDP program, but is now gone). The biggest exit wave occurred after the unintended subsidy cutbacks created by the Balanced Budget Act (discussed previously in the Medicare chapter). Nothing that looks at all like the dreaded death spiral has occurred in either program or appears at all likely to occur.

4

Cost Control

The "hot button" in comparing FEHBP and Medicare performance lies in their respective abilities to control cost increases over time. As the issue is most commonly set forth, if the unmanaged FEHBP can equal or better original Medicare's highly flawed, "one-size-fits-all" performance over time, then why shouldn't original Medicare be replaced by a premium-support system that allows consumers to make their own choices among plans? Why should we rely on the political and bureaucratic processes that overwhelmingly dominate Medicare decisions?

Dueling Estimates

The years have produced many competing and contradictory estimates of program performance for both Medicare and the FEHBP. These differences are easily created because conclusions depend heavily on the base year chosen for any comparison. For example, each program has had years in which its costs or premiums not merely stayed level, but decreased. A comparison ending in such a trough will likely show one program to be better than the other, whereas a comparison beginning in the same trough will likely show the opposite result.[1] Another variable affecting these comparisons lies in the ways they can use to measure costs. In particular, the FEHBP suffers because plans must predict future costs in setting their premiums. They can over- or underestimate over a several-year period, which can cause a readjustment in needed reserves and produce striking year-to-year changes. In the mid-1980s, after an OPM-forced benefit reduction, reserves grew so high that the OPM returned several billion dollars in reserves to the government (the primary payer) and to enrollees through cash rebates.[2] In 2007, after several years of unnecessarily high premium increases due to forecasting errors, most national plans were able to hold premiums level with 2006 by drawing down reserves. As a result, comparisons using weighted averages of premiums (as opposed to budgetary estimates of incurred costs) can be even more highly influenced by which years are selected as starting and ending points.[3]

The high (or low) point in such comparisons may have been reached in 2003 and early 2004, when six comparisons were published that, in effect, declared the issue of comparative cost control between original Medicare and the FEHBP settled. Three of these said that Medicare controlled costs better than private plans, singling out the FEHBP, and implied that the advocates of plan choice and premium support should quietly depart. Three said the opposite. It is unlikely that this flurry of activity (the results of which are summarized below) was a coincidence, given the then-recent furor over the imminent, but by no means settled, passage of the Medicare Modernization Act.[4] It has started again, in fact, with the salience of health reform. One recent analysis by an advocate for a "public plan" argues that Medicare controls costs better than private plans, while the blog's title nakedly displays the author's appraisal of more accurate estimates suggesting the opposite: "Dangerous Confusion on Medicare Cost Control" (White 2009).[5]

The history of Medicare/FEHBP comparisons is venerable. We can start, however, with the first comprehensive set of long-term cost control estimates, published in an essay in Robert Helms's *Health Policy Reform: Competition and Controls* (Francis 1993). Francis compared the two programs' cost control performances over time by comparing combined Medicare Part A and B costs to FEHBP premiums, from 1975 through 1993.[6] Francis chose to compare results only if they covered ten years or more, and to cover every available ten-year period ending from 1985 through 1993, to avoid biased base years. His analysis showed that both programs had been able to reduce annual cost increases from the double-digit to the single-digit range during this period. He concluded that Medicare slightly outperformed the FEHBP in nominal cost increases. For the latest available ten-year period, ending in 1993, he showed an average 9.1 percent rate of increase in FEHBP premiums, compared to 8.3 percent for Medicare costs.[7] These comparisons did not, however, include benefit improvements, which were almost nonexistent in Medicare but demonstrated by Francis to be substantial in the FEHBP. Hence, he concluded that, taking into account the effects of benefit improvements on premiums, the FEHBP outperformed Medicare in cost control.

A decade later, as the prospects for free-market surgery on Medicare grew, the first of the 2003 estimates, by Cristina Boccuti and Marilyn Moon of the Urban Institute, appeared in the March/April issue of *Health Affairs* (Boccuti and Moon 2003). This analysis of the period 1970–2000 used National Health Accounts data to compare private plans to Medicare over time. While it did not present any data on the FEHBP (which, several studies have shown, performs better than the private-sector average), it made specific references to the FEHBP program in criticizing the "assertions that the private sector is better able to constrain spending" (230), in pointed juxtaposition to a citation to testimony proposing the FEHBP as a model for Medicare reform. This study attempted to deal with the point that private plans covered prescription drugs while original Medicare did not. The comparisons of total growth in per-enrollee payments showed Medicare winning hands down, but when "like services" were compared, the trend lines were far closer. The study did not offer any detail on its data or calculation methods, and presented all its quantitative conclusions in graphs; hence, it was something of a "black box." It rather glowingly referred to "Medicare's success" and to the Davis finding, rebutted earlier in this analysis, that "Medicare beneficiaries are generally more satisfied with their health care than are privately insured people under age 65" (ibid., 235).[8]

Next to join the debate was Mark Merlis, an independent consultant commissioned by the Kaiser Family Foundation. Merlis correctly emphasized that "annual changes in FEHBP premiums can be deceptive" (Merlis 2003, 8). Nonetheless, he used a short time period to compare programs, from 1996 through 2003—a period including the years in which effects of the Balanced Budget Act of 1997 on Medicare spending were most pronounced. The result was, in effect, a "peak to trough" estimate of Medicare spending trends. Of course, Merlis was writing in 2003, and hence had little choice in the matter of the end year. He used two measures of FEHBP spending, one from premiums and one from the federal budget, showing that FEHBP over this period averaged either 5.3 percent or 7.2 percent in annual growth rate, depending on the data used, compared to an average 4.2 percent growth rate for Medicare spending. Merlis made a valiant but modest attempt to control for the generous coverage of drugs in the FEHBP by using OPM data that were, unfortunately, available only for two years, arguing that the Medicare advantage would have been reduced, but still present, after making this adjustment.

Following Merlis with the third set of estimates was Joe Antos of the American Enterprise Institute (U.S. Senate, Special Committee on Aging 2003). In an attempt to incorporate changes in insurance benefits systematically, Antos focused on changes in the generosity of private insurance benefits, using estimates from the National Health Accounts of reductions in private out-of-pocket spending over time as a measure of increasing plan generosity. He found that the percentage of spending paid by private health insurance plans had risen from about 60 percent in 1970 to about 85 percent in 1999. He agreed with Boccuti that, overall, unadjusted spending increases had been much higher for private insurance than for Medicare. Like the authors of other studies covering both earlier and later periods, he found that the early years favored private plans and the later years tended to favor Medicare. In his most important finding, however, Antos concluded that "although private insurance spending has risen faster than Medicare spending over the past 30 years, the *value* of private insurance has risen just as rapidly. These data suggest that Medicare does *not* have an advantage over the private sector in limiting the growth of health care spending" (ibid., 2, emphases in the original).

In June of that same year, Mike O'Grady of the U.S. Congress Joint Economic Committee produced the fourth set of estimates and expanded the comparison to include the California Public Employees Retirement System (CalPERS), which is second only to the FEHBP in size among employer programs, and which better meets Enthoven's preferred design parameters for managed competition (U.S. Senate, Joint Economic Committee 2003). Like Francis and Merlis, O'Grady emphasized the importance of the time period and base years used for comparison. In particular, he pointed out that the influence on such comparisons of the BBA and inclusion in the analysis of the years immediately preceding or following it was profound. O'Grady systematically assessed the effect of drug spending on comparative cost performance over the entire period since 1983. He found that without adjusting for this benefit differential, Medicare slightly outperformed the FEHBP in later years, but vice versa in earlier years, and that the two programs essentially tied in rate of growth over two decades. When he adjusted for drugs, the FEHBP outperformed Medicare by an average of just under one percentage point (5.8 percent versus 6.7 percent). He also found that CalPERS almost matched the FEHBP in performance, and that both programs substantially outperformed private health insurance as a whole.

> Hopefully, the last word.
> Jeff Lemieux, referring to the O'Grady analysis
> "Medicare vs. FEHBP Spending: A Rare, Reasonable Analysis"

In the fifth of the 2003 studies, Francis updated his 1993 estimates (Francis 2003a). He found that with updates through 2003, original Medicare and the FEHBP had tied in overall growth over the previous ten years, at 6 percent each. Since this comparison did not control for prescription drugs or changes in benefit generosity over time, he again concluded that the FEHBP still outperformed Medicare in cost control.

The sixth study appeared in January of 2004, when the "Health Accounts Team" at CMS presented its annual update on health spending in the U.S. economy (Levit et al. 2004). In a departure from its usual practice, the team compared Medicare, FEHBP, and overall private health insurance cost increases over time, specifically mentioning the policy debate over the merits of moving Medicare to a competitive model, and citing the recent work by Antos and O'Grady. This analysis of annual data through 2002 controlled for drug spending but not for changes in benefit generosity. It found that, calculated on either an unadjusted basis or controlling for drugs, Medicare outperformed both the FEHBP and private insurance in general. Excluding drugs, it found that over thirty years, Medicare's costs increased an average of 9.1 percent annually, compared to 9.6 percent in the FEHBP and 10.1 percent in private plans. In the most recent seventeen years (starting when the prospective payment system was imposed on hospitals and, hence, starting from a "peak"), it found rates of 5.8, 7.3, and 7.4 percent, respectively.

Of the six studies we have described, none used precisely the same methodology, and few presented any real detail on their data measurements

continued on page 118

TABLE 4-1

MEDICARE AND FEHBP COST CONTROL OVER TIME, UNADJUSTED

Year	————————————Original Medicare————————————				
	Part A cost ($)	Part B cost ($)	Average cost per enrollee ($)	Annual increase (%)	Ten-year average increase (%)
1975	462	180	642	NA	NA
1976	526	213	738	15.0	NA
1977	589	245	834	13.0	NA
1978	691	293	984	18.0	NA
1979	793	342	1,135	15.3	NA
1980	895	390	1,285	13.2	NA
1981	1,027	466	1,492	16.1	NA
1982	1,159	541	1,700	13.9	NA
1983	1,290	617	1,907	12.2	NA
1984	1,422	692	2,115	10.9	NA
1985	1,554	768	2,322	9.8	13.7
1986	1,591	831	2,422	4.3	12.7
1987	1,592	969	2,561	5.7	12.0
1988	1,630	1,070	2,700	5.4	10.7
1989	1,765	1,158	2,923	8.3	10.0
1990	1,963	1,304	3,267	11.8	9.8
1991	2,009	1,381	3,390	3.8	8.6
1992	2,315	1,445	3,760	10.9	8.3
1993	2,546	1,524	4,070	8.2	7.9
1994	2,783	1,658	4,441	9.1	7.7
1995	3,130	1,823	4,953	11.5	7.9
1996	3,412	1,900	5,312	7.2	8.2
1997	3,616	1,996	5,612	5.6	8.2
1998	3,483	2,071	5,554	−1.0	7.5
1999	3,322	2,180	5,502	−0.9	6.6
2000	3,272	2,381	5,653	2.7	5.7
2001	3,559	2,646	6,205	9.8	6.3
2002	3,743	2,922	6,665	7.4	6.0
2003	3,733	3,209	6,942	4.2	5.6
2004	4,039	3,450	7,489	7.9	5.4
2005	4,262	3,756	8,018	7.1	5.0
2006	4,392	4,113	8,505	6.1	4.9
2007	4,573	4,312	8,885	4.5	4.8
2008	5,091	4,433	9,524	7.2	5.6
2009 est.	5,314	4,508	9,822	3.1	6.0

SOURCES: Medicare data from annual U.S. Boards of Trustees 2009 and prior years, with some earlier years interpolated or from the U.S. House of Representatives, Committee on Ways and Means *Green Book*, 2004 and prior years. FEHBP data from U.S. Office of Management and Budget 2009 and prior years, with some years from the U.S. Office of Personnel Management Insurance Report 1982 and prior

		FEHBP		
Program costs ($M)	End-of-year enrollment (K)	Average cost per enrollee ($)	Annual increase (%)	Ten-year average increase (%)
1,753	3,147	557	NA	NA
2,239	3,226	694	24.6	NA
2,600	3,297	789	13.6	NA
2,808	3,393	828	4.9	NA
3,150	3,491	902	9.0	NA
3,674	3,598	1,021	13.2	NA
4,653	3,684	1,263	23.7	NA
4,980	3,729	1,335	5.7	NA
5,525	3,641	1,517	13.6	NA
6,583	3,689	1,784	17.6	NA
6,482	3,768	1,720	–3.6	12.2
5,723	3,847	1,488	–13.5	8.4
7,714	3,909	1,973	32.7	10.3
9,016	4,010	2,248	13.9	11.2
10,169	4,050	2,511	11.7	11.5
10,922	4,041	2,703	7.6	10.9
12,657	4,077	3,104	14.9	10.1
14,024	4,074	3,442	10.9	10.6
14,546	4,077	3,568	3.6	9.6
15,218	4,096	3,715	4.1	8.2
15,515	4,053	3,828	3.0	8.9
16,148	4,159	3,883	1.4	10.4
16,557	4,133	4,006	3.2	7.4
17,161	4,120	4,165	4.0	6.4
18,654	4,123	4,524	8.6	6.1
19,662	4,084	4,814	6.4	6.0
21,143	4,075	5,188	7.8	5.3
22,820	4,046	5,640	8.7	5.1
25,278	4,052	6,238	10.6	5.8
27,366	4,035	6,782	8.7	6.2
29,757	4,007	7,426	9.5	6.9
31,180	4,024	7,749	4.3	7.2
33,922	4,012	8,455	9.1	7.8
35,922	4,027	8,920	5.5	7.9
37,763	4,039	9,350	4.8	7.5

years. Medicare data primarily calendar year; FEHBP data primarily fiscal year.
NOTE: FEHBP amounts do not exactly equal annual premium changes because of changes in reserves and open season shifts.

continued from page 115
(for instance, just what dollar number was used for Medicare costs in year X was available only from Francis and Merlis). In broad outline, however, they agreed on several points, the most important two being that, first, the FEHBP and private plans generally were stronger in the earlier periods, but Medicare improved its relative performance after the payment reforms and reductions of the most recent two decades; and, second, the performance of the FEHBP and private plans relative to Medicare's was improved by taking into account prescription drug coverage. A third important point was addressed quantitatively only in the Antos study but rebutted by none— namely that, taking into account overall benefit generosity (not just drugs), private plans' performance in controlling costs was clearly equal to Medicare's.

Where the studies disagreed was in the "sound bite" bottom line as to whether, in fact, Medicare outperformed the FEHBP in cost control, or vice versa. The Levit and O'Grady studies stood in sharpest contrast, since they both attempted the identical adjustment—for prescription drug costs—and came to different conclusions.[9] Leaving aside that disagreement, the Antos study provided the most comprehensive and, arguably, the most thorough correction to the raw data in its comparison of Medicare to private health plans, taking into account improvement in private plans' insurance generosity over time.

Reacting in understandable puzzlement, the Office of the Assistant Secretary for Planning and Evaluation in the U.S. Department of Health and Human Services asked the Actuarial Research Corporation (ARC) to take a look at the controversy, focusing on the Boccuti and Moon and Francis analyses (Peppe et al. 2005). The unpublished report created a variety of comparisons using National Health Accounts and other data and essentially concluded that both analyses were accurate, despite minor differences in data, analysis, and presentation: "We therefore agree that the difference in growth rates between the two programs . . . is negligible" (ibid., 9). Since this comparison, like those it reviewed, did not measure benefit improvements, it left intact the point that the FEHBP had outperformed Medicare in benefit-adjusted cost control. The review also disclosed a methodological point that had not been clearly stated previously: The Boccuti and Moon analysis used a per-covered-life measure of enrollment (including children), whereas the Francis analysis used a per-contract (household) measure of enrollment. Since substantial aging of the federal workforce took place in this period, and "empty nesters" have much higher per-capita costs than young families, this is an implicit source of bias against the FEHBP in the comparison, analyzed below. That said, the ARC study did agree with Boccuti and Moon that, taken as a whole, Medicare had outperformed private-sector insurance substantially over an extended period; and it agreed with both analyses that in the most recent years, Medicare had outperformed the FEHBP (again, not controlling for benefit improvements).

All these studies are now somewhat dated. We can now take another look, building on their strengths and weaknesses as well as on a longer time series. Table 4-1 presents historical data covering the last third of a century, including data points and calculation details.

These data show no marked superiority of one program over another in controlling per-enrollee costs over the entire period of time, except for the last decade. They show a strong tendency for both programs to improve performance over time. Some results can be attributed to known causes. For example, Medicare shows a marked improvement in cost control in the years following enactment of prospective payment for hospitals, and again in the years following BBA enactment. The FEHBP shows some gyrations in the 1980s relating to a period of cost growth, OPM-directed benefit reductions to reduce costs, and subsequent benefit improvements when the OPM relented. The FEHBP also shows a period of remarkably low growth rates in the early and middle 1990s, when HMO enrollment was growing fast and before the HMO backlash not only reversed this trend but also reduced HMO-imposed utilization controls. These varying events, and the subsequent peaks and troughs, make even the ten-year comparisons follow otherwise unpredictable and inexplicable patterns. The other result of importance is that for the last ten years, these data seem to show that the Medicare program has decisively outperformed the FEHBP, with an average annual growth one and one-half percentage points lower. Note, however, that as recently as 2003, the ten-year record of the two programs was essentially tied, based on these unadjusted cost data.

Another way to view these same data is in terms of cumulative growth over time, showing the per-enrollee cost for each program as a multiple of the cost in the base year 1975. Figure 4-1 shows that as recently as the year

FIGURE 4-1

CUMULATIVE GROWTH IN PER-ENROLLEE COST
IN MEDICARE AND THE FEHBP, UNADJUSTED

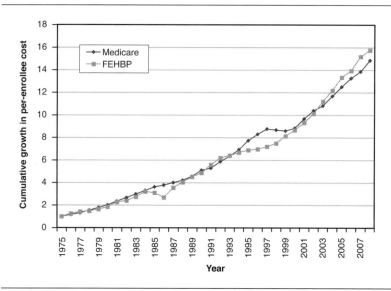

Source: Table 4-1.

2002, the cumulative growth in per-enrollee cost for Medicare (10.4) was higher than for the FEHBP (10.1). By 2009, however, Medicare (15.3) was more than a full multiple below the FEHBP (16.8).

These results do not control for five important variables. First, FEHBP benefit generosity has improved markedly over time. Second, Medicare has in recent years increasingly shifted payment of its enrollees' costs to private insurers through the Medicare Secondary Payer program, which artificially reduces Medicare's costs and raises private costs correspondingly. Third, the federal workforce has aged greatly in recent decades, resulting in a large increase in costly retirees as a fraction of total enrollment. Fourth, there is reason to believe, and some evidence, that Medicare Advantage and PDP plans have major effects in reducing the costs of original Medicare. All four of these factors penalize the FEHBP in comparison to Medicare. The fifth variable, the role of Medicare as primary insurer for most retirees over the age of sixty-five, has operated to reduce FEHBP cost growth, taking on increasing importance with the relative growth of the retiree population. We will explore these five variables in the sections below.

Benefit Generosity

The tale of the FEHBP, like that of employer-sponsored insurance (at least until recent years) is one of progressively increasing benefits over time. These manifest themselves most prominently as reductions in deductibles and coinsurance, and in conversion of coinsurance to copayments. It is very difficult to draw valid comparisons of health benefits over time, since the Consumer Price Index (CPI) can only generously be described as approximate in its measurement of health-care costs. Such problems in the medical-care portion of the CPI are well documented (Triplett 1999). More importantly, in recent decades the CPI has been modified in several areas, most notably automobile purchase, to take into account quality improvements over time. No such adjustments have been made to health-care spending. Longevity has improved so markedly in recent decades, with progress well documented in areas as diverse as emergency room treatment, prevention of stroke and heart attack, and cancer treatment, as to assure with certainty that health care has greatly improved its efficacy over time, despite well-documented problems of access and errors (Schuster et al. 2002). Nonetheless, nominal costs of health insurance offer some basis for comparisons over time, providing the insurance is compared equivalently, a conceptually much easier task (Pauly 1999).

Using the largest health plan in the FEHBP as an illustration, consider the progression of benefits in the Blue Cross standard option shown in table 4-2.

As these data show, this plan eliminated hospital day limits and benefit maximums, while adding a catastrophic protection benefit that, in real terms, has steadily improved.[10] Likewise, as measured either by federal pay or the CPI, the deductible has been greatly reduced in real terms from the levels it would otherwise have reached. Interestingly, in 1970 the deductible was higher than the total cost of the policy. The Blue Cross benefit progression is typical of national plans in the program. HMOs, which have always had more generous benefits than FFS plans, have increased their benefits less.

TABLE 4-2

BLUE CROSS STANDARD OPTION BENEFIT IMPROVEMENT OVER TIME

Year	Total premium (self only)	Nominal deductible	Hospital confinement day limit
1970	$100	$150	30
1975	$110	$150	90
1980	$210	$200	30
1985	$780	$250	None
1990	$1,760	$250	None
1995	$2,110	$200	None
2000	$2,830	$200	None
2005	$4,730	$250	None
2006	$5,130	$250	None
2007	$5,180	$250	None
2008	$5,390	$300	None
2009	$5,600	$300	None

Sources: Benefits from Blue Cross brochures; premium data from the OPM; pay and CPI data from Patrick Purcell, Congressional Research Service 2009a.

The cumulative effect of benefit increases has been major. These increases have occurred both in the plans themselves and in the choices of enrollees among plans, most notably in the movement toward HMOs from FFS plans. Table 4-3 adjusts for these changes. It uses an enrollment-weighted estimate of out-of-pocket costs, as measured by *CHECKBOOK's Guide* for non-aged employee enrollees in all plans (Francis et al. 2008 and prior years). While these costs differ from those of retirees in any given year, they change almost identically over time.[11]

The table shows that out-of-pocket payments by enrollees have decreased from about 40 percent of total payments under the average plan (enrollment-weighted) to about 13 percent over the last third of a century.[12] These percentages would be slightly different for retirees below age sixty-five, but the trends would be the same. As discussed below, they would be significantly different, and far lower, for retirees with Medicare. Note that these estimates include both prescription drug and dental expenses, the

Maximum outpatient benefit limit	Catastrophic protection limit	Deductible if indexed to federal pay	Deductible if indexed to CPI
$20,000	None	$150	$150
$150,000	None	$190	$190
None	$8,000	$280	$430
None	$2,750	$330	$690
None	$3,150	$380	$830
None	$3,950	$450	$770
None	$3,750	$530	$870
None	$4,000	$650	$1,220
None	$4,000	$670	$1,260
None	$4,000	$680	$1,300
None	$4,500	$710	$1,630
None	$5,000	$730	$1,630

methodology used in *CHECKBOOK's Guide* (Francis et al. 2008 and prior years). That methodology is revised slightly every year, and in some years more than in others, and measured changes in out-of-pocket costs reflect those small alterations.

Adjusting for benefit generosity greatly improves the measured performance of the FEHBP in controlling costs over time. In most years it reduces the annual percentage rate of increase by one or two percentage points. In recent years, however, benefit improvement has slowed and ended, largely as the result of three factors. First, HMOs have better benefits, and the earlier migration to HMOs has been halted and slightly reversed. Second, as levels of out-of-pocket costs approach zero, the relative scope for improvement is greatly reduced. Third, plans know perfectly well that some level of cost-sharing is necessary to restrain utilization and are reluctant to eliminate it entirely, except for hospitalization. In 2008 and 2009, the trend actually reversed slightly, in part because the largest single plan, Blue Cross standard option, slightly increased cost-sharing.

continued on page 127

TABLE 4-3

FEHBP COST INCREASES ADJUSTED FOR BENEFIT IMPROVEMENTS

Year	Average cost per enrollee ($)	Annual increase (%)	Ten-year average increase (%)
1975	557	NA	NA
1976	694	24.6	NA
1977	789	13.6	NA
1978	828	4.9	NA
1979	902	9.0	NA
1980	1,021	13.2	NA
1981	1,263	23.7	NA
1982	1,335	5.7	NA
1983	1,517	13.6	NA
1984	1,784	17.6	NA
1985	1,720	−3.6	12.2
1986	1,488	−13.5	8.4
1987	1,973	32.7	10.3
1988	2,248	13.9	11.2
1989	2,511	11.7	11.5
1990	2,703	7.6	10.9
1991	3,104	14.9	10.1
1992	3,442	10.9	10.6
1993	3,568	3.6	9.6
1994	3,715	4.1	8.2
1995	3,828	3.0	8.9
1996	3,883	1.4	10.4
1997	4,006	3.2	7.4
1998	4,165	4.0	6.4
1999	4,524	8.6	6.1
2000	4,814	6.4	6.0
2001	5,188	7.8	5.3
2002	5,640	8.7	5.1
2003	6,238	10.6	5.8
2004	6,782	8.7	6.2
2005	7,426	9.5	6.9
2006	7,749	4.3	7.2
2007	8,445	9.1	7.8
2008	8,920	5.5	7.9
2009 est.	9,350	4.8	7.5

SOURCES: Previous table for unadjusted FEHBP cost estimates; *CHECKBOOK's Guide* estimates of out-of-pocket costs for each plan for self-only employees (Francis et al. 2008 and prior years), weighted

Out-of-pocket percentage of total cost	Adjustment for out-of-pocket costs ($)	Adjusted cost ($)	Annual increase (%)	Ten-year average increase (%)
39.5	364	921	NA	NA
38.5	434	1,129	22.6	NA
37.5	473	1,262	11.8	NA
36.5	476	1,303	3.3	NA
35.5	497	1,399	7.3	NA
34.5	538	1,559	11.4	NA
33.5	636	1,899	21.8	NA
32.5	643	1,978	4.2	NA
31.5	698	2,215	12.0	NA
30.5	783	2,568	15.9	NA
29.5	720	2,440	−5.0	10.5
27.7	571	2,059	−15.6	6.7
26.0	693	2,666	29.5	8.5
24.2	719	2,967	11.3	9.3
22.5	727	3,238	9.1	9.5
20.7	706	3,408	5.3	8.8
19.6	757	3,861	13.3	8.0
18.5	781	4,224	9.4	8.5
17.4	752	4,319	2.3	7.5
16.3	724	4,439	2.8	6.2
15.2	686	4,514	1.7	6.9
14.9	678	4,560	1.0	8.6
14.5	680	4,687	2.8	5.9
14.2	688	4,854	3.6	5.1
13.8	727	5,251	8.2	5.0
13.5	751	5,566	6.0	5.1
14.3	866	6,054	8.8	4.6
14.3	940	6,580	8.7	4.6
14.9	1,092	7,331	11.4	5.5
14.9	1,186	7,968	8.7	6.1
13.4	1,149	8,575	7.6	6.7
12.8	1,137	8,886	3.6	6.9
12.5	1,208	9,663	8.7	7.5
13.1	1,345	10,265	6.2	7.8
13.0	1,397	10,747	4.7	7.4

for enrollment using unpublished "Head Count" data from the OPM Office of Actuaries.
NOTE: Some years interpolated.

TABLE 4-4

MEDICARE AND FEHBP COST CONTROL OVER TIME,
ADJUSTED FOR BENEFIT IMPROVEMENT

| Year | ———Original Medicare——— | | ———FEHBP adjusted——— | |
	Annual increase (%)	Ten-year average increase (%)	Annual increase (%)	Ten-year average increase (%)
1975	NA	NA	NA	NA
1976	15.0	NA	22.6	NA
1977	13.0	NA	11.8	NA
1978	18.0	NA	3.3	NA
1979	15.3	NA	7.3	NA
1980	13.2	NA	11.4	NA
1981	16.1	NA	21.8	NA
1982	13.9	NA	4.2	NA
1983	12.2	NA	12.0	NA
1984	10.9	NA	15.9	NA
1985	9.8	13.7	−5.0	10.5
1986	4.3	12.7	−15.6	6.7
1987	5.7	12.0	29.5	8.5
1988	5.4	10.7	11.3	9.3
1989	8.3	10.0	9.1	9.5
1990	11.8	9.8	5.3	8.8
1991	3.8	8.6	13.3	8.0
1992	10.9	8.3	9.4	8.5
1993	8.2	7.9	2.3	7.5
1994	9.1	7.7	2.8	6.2
1995	11.5	7.9	1.7	6.9
1996	7.2	8.2	1.0	8.6
1997	5.6	8.2	2.8	5.9
1998	−1.0	7.5	3.6	5.1
1999	−0.9	6.6	8.2	5.0
2000	2.7	5.7	6.0	5.1
2001	9.8	6.3	8.8	4.6
2002	7.4	6.0	8.7	4.6
2003	4.2	5.6	11.4	5.5
2004	7.9	5.4	8.7	6.1
2005	7.1	5.0	7.6	6.7

continued on the next page

Table 4-4, continued from the previous page

| | —————Original Medicare————— | | —————FEHBP adjusted————— | |
Year	Annual increase (%)	Ten-year average increase (%)	Annual increase (%)	Ten-year average increase (%)
2006	6.1	4.9	3.6	6.9
2007	4.5	4.8	8.7	7.5
2008	7.2	5.6	6.2	7.8
2009 est.	3.1	6.0	4.7	7.4
All-year avg.	8.4	7.8	7.8	7.1
1975–2001 avg.	9.2	8.9	7.9	7.3
2002–2009 avg.	5.9	5.4	7.4	6.6

SOURCE: Table 4-1 and table 4-3.

continued from page 123

The result of controlling for increasing FEHBP benefit generosity in comparing FEHBP and Medicare performance over time is shown in table 4-4, which combines table 4-3 results with the same Medicare data used in table 4-1. I have made no attempt to adjust Medicare benefits for generosity, as those changes are relatively small and there are no time series data to capture their effects on out-of-pocket payments.[13]

With the comparison adjusted for benefits improvement, the FEHBP demonstrates decisively superior cost control performance over the entire period of time, particularly in the earlier twenty-five years. Even with the adjustment, however, Medicare shows a marked relative improvement, and absolutely better results, in the last half-dozen years. These are due in part to BBA-created payment reductions, and in part to the effects on the FEHBP of unusually high increases in prescription drug prices in most of the last decade. They are likely also due to the effects of Medicare Advantage plans in reducing the costs of original Medicare in the areas in which they attract substantial enrollment (see Chernew et al. 2008, Zhang et al. 2009, my discussion of competitive Medicare below, and my evaluation of Medicare Advantage in the concluding section). It appears that Medicare Advantage plans have an independent effect on reducing costs in original Medicare not just by reducing costs to enrollees they attract, but also by reducing costs of original Medicare enrollees in the same geographic areas through effects on

FIGURE 4-2

CUMULATIVE GROWTH IN PER-ENROLLEE COST IN MEDICARE
AND THE FEHBP, ADJUSTED FOR BENEFIT IMPROVEMENTS

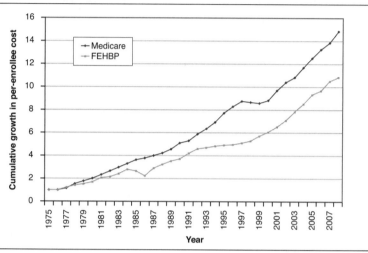

SOURCE: Table 4-2.

physician practices. The OPM estimates that almost one-fifth of FEHBP total spending is on prescription drugs, due in large part to drug utilization by those over age sixty-five.[14] Medicare, as a latecomer to drug coverage, has suffered virtually none of that cost increase. Most important was the blow delivered to the FEHBP's competitive model by premium conversion (as was discussed in chapter 2, above). Savings to enrollees from choosing lower-cost plans were cut by a third, from an already low maximum of 25 percent to a paltry 16 or 17 percent among plans with lower premiums, and the penalty for choosing higher-cost plans was cut by a third, from the entire cost of the higher premium to only about two-thirds of it.

With these four factors in Medicare's structural favor occurring more or less simultaneously, it is impossible to separate out their independent effects. They clearly show in the figures for 2002–7, however. Without reforms addressed later in this analysis, the FEHBP is unlikely ever again to match or beat Medicare performance in cost control.

Nonetheless, as indicated in the benefit-adjusted graph in figure 4-2, the cumulative effect of annual increases over time still shows a clear superiority for the FEHBP.

Medicare Secondary Payer

One major potential adjustment to the Medicare data arises because, quite apart from original Medicare's performance in controlling costs in its own operations, Congress has passed regulatory legislation that makes it illegal for private plans (including FEHBP plans) to pay after, rather than before, Medicare pays for the working aged and several other categories of Medicare enrollees. Prior to 1982, it was common practice for older workers to sign up for Medicare at age sixty-five, and for their employer's plan to become the secondary payer after Medicare for medical costs. Medicare was the universal entitlement program for all persons over age sixty-five. Then, in a fit of budget discipline, the Medicare Secondary Payer (MSP) program was created in 1982 through the Tax Equity and Fiscal Responsibility Act (TEFRA, Public Law 97-248) as a scheme to force employers—really, as all economists agree, workers—to subsidize even more of the cost of original Medicare. MSP imposed a panoply of legal requirements to compel acquiescence. For example, it became illegal for workers to purchase Medigap policies upon turning sixty-five. It is also illegal under MSP for employers not to provide age-sixty-five workers the identical policies they provide to age-sixty-four workers—that is, MSP prohibits employers from relying on Medicare entitlement as primary coverage for their aged workers. But the essential change was to make Medicare a conditional rather than absolute entitlement for age-sixty-five workers and thereby eliminate almost all Medicare payments on behalf of those "enrollees."[15]

For some years MSP had relatively little effect. Employers readily skirted its rules, and, even when they couldn't, the government had only ineffective tools to identify which workers over age sixty-five had group health insurance from their employers (Glied and Stabile 2001, Goda et al. 2007, Chaikind for the U.S. Congressional Research Service 2008). The GAO periodically fulminated at the lack of progress (U.S. General Accounting Office 1995). Nonetheless, substantial advances were made over time due both to legislative accretions and executive branch efforts. For example, the Office of the Inspector General of the Department of Health and Human Services became a diligent reviewer (a June 2009 search within www.hhs.gov/oig for the term "MSP" resulted in 236 hits). The only enforcement mechanism was for years a questionnaire sent to all newly enrolled Medicare beneficiaries asking if they

TABLE 4-5

MEDICARE SECONDARY PAYER DATA

Year	Number of MSP cases (thousands)					
	Working aged	Auto insurance and workers comp	Working disabled	All others	Total cases	Percentage of Medicare enrollment
1996	659	376	346	146	1,527	4.0%
1997	919	443	455	194	2,011	5.2%
1998	946	484	491	221	2,142	5.5%
1999	1,019	524	538	242	2,323	5.9%
2000	1,184	567	571	248	2,570	6.5%
2001	1,294	593	601	276	2,764	6.9%
2002	1,390	629	624	300	2,943	7.2%
2003	1,511	671	656	324	3,162	7.7%
2004	1,586	719	680	346	3,331	7.9%
2005	1,735	764	720	365	3,584	8.4%
2006	1,798	799	713	385	3,695	8.5%

SOURCES: Unpublished data from the CMS Medicare Denominator File, courtesy of the Office of Research, Development, and Information.

had any other health insurance. Using authority added in the Omnibus Budget Reconciliation Act of 1989 (Public Law 101-239), the CMS also now uses a data match program involving Social Security Administration and Internal Revenue Service records to identify employers who might sponsor insurance subject to MSP. As another reform, in 2001 the agency placed primary enforcement responsibility in the hands of a single coordination of benefits contract. In 2007, in the Medicare, Medicaid, and SCHIP Extension Act (Public Law 110-173), Congress sought to improve MSP enforcement even further by expanding legal requirements that most health plans in America report enrollment information to enhance the CMS's ability to make collections.

With all this effort, and with expansions to cover additional groups, including the working disabled below age sixty-five, MSP has over the years covered an increasing percentage of Medicare beneficiaries. Although HHS has apparently not published any data on either covered enrollees or monies saved, some pieces of information are available, as shown in table 4-5.

These data show that as of 2006, some 3.7 million Medicare enrollees—over 8 percent of total Medicare enrollment—were subject to MSP. This is an increase from about 4 percent a decade ago. About half of these persons are working aged, a category likely to grow substantially in future years. A large number are working disabled, reflecting strenuous efforts in both the Bill Clinton and George W. Bush administrations to provide incentives and assistance to disabled Americans to return to the workforce.

MSP payment rules are draconian. It is very difficult for a Medicare enrollee to obtain any Medicare compensation after his private policy has paid his primary benefit. Accordingly, MSP creates a Medicare windfall currently on the order of $30 billion a year (perhaps as much as $10,000 per enrollee). It would be higher but for workers being allowed penalty-free discretion as to whether to sign up for Part B upon turning age sixty-five if they are still working and covered by group insurance.[16] Although few likely realize that Part B provides essentially zero benefits in their situation, some fraction of them decline to enroll, which limits potential MSP savings to hospitalization cost under Part A. It is also likely that the sickest and most expensive retire (immediately making Medicare primary) while the healthier (on average) continue to work.

It is, therefore, unclear how much the regulatory MSP program artificially reduces the amounts of money attributed to original Medicare costs, and how much it would raise the average per-enrollee costs of original Medicare were this adjustment to be made. My rough calculations suggest, however, that an assumption that MSP saves 80 percent of what Medicare would otherwise pay would increase the annual rate of increase in original Medicare spending by about three-tenths of 1 percent. This is not enough to change our quantitative conclusions substantially, but it does reinforce the pattern already described. Table 4-6 shows what the comparison adjusted for FEHBP benefit improvements would be, taking into account MSP.

These data should be viewed as suggestive rather than certain, since they rest on very little hard information about MSP. Assuming, however, that these adjustments are reasonably accurate, they both confirm and solidify the findings that over the entire period the FEHBP has decisively outperformed original Medicare in cost control, that this superiority was

TABLE 4-6

MEDICARE AND FEHBP COST CONTROL OVER TIME, ADJUSTED FOR MEDICARE SECONDARY PAYER AND BENEFIT IMPROVEMENT

Year	Medicare adjusted for MSP Annual increase (%)	Medicare adjusted for MSP Ten-year average increase (%)	FEHBP adjusted for benefits Annual increase (%)	FEHBP adjusted for benefits Ten-year average increase (%)
1975	NA	NA	NA	NA
1976	15.0	NA	22.6	NA
1977	13.0	NA	11.8	NA
1978	18.0	NA	3.3	NA
1979	15.3	NA	7.3	NA
1980	13.2	NA	11.4	NA
1981	16.1	NA	21.8	NA
1982	13.9	NA	4.2	NA
1983	12.5	NA	12.0	NA
1984	11.1	NA	15.9	NA
1985	10.1	13.8	−5.0	10.5
1986	4.6	12.8	−15.6	6.7
1987	6.0	12.1	29.5	8.5
1988	5.7	10.8	11.3	9.3
1989	8.5	10.2	9.1	9.5
1990	12.0	10.0	5.3	8.8
1991	4.0	8.8	13.3	8.0
1992	11.2	8.6	9.4	8.5
1993	8.5	8.2	2.3	7.5
1994	9.4	8.0	2.8	6.2
1995	11.7	8.2	1.7	6.9
1996	7.4	8.4	1.0	8.6
1997	6.7	8.5	2.8	5.9
1998	−0.8	7.9	3.6	5.1
1999	−0.6	6.9	8.2	5.0
2000	3.2	6.1	6.0	5.1
2001	10.1	6.7	8.8	4.6
2002	7.7	6.3	8.7	4.6
2003	4.5	5.9	11.4	5.5

continued on the next page

Table 4-6, continued from the previous page

	Medicare adjusted for MSP		FEHBP adjusted for benefits	
Year	Annual increase (%)	Ten-year average increase (%)	Annual increase (%)	Ten-year average increase (%)
2004	8.1	5.8	8.7	6.1
2005	7.4	5.4	7.6	6.7
2006	6.1	5.2	3.6	6.9
2007	4.5	5.0	8.7	7.5
2008	7.2	5.8	6.2	7.8
2009 est.	3.1	6.2	4.7	7.4
All-year avg.	8.7	8.1	7.8	7.1
1975–2001 avg.	9.4	9.2	7.9	7.3
2002–9 avg.	6.1	5.7	7.4	6.6

SOURCE: Author's calculations.

pronounced from 1975 to 2001, and that during the last decade the pattern reversed, with Medicare demonstrating a slight performance edge.

Aging Federal Enrollees

The third major variable we have noted as still uncontrolled in the comparison above is the aging of the federal workforce and growth in the retiree population as a proportion of FEHBP enrollees. The federal workforce has grown progressively and markedly older over the last two decades. Unfortunately, no age data are extant that cover the last third of a century, plus postal as well as general schedule employees, plus retirees. Data from the OPM on nonpostal civilian employees, however, show a massive deterioration in the relative proportion of lower-cost younger employees compared to older employees and retirees. From 1985 to 2006 the average age of these federal employees increased from forty-two to forty-seven years, as shown by the data in figure 4-3.

While it is a commonplace that health-care costs rise with age, it is always well to be reminded of the extent to which this occurs. Data from

FIGURE 4-3

AGE DISTRIBUTION OF FEDERAL EMPLOYEES

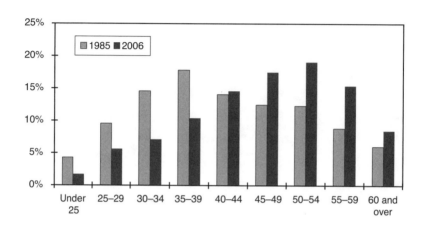

SOURCE: U.S. Office of Personnel Management, Office of Workforce Information n.d.
NOTE: Data include only full-time permanent civilian employees and exclude postal employees.

FIGURE 4-4

HEALTH CARE SPENDING BY AGE

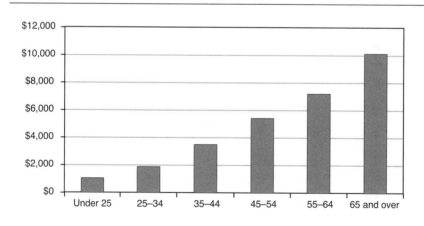

SOURCE: Pooled Medical Expenditure Panel Survey (MEPS) data for 2003–5, adjusted for inflation,
provided to the author by the Agency for Healthcare Research and Quality of the U.S. Department of
Health and Human Services.

the Medical Expenditure Panel Survey for recent years demonstrate just how severely the FEHBP has been affected, as shown in figure 4-4.

Other demographic trends also influence costs. In recent decades, families have been getting smaller, and older employees are most commonly "empty nesters," two factors that mean the proportion of children covered by the program has been decreasing. The cost-per-"contract"-enrollee measure used in almost all analyses comparing the FEHBP and Medicare does not control for this omitted variable, the net effect of which, if measured, would slightly offset the increase in cost due to the aging of the parents.[17] Another variable on which we do have data is the relative proportion of self-only to family enrollments. The former have been rising as a proportion of total enrollment, from about 39 percent in 1990 to about 47 percent in 2008. This is financially significant, as family premiums average slightly more than twice as much as self-only premiums in the FEHBP. Of course, this change primarily reflects the growth in older and divorced or widowed enrollees, and hence also simply offsets part of the unmeasured effect of aging on cost. Without an appropriate set of data on the demographics of enrollees, it is hard to reach any conclusion other than the obvious one that the aging effect tilts the comparison substantially, and that were age and family composition to be appropriately adjusted, the comparison results would be even more strongly in the FEHBP's favor than those produced simply by making the benefit adjustment.

Competitive Medicare

A fifth variable that affects the cost comparison is the effect of competitive Medicare on the costs of original Medicare. As we shall discuss at greater length, there are theoretical grounds, and some evidence, suggesting that both Medicare Advantage and prescription drug plans reduce the cost of original Medicare from what it would otherwise have been. A recent study on "The Effect of Medicare Part D on Drug and Medical Spending" (Zhang et al. 2009) found offsetting reductions in medical (hospital and doctor) spending that roughly equaled the cost of increases in drug spending among those who had little or no prior drug coverage. This study's sample was limited to those in a Medicare Advantage plan, but its results are likely generalizable to the broader Part D population, including those in stand-alone PDP plans, subject to the caveat that an MA plan has incentives and tools to manage care not available to those in original Medicare. Other studies (Chernew et al. 2008, Atherly and Thorpe 2005) also suggest strong effects on spending on original Medicare from MA plans, either directly or because they reduce Medicaid participation and, hence, the overutilization due to Medicaid. Also, although there is as yet no quantitative study, the role of MA in reducing Medigap enrollment has undoubtedly led to substantial savings in original Medicare through increased cost-sharing.

These results are discussed later in the analysis as part of our overall appraisal of competitive Medicare. For present purposes, the key point is that the MA and PDP programs, operating independently, create savings for original Medicare that it could not have achieved on its own, given its inherent design. These effects have been strongest in the last decade (with Medicare Advantage and its predecessor reaching all-time high levels of enrollment, and the creation of Part D), precisely the period in which, for the first time in five decades, original Medicare showed a cost advantage over the FEHBP.

Medicare and FEHBP Interaction

Were the analysis to stop here, the conclusion on comparative cost control would be unambiguously in favor of the FEHBP. It is likely that even in the last decade, and despite the introduction of tax-preferred enrollee premiums, the FEHBP has outperformed original Medicare in cost control. There is, however, the fifth major variable we have mentioned above: A large fraction of what would otherwise be FEHBP costs are paid by Medicare. If Medicare enrollment were constant as a proportion of FEHBP enrollment over the years, this would not affect the direct comparison. We do know that ever since the inception of Medicare, the FEHBP national plans have sought to persuade enrollees to join Medicare. National plan brochures have, since the 1960s, pointedly stated that when Medicare is primary for hospital and physician costs, the FEHBP plan guarantees that the enrollee bears no cost-sharing for those services. Even before Medicare Part A coverage for federal retirees was guaranteed to those retiring after 1983, a fraction obtained Part A coverage through private employment before or after federal service.

FIGURE 4-5

**PLAN COST BY AGE AND MEDICARE STATUS
WHEN MEDICARE PAYS FIRST, 2006**

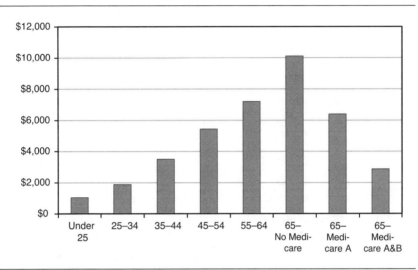

SOURCES: Pooled Medical Expenditure Panel Survey (MEPS) data for 2003–5, adjusted for inflation, provided to the author by the Agency for Healthcare Research and Quality of the U.S. Department of Health and Human Services; U.S. Department of Health and Human Services, Centers for Medicare and Medicaid Services 2006a, table 21.

Part B has always been available to all federal retirees on the same basis as private retirees, and until recent years was a reasonably desirable supplement to FEHBP coverage.[18] However, although the proportion of enrollees ages sixty-five and over who have Medicare coverage does not appear to be changing substantially over time (as shown previously in this analysis), the proportion of enrollees ages sixty-five and over to total enrollment has grown. Hence, the pattern shown in figure 4-5 becomes important. This figure shows the average cost for which FEHBP plans are responsible for various categories of age and Medicare status. It shows that older workers and younger retirees in the age range of fifty-five to sixty-four are the second-worst risk category for plans, with costs more than double those of workers ages twenty-five to forty-four.[19] Retirees with Medicare parts A and B present costs, after Medicare pays first, just about the same as those for these younger workers.

While these data are not specific to the FEHBP, they do take into account both prescription drug and dental spending, and a similar calculation for the FEHBP would undoubtedly show an almost identical pattern, except for the utilization effects discussed below. Hence, it is likely that Medicare coverage largely but not entirely offsets the effects of an aging workforce with respect to at least the retiree population.

Yet another potentially cost-reducing connection illustrates the "joined-at-the-hip" situation of these two programs. Congress enacted statutes in 1990 for inpatient hospitals, and in 1993 for physician services, that prohibited charges for FEHBP enrollees ages sixty-five and over higher than the charges allowed under Medicare inpatient and outpatient fee schedules, respectively. This limitation on costs applies whether or not the retiree is enrolled in Medicare Part A or Part B. Hence, while not, strictly speaking, a Medicare coordination benefit, the law now mandates a noncompetitive rate for this group of enrollees and has undoubtedly reduced their FEHBP costs below the levels that the plans were able to negotiate with preferred providers. Because this limitation on hospital and physician charges applies to all hospitals and physicians participating in Medicare, however, not just to plan-preferred providers, it effectively prevents plans from applying panel restrictions to these enrollees, unless the plan provides no out-of-network coverage.

This elimination of network limitations presents yet another factor. The combination of Medicare and a national FEHBP plan provides essentially free hospital and physician care, in the United States or abroad, similar to the combination of Medicare and the most generous Medigap plans. Because dual coverage creates a 15–25 percent increase in utilization and costs for FEHBP enrollees compared to those of comparable age who are not enrolled in parts A and B, much of the apparent savings to the FEHBP from dual enrollment is dissipated (Medicare, as primary payer, bears the brunt of the cost increase, but even a program as large as the FEHBP would have little effect on overall Medicare cost averages).

Cost-Shifting

Still missing from the analysis is cost-shifting. Were cost-shifting from Medicare (and Medicaid) to private insurance neutral in proportion over time, and attributable largely to the original enactment of hospital prospective payment, it would have little effect on performance comparisons for recent decades. Or, if cost-shifting were really quite small, it would have little effect. There are unsettled questions (see Dobson et al. 2006 for one perspective, Morrisey 2003 and 1994 for another). But there is no reason to accept these predicates uncritically. Cost-shifting effects are likely to be largest when Medicare payment rules are the most stringent. The principal effects of prospective payment in the early years were those on hospital incentives. Shorter lengths of stay became profitable when reimbursement shifted from paying all hospital costs, however high at any particular hospital, to fixed fees for episodes of care. Prospective payment provided a cost reduction engine that benefited public and private payers almost alike.

But when payment rates grow ever tighter, as they have since the BBA was enacted, the magnitude of cost-shifting is likely to become stronger. This clearly disadvantages the FEHBP in any cost comparison, and potentially very substantially. One recent industry-sponsored and crude estimate pegs the annual effects of cost-shifting due to "underpayments" by Medicare and Medicaid compared to private payers at almost $90 billion annually, and about $1,500 in additional premium for an average family (Fox and Pickering 2008). Even if the underlying reality is only a small fraction of estimates such as these, the FEHBP-to-Medicare cost comparisons would change radically with even relatively small adjustments. Cost-shifting, by definition, is not cost control. To the extent that original Medicare's accounting costs are artificially reduced by having its real costs paid by others, any conventionally measured costs are a misleading measure to that same extent. Any substantial cost-shifting during the last decade would reverse the seeming improvement in relative Medicare performance over that decade. For example, cost-shifting on the order of $35 billion would reduce the average conventionally measured per-enrollee cost of original Medicare by about 10 percent from its real level. It would also raise the cost of a private plan, such as those in the FEHBP, by several percent.

Among the conditions necessary for cost-shifting to occur is for original Medicare to exercise a considerable degree of monopsony power. Undoubtedly, Medicare has such power. Although the law does not compel participation in Medicare, it is hard to see how a hospital could survive financially or in the court of public opinion were it to refuse to take Medicare patients. Suppliers of medical equipment would face a similar constraint, as would physicians whose specialties lead to a predominantly elderly patient load (for instance, open-heart surgery). Without better and better-accepted measures of cost-shifting, including changes over time, these effects cannot be shown in our comparison tables.

Displacement and Crowd-Out

Displacement is one of the most neglected aspects of program performance.[20] "Displacement" refers to the tendency of any recipient of earmarked funds to use those funds to displace monies it would otherwise have spent from its own revenues. The phenomenon is pervasive in federal grants-in-aid programs for states and localities, and in federal transfer payments to individuals. For example, federal highway grants "free up" money that states would otherwise have spent to build highways, with the result that the net effect of these grants is less increased spending on highways than the accounting measures of program spending suggest. Likewise, food stamps displace some money that recipients would otherwise have spent on food from their other resources, however meager.[21] Again, the accounting trail shows that the money is spent on food at the grocery store, but does not include the money that would otherwise have been spent on food.

Many factors affect displacement. For example, very-low-income persons have fewer of their own resources, and studies have found that food stamps are very efficient in improving dietary intake for the very poorest. But recipients with higher (though still low) incomes increase their dietary intake by much less than the value of the food stamps they receive. In effect, the food stamp subsidy for food allows them to spend more on other valued consumption. Displacement is higher when programs fund activities that are highly valued by recipients and lower when the activities are lower priorities of recipients. Cost-sharing ("matching") also substantially affects spending incentives and displacement.

Congress can and sometimes does adjust program design to attempt to reduce displacement. For example, it is common for discretionary grant programs to require states and localities to maintain existing spending levels ("maintenance of effort"). These requirements are almost always ineffectual over time because they do not include an inflation adjustment. The Medicaid program involves displacement at two levels—both substituting for some state spending and substituting for some enrollee spending. Congress has tried to reduce the former with a variable match rate favoring the poorest states, but the matching formula is highly flawed and fails to achieve this objective (Helms 2007).

Displacement has been recognized as a major factor in health insurance subsidies to individuals under the descriptive term "crowd-out," used in this context to describe individuals' choices to drop (or decline) private insurance to get publicly subsidized insurance instead. Crowd-out is difficult to measure, and econometric studies of Medicaid and the State Children's Health Insurance Program have, over time, resulted in varying estimates (Gruber and Simon 2008). A careful synthesis and reanalysis of the available data, however, have led to the conclusion that in these two programs, crowd-out rates are on the order of 60 percent. That is, more than half of those covered would purchase their own insurance (usually with an employer contribution) if they were not offered the public program. The result is that the taxpayer cost per person enrolled is roughly double the accounting cost figures that ignore this displacement effect.

There do not appear to be any studies of displacement in either original Medicare or the FEHBP. With the taxpayer share of average per-enrollee Medicare costs at almost 90 percent, however, and the revealed willingness of enrollees to pay for Medigap insurance from their own funds, it seems obvious that most enrollees are being unnecessarily subsidized for a substantial portion of the costs that they could and would pay from own funds if their premium cost-sharing for parts A, B, and C were increased. (Recall that the lowest income enrollees pay no "premium" cost—a subsidy that would presumably continue if premium cost-sharing were raised for those with average or higher incomes.) This suggests that displacement in the broadest sense (not crowd-out, as more narrowly defined in terms of an all-

or-nothing purchasing decision) is substantial in original Medicare and, by extension, Medicare Advantage. Substantial displacement undoubtedly occurs in Medicare Part D, and one study estimates this to be on the order of 70 percent—even higher than for Medicaid and SCHIP (Lichtenberg and Sun 2007). Estimates of this magnitude are obviously plausible because so many of the elderly had coverage through Medigap plans, whose premiums they paid from own funds prior to the enactment of Part D.

In contrast, the employer (taxpayer) share of the FEHBP premium involves no displacement in the conventional sense. This spending is part of total compensation to the employee for work performed, not a subsidy or grant. There is, however, a targeted subsidy in the income tax exclusion for health insurance premiums which affects virtually all public and private employees and undoubtedly involves displacement effects. That is, a dollar spent on the individual income tax exclusion does not buy an additional dollar of health insurance spending, but some lesser amount.[22]

In the absence of econometric studies, it is impossible to compare the relative performance of Medicare (both original and competitive Medicare) and the FEHBP in terms of unnecessary waste of taxpayer funds through displacement. Since the tax exclusion is a far smaller fraction of total premium cost in private plans than is the taxpayer fraction of Medicare costs, displacement effects are undoubtedly far larger in Medicare. Displacement is primarily a "transfer" effect, however, rather than a "real" effect (as economists use these terms).[23] Hence, any displacement assessment would ultimately lead to issues of fairness and equity, as well as to issues of alternative uses of taxes, rather than to a showing that one program or the other was better at real cost control.[24] On the other hand, one could argue that since the accounting framework used in almost all contemporary analysis of these programs focuses primarily on government (taxpayer) costs, it would not be unreasonable to evaluate these programs' displacement effects in terms of "bang for the taxpayer buck." Presumably, the FEHBP would win such a comparison hands down.

The Bottom Line for Cost Control Performance

My own judgment, which is necessarily partly qualitative as well as quantitative, is that the "bottom line" is not a close question historically, but open for the future. The FEHBP has demonstrably outperformed Medicare in cost control over most of the history of these two programs, simply taking into account benefit improvements in the FEHBP. This conclusion is robust without even making demographic, cost-shifting, or displacement adjustments which, were they empirically feasible, would all substantially benefit the FEHBP side of the comparison, on balance.

In a sense, however, the debate over dueling cost control comparisons is both sterile and loaded in favor of the FEHBP. The federal government has the power of coercion over the amounts it pays to health-care providers under original Medicare. To date, the velvet glove has not been removed from that iron fist. Even the option once available to physicians to "balance-bill" Medicare patients has been legislated to amount, in essence, to an "all-or-none" opt-out decision. Obstetricians and pediatricians aside, few physician specialists can reasonably decide to forfeit almost half the market (and, for many specialists, far more), as measured by service volume. So long as original Medicare pays at least what economists call the "marginal cost" of services, virtually all hospitals and the great majority of physicians will participate in the program.

Despite the Balanced Budget Act cuts and the ostensible reductions in physician payments under "sustainable growth rate" (SGR), it is unlikely that Medicare's payment reduction economic limits have been approached.[25] Congress has been unwilling to implement the statutorily mandated SGR cuts since 2003, and physician participation remains high (U.S. Medicare Payment Advisory Commission 2009). Ultimately, of course, reductions in Medicare payment rates reflect decisions subject to the political calculus. No one knows where the political limits lie. In the past, providers have, by and large, been successful in obtaining relief from payment levels that were, arguably, painfully low. In the future, as Medicare insolvency comes ever closer, the politically tolerable payment limits will inexorably fall.

In the meantime, what is by far the most striking feature of the FEHBP's ability to equal or exceed Medicare cost control is that this achievement has been politically painless and virtually without "rent-seeking" payments to

5

Premiums and Benefits

In general, the premiums for most kinds of insurance (auto, life, and house) are paid fully by the purchaser. Health insurance was paid fully by purchasers until, as explained earlier, World War II brought a radically different pattern to workers and the Great Society to the elderly and disabled (Medicare) and the poor (Medicaid).[1] But quite apart from who pays what share is the question of premium design. There is a huge difference in incentives for both plans and enrollees if the employer or sponsor pays 72 or 75 percent of the cost of every insurance plan, as opposed to a dollar amount equal to 72 or 75 percent of the average plan cost and nothing more for plans that cost more than this subsidy level. Both systems result in spending the same amount (in the first year) but the implications for enrollees are very different (Feldman et al. 2002). Quite apart from incentive effects, the first model requires all enrollees to pay substantial amounts for insurance no matter what plan they buy, while the second allows prudent buyers to get insurance for free. If purchasers get to keep the money they save by buying insurance that costs less than 72 or 75 percent of the average, yet another set of incentives and implications arises. The first of these three models is roughly the same as original Medicare's 75 percent premium subsidy for Part B. It is also the model used by most employers. The third model is roughly the same as that used by Medicare Part D (75 percent) and the FEHBP (72 percent).

Likewise, insurance benefits of actuarially equal (and high) value can have very different implications for both cost-sharing and incentives. Insurance plans differ hugely depending, for example, on whether the enrollee pays 20 percent coinsurance for all doctor charges without limit (Medicare Part B), a copay of (say) $20 a visit for all visits without limit (a typical HMO in Medicare Advantage or the FEHBP), or either of these amounts with a limit on out-of-pocket exposure of (say) $4,000 or $5,000 (most MA and FEHBP PPO plans).

This chapter analyzes the premium and benefit designs in original Medicare, competitive Medicare, and the FEHBP in terms of direct impact and behavior incentives over time.

Premium Design

In an environment where only a single health plan is allowed, many variations in premium design will function without unintended, negative side effects. For example, a private employer sponsoring a single plan could "contribute" a fourth, a half, three-fourths, or all of the premium. Because that contribution does not count as taxable income, arguably the most beneficial arrangement to employees would be the 100 percent contribution, coupled with minimal cost-sharing or tax-free alternatives such as flexible spending accounts. On both theoretical and empirical grounds, however, economists uniformly judge health insurance to be employee compensation, in lieu of cash wages. In other words, employee enrollees pay the full cost of their insurance, regardless of employer share. Therefore, tying a large proportion of wages to health insurance involves nontrivial economic "welfare" losses to employees who prefer to spend more of their compensation on housing, food, transportation, or other goods and services.

At the opposite end of the spectrum, employer or sponsor payments below perhaps half of premiums generate substantial potential risk selection. In the last chapter, figure 4-4 showed that employees of different ages present very different cost profiles, on average. If all age groups are in a single insurance pool and all pay the same premium, this is a recipe for adverse selection (and moral hazard as well, if the employer sponsors multiple plans and has an annual open season). Why should a young employee at age twenty-five pay (say) a 50 percent share of a $4,000 premium when his own expected cost, which is roughly the value of the insurance to him, is likely to be $1,000? However, if the employer share is (say) 75 percent, then the insurance purchase for the twenty-five-year old is not a bad deal, and for those older than thirty-five it becomes a very good deal.[2] The same kind of calculus arises when people sort themselves out by expected health expenses on any basis, not just age. The premium subsidy in original Medicare, competitive Medicare, and the FEHBP is high enough to avoid most but not all such risk selection, though it is unlikely this was originally understood except in the case of Medicare Part D, where a great deal of attention was paid to potential risk selection when the program was created.

A failure to get the subsidy to a level high enough to avoid age-related risk selection occurs in the Federal Employee Group Life Insurance (FEGLI) program. This program is managed in the same bureau within the OPM as the FEHBP. In the FEGLI, like the FEHBP the product of an antiquated (but in this case hugely flawed) design that has been unchanged in its essentials for decades, the government pays only one-third of the cost of basic term insurance, and all employees of all ages are in the same risk pool for basic insurance. Private market prices for term insurance for younger employees are far lower than the resulting pooled premium, and most younger employees decline this insurance (thereby raising the pooled premium even higher).[3] The government partially controls the resulting moral hazard by allowing enrollment only upon being hired and holding only very infrequent and unscheduled open seasons, but only at the cost of denying employees the ability to obtain subsidized insurance in response to changes in family needs, such as the birth of a child.

Original Medicare largely avoids the risk selection problem by dint of its extremely low enrollee share of program costs, and a substantial penalty of 10 percent a year for every year after age sixty-five that goes by without enrollment. For whatever reasons, however, about 7 percent of Medicare enrollees accept the "free" Part A insurance but decline paying one-fourth of the costs of Part B (U.S. Boards of Trustees 2009, 37). Some of these, of course, have other sources of insurance (such as the FEHBP) but many do not. The FEHBP's main buttress against this problem lies in its reasonably generous and unintentionally ingenious premium-support formula, which pays three-fourths of the cost of frugal plans while penalizing the choice of "Cadillac" plans (Florence and Thorpe 2003). Perhaps one in twenty federal employees (typically younger and lower paid), however, declines to enroll in the FEHBP while having no other insurance.

Original Medicare, while in its own terms a single health plan, is financed largely by working taxpayers (five-sixths) rather than retired enrollees (one-sixth), even outside of the means-tested upper and lower retiree segments.[4] Implicit in this very generous financing model is the notion that the elderly are largely unable to finance their own insurance, and that it should instead be paid for by current employees (who, in addition, pay for their own insurance), regardless of relative income levels. It is beyond the scope of this analysis to deal in the metaphysics of proper or "fair" premium contribution design for social insurance programs, but Medicare presents such issues. For example, a recent analysis condemns the means-testing of the Medicare Part B premium at higher income levels as contrary to the principles of social insurance (Hacker and Marmor 2004).[5] Henry Aaron and Jeanne Lambrew (2008) make a similar point in their chapter on the option of reforming Medicare as a social insurance program.

Viewed from the prism of the modern economy writ large, however, the financing of "insurance" through intergenerational transfers by payments from current taxpayers verges on the bizarre. It certainly creates the conditions for the coming insolvency of Medicare, as predicted by the Boards of Trustees for Social Security and Medicare (U.S. Boards of Trustees 2009), the Congressional Budget Office, and many other distinguished critics (Rivlin and Antos 2007). The current premium and benefit structure of original Medicare taken together, moreover, create the means as well as the near necessity for most retirees to purchase wasteful Medigap insurance at great expense to themselves and far more to the program.

Competitive Medicare presents a substantially different story. Just as in original Medicare, costs of both the Part D and Medicare Advantage programs are paid largely by current taxpayers. That payment is, however, essentially capped at a level near the average amount spent on all enrollees nationally (Part D) or in the local area (Medicare Advantage). Those who join plans with higher costs for either core or extra benefits pay essentially the full marginal cost of their choices. Recipients who join plans whose costs are below average retain 75 percent of the savings (Medicare Advantage) or all of the savings (Part D), either in reduced premiums or a combination of lower premiums and richer benefits.[6] The two programs' "benchmark" and premium calculations differ in myriad ways, most fundamentally in that MA benchmarks are still based largely on the costs of original Medicare in each area, while Part D benchmarks are based largely on the national average costs of competing prescription drug plans.

While there are many additional complexities, the bottom line is that in these programs enrollees get most of the savings from choosing lower-cost plans and pay almost all of the extra costs from choosing higher-cost plans. Low-income enrollees are exempted from paying most or all of the premiums in both programs, but for the great majority of enrollees premium amounts follow plan choices, and marginal incentives are set in a market-like way. Competing plans have equally substantial incentives to compete for business by finding the most attractive mix among lower costs, benefit generosity, and customer service. Of particular importance, the one-year enrollment requirement and annual open enrollment period provide both enrollment stability and the ability to "vote with one's feet" among competing plans to obtain better value.[7]

The FEHBP once had a similar system in terms of marginal costs and incentives to both plans and enrollees. Even at its best, however, the incentives were substantially inferior to those in competitive Medicare because the government retained 75 percent of the savings from decisions to join lower-cost plans, leaving only 25 percent to enrollees—the opposite of the Medicare Advantage and Part D schemes. Since the advent of premium conversion, even these competitive incentives have been drastically reduced in the FEHBP. With tax preferences, today the enrollee retains only about two-thirds of the nominal 25 percent, or 16 percent, of the savings from joining a lower-cost plan, and pays only about two-thirds of the cost of joining a higher-cost plan. With consumer incentives so muted, plans have correspondingly lower incentives to keep costs down, but they retain substantial incentives to improve benefits and service.

Both the FEHBP and Medicare Advantage programs arguably create unduly weak incentives for the plans themselves to reduce costs. In the FEHBP, the national plans and some HMOs operate on an "experience-rated" model that tightly restricts profits to a few percent of expenses. Perversely, the better a plan is at reducing costs, the lower the profits it earns. While competition for enrollees still creates substantial incentives to hold costs down (a plan makes up in volume what it cannot make in margin), the overall design is not tilted toward minimizing costs. Medicare Advantage suffers from a similar problem. Because the government requires that three-fourths of all savings below the benchmark be spent on increased benefits or premium reductions, the plans face strong disincentives against aggressive frugality. Medicare Part D operates similarly. The incentives for cost reduction are, however, stronger than those in experience-rated FEHBP plans. Moreover, since all premiums are paid with "real" rather than tax-discounted dollars, enrollee incentives are markedly stronger.

One group of FEHBP enrollees still faces the program's original incentive structure. Retirees do not receive tax subsidies on the enrollee share of premiums. Hence, they retain 25 percent of premium costs for frugal plan choices and pay 100 percent of the additional premium in higher-cost plans. Whether or not this will endure is uncertain, however. The National Association of Retired and Active Federal Employees, the principal advocacy group for federal retirees, has for years actively campaigned to extend to its members the same tax subsidies provided to active employees. This would be a radical breach of accepted tax policy norms, since the tax preference for the enrollee share of employment-based health insurance has been limited in both the public and private sectors to current employees. Moreover, it would create a precedent for extending such favored treatment to all other retired Americans, who face the identical disjuncture between pre- and postretirement tax treatment. According to this line of reasoning, why shouldn't even the Medicare parts B and D premiums become tax-preferred, along with Medigap premiums and retiree premiums in employer-sponsored plans? About half of the House Ways and Means Committee members have reportedly endorsed this tax subsidy proposal (Barr 2007b). This may, however, and likely does, just reflect token support by members who find it easy to endorse a poor idea they know will never be enacted.

If these retirees were, however, to obtain from the tax committees the subsidy they seek, it would eliminate the last substantial incentives to restrain premiums in the FEHBP. Of course, any given level of desired premium cost reduction for retirees and other annuitants could be achieved simply by providing them with a more generous government share of premiums than that given to employees, while retaining existing tax treatment. But this alternative would require violating the "all-are-treated-alike" norm that has governed premium calculation in the FEHBP for almost half a century. In the paranoid world of entitlement program politics, such a change would likely be regarded as a breach of principle and condemned as a precedent for future dreadful deeds. Another and even simpler alternative that avoids this problem would be to raise annuity checks by a comparable amount, but this would likely be outside the customary tunnel vision circumscribing what options are considered.

In summary, competitive Medicare has far better premium incentives than the contemporary FEHBP, leaving aside questions as to which taxpayers pay the "government share" subsidy and whether that subsidy is "too high," "too low," or well targeted in original Medicare, competitive Medicare, or the FEHBP. There is every reason to believe that MA and Part D plans will vigorously compete in the future to attract enrollees by controlling costs, and little reason to believe that competitive forces within the FEHBP will ever again be as strong or effective as they were in the first forty years of the program. What little competitive pressure remains in the FEHBP is under direct political threat that emphasizes near-term benefits to enrollees over options that would serve them far better over time.[8]

Benefit Levels and Design

While optimal premium design has substantial effects on the performance of health insurance programs over time, optimal benefit design is of even greater importance. There is a good deal of evidence that Americans on very tight budgets skimp on necessary health care, such as medicines that control their diabetes or blood pressure or cholesterol. At the same time, the cost of health care in America has been rising for decades at a rate about two percentage points higher than the rate of growth in gross domestic product (GDP) or personal income. Clearly, one of the primary reasons for this is that the price most Americans pay for medical care, once the insurance bill is paid, is somewhere between zero and 20 percent of what it actually costs. "Moral hazard" says that the result is the entirely predictable overuse of health care. And we have a good deal of evidence that overuse of health care is exactly what is happening, not just in original Medicare, but in most places, for most people, regardless of which insurance policy they have.

Optimal Benefit Levels and Cost-Sharing. An extensive literature documents the magnitude of potential savings from well-designed cost-sharing features in health plans. The "gold standard" for large-scale social research was the famous RAND health insurance experiment, which documented potential savings of as much as 40 percent simply through the use of substantial deductibles and coinsurance. Many other studies have been conducted since, with substantially consistent results.[9] The original RAND results and the later research also demonstrate that—with the important exception of low-income persons—reduction in utilization involves no consequential adverse health effects. In other words, even a modest amount of cost-sharing can eliminate a great deal of wasteful overutilization. Meanwhile, another body of literature (for example, Wennberg, Fisher, et al. 2007 and Wennberg, O'Connor, et al. 2007) emphasizes the scale of unnecessary care to be reduced.

> I have some friends who believe that cost sharing is evil. It causes people to underuse medical care, which then ruins their health. . . . There are other people I know who sound just as reasonable when you talk to them in polite company . . . [who] say that cost sharing is virtuous. It causes people to be frugal and wise in their use of medical care.
>
> Mark V. Pauly
> "The Truth about Moral Hazard and Adverse Selection"

Unfortunately, the literature contains a good deal more theoretical than practical analysis. Even so, some broad conclusions are clear. Cost-sharing matters, and it matters a lot, even though price elasticities of demand are low. Cost-sharing is particularly effective for outpatient services. And, except for low-income persons, cost-sharing does not ordinarily have adverse effects on health. Even for low-income persons, these adverse effects are, on average, quite small.

Viewed as a standalone program, original Medicare has a reasonably adequate insurance design by these standards. Coinsurance of 20 percent for physician costs is substantial enough to discourage a great deal of unnecessary utilization. Cost-sharing for hospitalization is, after the deductible, zero for almost all episodes. This is also near optimal, as hospital utilization is hardly likely to increase simply because cost-sharing is low—people don't enjoy those visits. The erosion in real terms of the Part B deductible over time is a bad design feature, recently and belatedly rectified in a small way by indexing it to inflation. The Part B deductible level is now $135, hardly more than a token. Low-income enrollees are also eligible for Medicaid, in which case both premiums and cost-sharing for them are reduced to near zero, a good design feature based on the research findings.

The FEHBP plans used to have even higher cost-sharing (on average), but that was, as previously explained, greatly reduced over time. A major part of the reduction came from the growth of capitated HMOs, which arguably do an even better job than cost-sharing in controlling excess utilization, despite their nominal copayments. However, since roughly 1990 (varying by plan), the national FFS plans have virtually all become primarily PPO plans. In doing so, they have largely dropped coinsurance and replaced it with copayments. There are interesting theoretical arguments as to the desirability of decreasing cost-sharing as expenses rise—an effect inherent in the copayment model—but FEHBP copayments have been low, typically in the range of fifteen to twenty-five dollars for outpatient services, and a few hundred dollars for inpatient services. Hence, their ability to inhibit excess utilization is far less than that of original Medicare, of the FEHBP as it was two decades ago, or of HMOs in either program. The FEHBP has no provision for better benefits or reduced premiums for low-income enrollees, but there are, as a practical matter, few such persons in the federal employee and retiree pools, and virtually none who are not eligible for Medicaid or free or reduced-cost Medicare.

Arguably, then, original Medicare has a modestly better benefit structure for equitable cost control of inpatient and outpatient medical benefits than does the present FEHBP.

Of course, the story does not stop there. The failure of original Medicare to cover prescription drugs, or to provide catastrophic limits on financial risk, means that it has been grossly inferior as an insurance program virtually since its inception. As previously shown, the not atypical Blue Cross standard option did away decades ago with hospital benefit maximums that remained in original Medicare after a half-century, instituted a catastrophic limit protection, and covered prescription drugs. It is fair to say that not a single FEHBP plan for at least the last three decades has been as weak as original Medicare is today.

Even worse, Medicare's gaps were so substantial as to induce many former employers (including the federal government) to provide wraparound benefits to their retirees to fill those gaps, or to induce enrollees to join Medigap plans if former employer coverage was not available. The moral hazard and excess utilization resulting from the failure of the program to provide a competent and adequate insurance benefit have arguably been the biggest engine driving Medicare costs for its entire history.[10]

Prescription Drugs. The prescription drug benefit in original Medicare (standing alone) was and remains essentially nonexistent.[11] It is of interest, however, to compare and contrast the drug benefits in FEHBP plans with those of Medicare Part D.

For the past dozen years, FEHBP plans have been struggling to cope with accelerating increases in prescription drug costs and progressively instituting cost-saving measures through benefit redesign. In 1994, for example, the Blue Cross standard option charged enrollees 20 percent of the cost of prescription drugs, after a $50 deductible. Medicare A and B enrollees in Blue Cross paid nothing for prescription drugs. Today, Blue Cross requires enrollees to pay 25 percent at retail, but only $10 for generics (waived for the first four prescriptions), and only $65 for a ninety-day supply (by mail order) of brand-name drugs. Medicare enrollees pay the same as all others. During this same period, all the other national plans made similar changes. Meanwhile, most HMOs were already using a tiered payment model, but they substantially raised copayments in the third tier ("nonformulary" brand-name drugs) and created three new tiers for mail order.

These kinds of cost-sharing changes drastically reduce spending on drugs, by a fourth or more for the kinds of tiering used in most FEHBP plans (see Joyce et al. 2002). They were adopted painlessly in the FEHBP by the separate decisions of each plan as ratified by its customers, although a brief protest movement by independent pharmacists in the Washington, D.C., metro area did follow Blue Cross's decision to initiate discounted mail-order coverage. These pharmacists were able to persuade the state of Maryland to add a statutory mandate that no Maryland-based plan could provide a better rate for mail order than for retail outlet drugs. This rent-seeking, protectionist mandate has affected federal and nonfederal Maryland health plans and their enrollees adversely, but not the national FEHBP plans, which enjoy the protection of federal preemption.

In contrast, but in parallel, the Medicare Modernization Act provides for a "standard" Part D drug benefit within a competitive and flexible structure. The standard benefit uses an old-fashioned deductible and coinsurance model up to the doughnut hole, as the enrollee pays 25 percent coinsurance after the $295 deductible up to the coverage limit of $2,700 before the doughnut hole begins (U.S. Medicare Payment Advisory Commission 2008d, describing the 2009 Part D benefit levels, as adjusted for inflation from the original levels). The MMA allows plans to offer alternative benefits, however, provided they are actuarially equivalent to the standard benefit, or better. In practice, the great majority of plan offerings follow some version of the three- or six-tier benefit model rather than the standard benefit. In addition, Part D plans have created innovations, such as covering generic drugs for spending in the doughnut hole. They are also moving increasingly to a four-tier benefit model where the copay is even higher for expensive specialty drugs.

One can only imagine what Medicare drug coverage might look like today had Congress enacted a vintage 1980 or 1990 drug design plan, administered directly by the government through carriers or intermediaries based on published wholesale prices, a decade or two ago.[12] The Medicare Catastrophic Coverage Act of 1988, repealed stillborn because of political protest by middle- and upper-income seniors over huge means-tested premium increases, had a drug benefit that could not be administered as enacted. The statute called for computerized prescription drug records to be maintained by the Department of Health and Human Services on a real-time basis to check for drug interactions. This was in the days before the Internet, and it would have required a telephone call from a pharmacist's counter for each prescription. Congress neglected, however, to include in its parsimonious "dispensing fee" enough money to cover the cost of the long-distance phone calls needed to communicate with the HHS, which meant pharmacists would have lost money on every prescription.[13]

This particular problem would undoubtedly have been fixed sooner rather than later had the act not been repealed, but it would have been fixed by means of ever more careful and politically astute fine-tuning of dispensing fees and estimating methods for wholesale drug costs.[14] We would have today a library of GAO and MedPAC studies on just how much to pay pharmacists to handle dispensing of drugs covered by a single nationwide plan.[15]

One shudders to imagine the political fights that would have emerged over whether, and if so at what discounts, mail-order dispensing or three-tier drug pricing would have been created.

In any event, the delayed coverage of prescription drugs until the enactment of the MMA allowed for the management of drug benefits within private plans, rather than a "one-size-fits-all" micromanaged benefit. Under Part D, decisions on benefit design, while subject to the broad constraints of the statute, are made by professionals with major stakes in their ability to control costs while attracting customers. Hence, there is a wide range of benefit designs, adjusted each year, as plans and customers learn from experience. One of the major thrusts of plan designs has been to encourage generic substitutes for brand-name drugs, using a variety of carrot and stick incentives to enrollees. As a result, there has been a massive switch to generics over the last several year, which explains much of the difference between Part D costs as predicted and the far lower actual costs.[16]

Benefit Standardization. One of the recurring issues in the debates over FEHBP performance and the design of Medicare "premium support" has been the question of whether plan benefits should be standardized. The argument for standardization is twofold: that it will reduce both risk selection and consumer confusion (see Enthoven 1989 and Fox et al. 1999).

As we have seen, potential risk selection problems exist, but they are minor and controllable. To the extent that selection biases reflect preferences for prepayment of one kind of benefit rather than another and voluntary customer choice, they should not only be of little concern to program decision-makers, but a welcome characteristic of a multiplan system. As for consumer confusion, it is, as previously argued, a straw-man argument. In fact, it is arguably a good deal easier to make a choice among health plans than for almost any other major category of consumer purchase. In the real world, enrollees ask questions like, "Is my doctor in the plan?" "Am I willing to join an HMO?" "Does it have the coverage I need?" and "Can I save a lot of money on premiums?" If they can't readily find those answers, they ask friends or advisors for help. Increasingly, they use the Internet and tools such as the Medicare Planfinder tool (at www.medicare.gov) or CHECKBOOK's Guide (Francis et al. 2008 and prior years). If they are happy in their present plan, they stay put.[17]

A further point is that standardizing benefit design would be an extraordinarily complex task. Both plans and customers must balance many variables, including network size, cost-sharing in general, cost-sharing by type of benefit, utilization controls, and specific benefits, among others. Some of these categories are interdependent. For example, when "mental health parity" was mandated for private insurance, including the FEHBP, plans found it relatively simple to live with the moral hazard problem of nominally unlimited mental health benefits by imposing utilization controls on use (treatment plans administered by specialist firms) and by careful control of preferred provider panels. As another example, plans differ radically on their approach to network size and to allowing use of out-of-network providers. This is the essential distinction between most HMOs (and, within the HMO group, between the group model and the individual practice association model) and most PPO/FFS plans. But there are variations in each group, and different levels of cost-sharing for out-of-network providers. Standardizing on one model (whatever it might be) would create radical changes for many, and perhaps most, plans and consumers, and deny consumers preferring another model not only the ability to exercise that choice, but also to obtain either the additional benefit or lower cost of that choice.

Standardized benefits also require that someone do the standardizing. What Solomonic figure knows the answer as to whether all plans should adopt (say) the average HMO benefit package as opposed to (say) the average PPO package? Does this same figure have some divine information as to whether acupuncture and chiropractic should be covered at all, and, if so, for how many visits and at what rate? Would mental health benefits be truly unlimited or subject to plan approval, and, if the latter, what methods would be used to decide? Should generic drugs be free, cost $5, or cost $10, and should these prices be the same for local providers and for mail order? When Medigap benefits were standardized into nine plans, the body of experts involved undoubtedly made many wise decisions,[18] but one huge error was not to allow plans to offer catastrophic limits without also paying for first-dollar coverage. They thereby guaranteed that all Medigap plans would be the greatest force of moral hazard—through consumption of "free" medical services—ever created.[19]

The most notorious example of a single, standardized benefit package is the highly flawed design created by the U.S. Congress for original Medicare.

In any case, any standardized package (or even a set of standardized packages) created under any method necessarily suffers the obvious defects of all "one-size-fits-all" schemes. Famously, New Deal economist and brain-trust member Rexford Tugwell described his vision of retail food production, using canned peaches as an example of the process he envisioned for all food. A committee of housewives would debate and agree on the "best" size of can for canned peaches, and all food processing companies would be required by the government to produce all canned peaches in that size can, and no other. Consumers would never be confused, economies of scale in production would be realized, groceries would have fewer items to stock— the list of benefits to a tidy mind went on and on. If that size was less convenient for a single person than for a large family, or vice versa, or too heavy for shoppers who walked home and too light for those who drove, or led to wasted peaches from spoiled leftovers, that was a small price to pay for the perfection of the best-sized can as determined by "experts."

Some critics of benefit variation assert that plans could use their benefit-design powers to dissuade high-risk persons from joining. In neither the FEHBP nor competitive Medicare, however, would the oversight agencies allow a plan not to cover insulin, a favorite hobgoblin of critics, or otherwise discriminate against a broad category of high-cost enrollees. This is not to say that abusive design is impossible; simply that guarding against it is a fairly straightforward oversight task, and one in which any slackening would generate instant and effective public criticism.

The advantages of the original decision to allow FEHBP plans to design their own benefits subject only to broad oversight to prevent abuses are twofold. First, and obviously of great importance, it allowed for dynamic evolution of health plan offerings over time. HMOs came to the FEHBP decades before any "risk" plans were allowed to compete within Medicare, and they grew and remain far more popular in the FEHBP than in Medicare.[20] Preferred provider plans grew even more rapidly than HMOs in the FEHBP, but have only recently attracted large numbers of MA enrollees from original Medicare. Prescription drug benefit redesign was a substantial cost-saving reform. Hospice coverage was mandated in Medicare, and at first grew slowly in the FEHBP, but now is ubiquitous. Acupuncture now has a substantial presence in the FEHBP, and none in Medicare. Only in 2006 did Medicare finally start covering certain pancreatic transplants that most FEHBP plans had covered for almost a decade. The most important example of benefit improvement in both programs has been the creation of catastrophic expense limits on out-of-pocket costs. This never came to original Medicare (except through the purchase of Medigap plans, and the abortive enactment of MECCA), but has arrived equally painlessly and at far less expense through PFFS and other MA plans. In the FEHBP, all national plans have had catastrophic expense guarantees for decades, without fuss or bother.

As another comparison of benefit design in the FEHBP and original Medicare, consider outpatient psychiatric and other mental health care. "Parity" of mental health benefits to physical health benefits was mandated in the FEHBP by the OPM, starting in 2001. Prior to that, almost all national plans had imposed strict limits (for example, ten or twenty) on outpatient visits, and many had limited lengths of stay for inpatient mental health care. This reform was immediately beneficial to enrollees with major mental health problems, such as those requiring hospitalization. Mental health coverage is, however, peculiarly susceptible to moral hazard because there are no natural stopping points for outpatient care, which can reach a hundred or more visits a year and $30,000 or more a year in cost. Most health plans responded by making several major innovations, if these were not already in their benefit design (as they were for many HMOs). First, they tightly limited their preferred provider panels to mental health professionals that they knew would not provide unreasonably high numbers of visits of minor therapeutic value (this meant, as well, frugal per-visit payment levels). Second, they required treatment plans in which the medical value of specific interventions would have to be justified. Third, they hired "behavior management" firms to manage mental health benefits (this is sometimes called "carve-out"). As a result of the basic reform, mitigated by these steps, the costs of mental health care in the FEHBP rose by very little (Lichtenstein et al. 2004)—perhaps 1 percent of total premiums (Beavers and Mays 2005).

Meanwhile, the outpatient mental health benefit in original Medicare was significantly inferior to the regular Part B benefit for physical care, with coinsurance of 50 percent rather than 20 percent. The purpose of this discriminatory rate was obviously to limit overutilization. Nonetheless, Congress recently enacted a change to bring the mental health coinsurance down to 20 percent, over time, in the Medicare Improvements for Patients and Providers Act of 2008. Because (with the exception of provider payment limits) the provider panel and other tools available to FEHBP plans do not exist in original Medicare, it is quite likely that the cost of this benefit change will be substantially greater than in the FEHBP.[21] Luckily (or unluckily) for the taxpayer, the increase in costs is likely to be relatively small because Medicare enrollees with Medigap plans already have essentially unlimited free use of outpatient psychiatric care when using providers willing to accept the Medicare payment rates.

Equally if not more important, allowing benefit variations makes it extremely difficult for "rent-seeking" interest groups to obtain mandated benefits or preferred payment rates. In sharp contrast to Medicare, where all benefits are mandated in detail, the number of such mandates in the FEHBP can be counted on the fingers of one hand. In Medicare, where the focus of most benefit decisions is payment rates, almost every year provides yet another omnibus statute tinkering, with dozens or hundreds of provisions to benefit one group or subgroup over another. The reason for this is inherent in the differences in program design. When a provider group or "dread-disease" lobby approaches Congress to request a mandated benefit in the FEHBP, Congress has an "end-of-discussion" response to the effect that at least some plans cover the benefit, that pressure for change should focus on the plans rather than Congress, and that the decisions on which plans to join and, hence, whether to obtain that benefit, and at what level, are up to the enrollees. Original Medicare does not allow this answer, since all benefits, payments, and limitations are essentially uniform nationwide. These are subject to geographic adjustments to rates; but such adjustments are also subject to lobbying efforts and adjustments tailored to either group interests or "earmark" pork barrel.

Allowing plan-designed benefits offers even more advantages. The potential for both fraud and abuse is greatly reduced if every plan has its own unique coverages, its own unique payment methods, and its own unique provider profile methods. The "milk-the-system" approach to fraud or abuse that works with plan A may not work with plan B. Original Medicare offers a standardized target and a volume of business that can repay a great deal of effort devoted to figuring out how to maximize legal or illegal payments under that single system. Individual competitive Medicare and FEHBP plans provide far smaller and less remunerative targets.

Future Benefit Design Innovations. Currently projected cost increases in original Medicare are so large that they would require a doubling of federal income tax rates to pay. Far and away the most important hopes for restraining such cost increases are the laboratories provided by competitive Medicare and the FEHBP for natural experiments in innovative reforms. For example, it is possible in both the FEHBP and Medicare Advantage for individual plans to innovatively cover selectively (and change quickly over time) preventive and other "high-return" benefits with no deductible and no coinsurance, while maintaining higher levels of cost-sharing for less valuable benefits. It is almost inconceivable that Congress would enact cost-sharing changes in original Medicare to achieve such a result or that such changes, once enacted, could be quickly modified to reflect experience and other new information. An FEHBP or Medicare Advantage plan could institute virtually overnight three or four different cost-sharing levels for physician care (analogous to three-tiered drug benefits) to encourage both important care and cost restraint. Initiation by original Medicare of such an innovation would take years to accomplish as the slow legislative process dragged on: hearings, negotiations, draft bills, more hearings, modifications to accommodate special interests, revised draft bills, legislation in one chamber, legislation in the other chamber, statute enacted, proposed rule to implement drafted, public comment period, revisions to proposed rule, review by OMB and other agencies, final rule, contractor instructions, revisions to computer payment programs, and, finally, the change accomplished.[22] Most likely, a year or two later the reform would be found to be badly flawed by compromises made to accommodate particular stakeholders. Revising the initiative would take yet another cycle, complicated because new vested interests would have been created in the first round. Meanwhile, a private plan could have gone through three or four cycles of fine-tuning, finally getting the reform to work properly, and moved on to the next payment innovation.

Far and away the most important class of options for controlling or reducing future costs lies in benefit design, including not only coverage decisions but also cost-sharing decisions and care management decisions. For example, a recent analysis of alternative ways to reduce future Medicare costs includes a proposal to prohibit the purchase of Medigap insurance and to create a $5,000 deductible in original Medicare (Rettenmaier and

Saving 2007). While this is a drastic alternative unlikely to emerge in either program in the near term (before Medicare insolvency creates otherwise insuperable pressures on taxes), it suggests a range of possibilities that recognizes the potency of cost-sharing. Plans with such features already exist in the FEHBP as high-deductible plans.

In another approach, Joseph Newhouse has recently argued for using higher cost-sharing in combination with managed care (2004), and for departing from the principle of uniform cost-sharing over a category of services (such as physician visits) in favor of differential cost-sharing based essentially on the potential of a given service to reduce future costs (2006). This is conceptually similar to the "value-based" insurance design advocated by Michael Chernew and colleagues (2007). As it happens, very partial elements of such a model are in place today, in the FEHBP and other private plans that use high deductibles and health savings accounts, and in some HMOs. As allowed by U.S. Treasury Department regulations, the FEHBP's high-deductible plans all provide for high-value preventive services before the deductible kicks in. For example, in 2008 the Aetna Health-fund consumer-driven plan provided, without any copayment, an annual adult routine physical, well-child visits, a host of routine tests, including such expensive ones as colonoscopy and mammography, all standard child and adult immunizations, including the relatively new herpes zoster vaccine, and routine dental preventive care. Many HMOs have, of course, long waived copayments for some preventive services.

Interestingly, the Medicare Part D program arguably follows the "value-based" model implicitly, though crudely—in most Part D plans the deductible is waived, and the generosity of cost-sharing up to the $2,700 coverage limit (where the coverage gap begins in 2009) is more than sufficient to cover most costs of most maintenance drugs for almost all adults. Put another way, almost every Part D plan has three coinsurance levels: 0 percent or close to it; 100 percent during the coverage gap; and back to close to 0 percent above the catastrophic limit. A recent article (Chandra et al. 2009) finds significant benefits in reduced hospitalization from very low copayments for prescription drugs used by chronically ill and other at risk patients. These authors suggest that this means the Part D design is flawed because of the doughnut hole (33). I draw the opposite conclusion. Within the bounds of practical insurance design, the heavily subsidized first tier provides plans, physicians, and patients the opportunity to focus plan choice and prescription decisions on the most valuable drugs and to obtain these at low or minimal costs, either in generic versions or by selecting lower cost name brand drugs within therapeutic categories. $2,700 buys a lot of statins, diuretics, and most other maintenance drugs. Furthermore, low-income enrollees face no doughnut hole at all, and pay only token copays for both generic and name brand drugs.

The question then naturally arises, why not extend these existing models along the lines recommended by Newhouse and Chernew? For example, the "free" preventive benefit in high-deductible plans could cover selected additional services along the lines suggested by Newhouse, such as ACE inhibitors for diabetes, statins to lower cholesterol, and other therapies agreed to be of importance in preventing future morbidity and associated costs. In fact, there is evidence that this is happening in some health plans, though apparently not yet in the FEHBP (Freudenheim 2007). Likewise, nothing prevents Part D plans from including even name-brand ACE inhibitors for diabetes or statins in their most preferred tier of benefits. Similarly, Medicare Advantage plans have a clear incentive to make such changes, since they would benefit by keeping enrollees healthier and costing less.[23]

As another alternative, plans in both the FEHBP and competitive Medicare could decide to create tiered copayments for hospital choices, with hospitals that are less expensive to plans while providing effective treatment costing less to enrollees, even within the "preferred" group. Some private plans have tried this (Bennett 2002), and, if proved effective, it would be the kind of reform likely to find its way into competitive systems.[24]

Another technique used in a number of FEHBP plans, though normally in the context of posthospitalization costs, is for health plans to be authorized to offer selectively, at plan discretion, benefits that are not included in the contractual package. For example, an FEHBP plan might offer additional home health coverage or skilled nursing coverage to reduce the length of a hospitalization stay. This same idea could be extended to more modest interventions. (This is the kind of benefit that is impossible to handle in a defined-benefit plan, or government-run plan. By definition, providing a benefit to some and not to others violates the principle of guaranteed equal benefits for all.)

A much more ambitious idea has been advanced by Roger Feldman's *How to Fix Medicare: Let's Pay Patients, Not Physicians* (2008). Feldman suggests returning to indemnity-style payment (similar to the way automobile insurance is paid after an accident), coupled with what might be thought of as "lowest-cost-effective-alternative" payments (my term, not his). For the many medical procedures for which a cost-effective treatment package can be identified and priced, patients would get a payment for that amount. They would then be free to shop around, settling for an even more economical treatment and keeping the difference or, if so inclined, paying more out of pocket for a different but costlier treatment or for a provider who is charging more than is typical. For example, patients with certain back problems might be given an amount sufficient to pay for an extensive course of palliative and noninvasive treatments, but not enough for inpatient surgery. There are numerous implementation issues, and this scheme would not be suitable for all or even most procedures; but the basic idea involves potentially significant improvements in the medical-care market, as well as substantial savings. It is not an "all-or-nothing" idea, but could be combined with more traditional payment methods, evolving over time.

> General Surgeons are often asked to see patients with pain from gall-stones. If there aren't any complications—and there usually aren't—the pain goes away on its own or with pain medication. . . . But some have recurrent episodes, and need surgery to remove their gallbladder. . . . Increasingly, I was told, McAllen [Texas] surgeons simply operate. . . . And by operating they happen to make an extra seven hundred dollars.
>
> Atul Gawande
> "The Cost Conundrum"

For example, in the case of a diagnosis of gallstones, plans have a number of ways to discourage unnecessary surgery to alleviate what is often serious as well as frightening pain. By requiring prior approval or second surgical opinions, plans can discourage surgery until diet and medicines have been tried. A high deductible will certainly force both surgeon and patient to confront the fact that the surgery will likely cost the patient $700 and the alternative treatments a small fraction of this. The use of an indemnity payment for "gallbladder pain not yet proven unresponsive" of (say) $100 would reduce cost-sharing to zero until or unless the problem proved resistant to inexpensive treatments that are free to patients. Or plans can try what Atul Gawande recommends, which is attempting to develop a peer-driven culture of "accountability" for restraint in local medical communities, city by city and place by place, similar to the culture of the Mayo Clinic (Gawande 2009, 43–44).[25]

As these examples suggest, there are many ways to tailor benefits selectively to obtain many of the advantages of "first-dollar" coverage while still strongly discouraging excess utilization. Both the FEHBP and competitive Medicare offer natural and incremental approaches to changes in benefit design that plans could adopt to reduce costs without creating harmful pressures to avoid needed care. In the Medicare context, of course, the MA plans have the most to gain from such innovation, since they reap financial benefits by keeping their enrollees healthy and out of hospitals. In the FEHBP, plans also stand to gain, though to a lesser degree. Such discretionary flexibility would be unthinkable and impossible to administer in original Medicare.

More fundamentally, over the long run, the best two hopes for cost control in these programs lie in either

- the use of price and management mechanisms to structure consumer incentives to choose (or encourage physicians to choose) less costly and more effective services, or

- the use of capitation techniques to encourage plans to find cost-effective disease management strategies, large and small.

While disease management has yet to prove itself in replicable, large-scale practice (U.S. Congressional Budget Office 2004), there is near-universal agreement that the potential for both improving quality and reducing costs is huge. There are, of course, a broad range of potential reforms of these kinds, such as expanding use of "evidence-based" medicine and creating preferred provider panels using evidence on physician quality and cost control (for example, to identify physicians who keep patients out of hospitals). Meanwhile, we already have the evidence in hand that cost-sharing works in ways large and small to reduce unnecessary utilization.

Some of these prospective tools can be used in original Medicare, but some can only or best be used in private plans. Compared to private plans, original Medicare suffers from three crippling disadvantages. First, it cannot use the methods of incremental reform: trying an innovation, abandoning or modifying it as experience dictates, trying a new version, and so forth, until the innovation proves itself and secures a permanent place. Because Medicare operates on a "standardized benefit for all" model, with legal entitlements and due-process restrictions, and is modified through the politicized legislative process rather than through self-determined intraorganizational decisions by plan executives, it can generally operate only in far more lurching steps.

Second, Medicare cannot reasonably make changes until they are substantially proved in practice. For all practical purposes, binding Medicare decisions are "all-or-none" decisions that potentially affect all 35 million people in original Medicare. There are quasi-experimental demonstration projects funded through original Medicare (virtually all specified in law by Congress), and some coverage policy decisions now allow for testing particular procedures or devices in limited types of patients before expanding them to broader populations; but these innovations are both ponderous and few relative to the hundreds and thousands of potential decisions.

As an example, the CMS recently addressed whether it would cover "virtual" colonoscopies using computerized tomography ("CAT scans") rather than physical colonoscopy to detect colon cancer. Virtual colonoscopies are approved by the U.S. Food and Drug Administration (FDA) as safe and effective and are "better, safer, faster, cheaper" than physical colonoscopy (Pollack 2009). They have the added advantage of being acceptable to patients who are unwilling or unable (physically or mentally) to undertake an unpleasant, invasive test. When they detect polyps, however, they have the major disadvantage of having to be followed by a physical colonoscopy to determine whether those polyps are benign. Polyps are more prevalent among older patients, and in a large fraction of cases two procedures are needed to reach a diagnosis.

Clearly, there are arguments pro and con on this issue. Private insurance plans have come down on both sides. One option they have is to allow the virtual test only on those patients unwilling or unable to take the physical test. Original Medicare apparently cannot be so nuanced.[26] The CMS weighed the risks and benefits and decided against coverage (U.S. Department of Health and Human Services, Centers for Medicare and Medicaid Services, 2009b).

The third obstacle to Medicare's use of cost control tools is that some of the most promising innovations over the long run necessarily involve benefit cutbacks or constraints. For example, using the gallstone example cited by Gawande above, there are two simple solutions to waste that are likely to work in the vast majority of cases. Techniques of cost-effectiveness analysis could presumably show readily that for the vast majority of patients, the $100 pain relief and diet intervention is far superior to the $700 surgery. A health plan using either deductibles or coinsurance would provide the necessary prodding to lead to this (normally) most cost-effective solution, as the surgeon or patient or both contemplate the issue. Suppose the health plan has a 20 percent coinsurance rate. The lower-cost treatment will cost the patient $20 and the higher-cost treatment $140. This difference will not break many banks. But it will certainly focus attention.

Consider, however, the more draconian alternative of a "least costly alternative" payment standard, where the health plan will pay $100 and the patient will pay any excess over this for any more expensive treatment he chooses. Now the difference is $600, a more drastic signal. Original Medicare, without Medigap supplementation, could, in theory, support either alternative approach. But original Medicare is so badly flawed that it would require an act of Congress to prevent the Medigap supplementation that makes both alternative treatments "free" to the patient. It is virtually inconceivable that Congress would enact positive legislation to require this alternative even for gallstones, let alone for a life-threatening condition.[27] Consequently, the original Medicare model, as designed and practiced, is essentially incapable of disciplining benefit design excess.

6

Access, Fraud Control, and Governance

Other dimensions of plan performance are worthy of attention. I focus on three. Access is particularly important because it is so important to enrollees and so frequently mischaracterized by advocates. Fraud control is but one dimension of performance in cost control, but a particularly important one because of the magnitude of potential costs and the problems inherent in the design of original Medicare. Governance looms large because of the inherent tendencies of political systems, even—or especially—responsive democracies, to reward vested interests, procrastination, the status quo, and superficial reform over the solutions that actually work cleanly and quickly to the interests of consumers themselves. Paradoxically, we may only be able to achieve health reform through democratic processes which, while producing breakthroughs, may also impede or prevent the emergence of mechanisms that will enable those breakthroughs to work effectively and efficiently.

Access

Original Medicare, competitive Medicare, and the FEHBP differ greatly in the access their enrollees have to health-care providers. Of the three, the FEHBP provides by far the broadest access, as measured in terms of payment for services from any provider of choice. In the United States, all but one of the national plans offer both preferred provider organization and fee-for-service access in all plan options. These PPO networks in most cases cover half or more of all physicians and the great majority of hospitals and pharmacies. Under FFS, the precise plan payment provisions vary, but in general the plans promise to pay 70 or 75 percent of the plan network allowance (or in some cases usual, customary, and reasonable fees) toward

167

the cost of services delivered by any licensed provider. They also provide catastrophic guarantees, though usually inferior than when using preferred providers, toward FFS costs.

In practice, the FFS benefit is often lower than 75 percent, of course, because out-of-network providers have not agreed to accept the network rates or to charge what the plan regards as reasonable. In large cities with "Park Avenue specialists" or the equivalent, this can and does often mean that the plan will pay only about half the cost.[1] In most areas, however, coin-surance is usually about 25 percent, almost the same as original Medicare's. Unlike original Medicare, payment is not limited to Medicare "participating" providers (about 95 percent of all physicians) but extends to any licensed provider—100 percent of all physicians. The enrollee may have to file a claim, but usually half, and often three-quarters, of the cost of the service is paid. Outside the United States, FFS coverage extends worldwide in every national plan, and some plans (including the Blue Cross standard option) market themselves as providing excellent service and coverage everywhere in the world. Original Medicare offers no coverage abroad, not even emergency care, with minor exceptions in nearby Canada and Mexico.

FEHBP HMOs offer in most cases nothing more than plan network providers, plus emergency services anywhere in the United States or abroad. Some HMOs, however, also offer "point of service" FFS benefits using a deductible and coinsurance model similar to that in national plans. Others offer as well out-of-network coverage for college students away from home (another example of a benefit unlikely to find its way into the "one-size-fits-all" constraints inherent in any "standardized benefit" model). About 90 percent of federal employees and retirees have access to one or more HMOs (Florence et al. 2006).

Competitive Medicare offers a set of choices roughly comparable to those of the FEHBP, though usually limited to Medicare-participating providers and, in the case of HMOs, their networks. In many cases, includ-ing all Humana plans and most private fee-for-service plans, emergency care is covered worldwide. Few if any plans, however, offer worldwide FFS coverage comparable to that found in national FEHBP plans.[2]

Original Medicare, one of the few remaining "pure" FFS systems in the nation, is certainly broad in access, almost matching the scope of national FEHBP plans within the United States. In some respects it is superior, since about 95 percent of physicians agree to participate, while only about half of physicians participate in most national FEHBP plans as preferred providers (although the FEHBP extends payment to all licensed providers, as indicated above). The almost total lack of coverage abroad mentioned above is an understandable limitation in a program with tight constraints on administrative costs, but a severe one. It denies Medicare benefits entirely to the hundreds of thousands of retirees who live abroad, unless they make a special trip to the United States. With the diminished value of Part B, and the cost of travel, those retirees would essentially pay an exorbitant tax to remain in Medicare, and most do not.

All three programs offer substantial access to a vast array of physicians and other providers. For those who absolutely, positively, cannot do without some particular physician who is not in any network, FEHBP PPO plans offer the only assured payment, though likely only a fraction of what those physicians charge. For enrollees who want the broadest possible access to low- or no-cost physicians, original Medicare with Medigap offers the best access. For those who live abroad, the FEHBP is the only simple option. For those who want good access with both low premium and low cost-sharing, Medicare Advantage and FEHBP are best. In sum, on this dimension of performance one cannot "have it all" in any program, and all three offer more access to good providers than any one person reasonably needs in most circumstances.

Fraud Control

It may seem strange that a work devoted to evaluating competing health insurance models should include a focus on fraud. Substantial evidence indicates, however, that original Medicare (and Medicaid as well) is far more vulnerable to fraud than capitated health programs like the FEHBP and competitive Medicare. This vulnerability is inherent in both the design and financing of original Medicare. Fraud probably explains a great deal of the excess utilization (with no statistically observable patient benefit) that the Dartmouth researchers have documented as accounting for as much as a third of all spending in original Medicare (Fisher et al. 2003, mentioned in the introduction to part 2, above, and Wennberg et al. 2007, part 2).

In only a relative handful of instances in the past dozen years has the federal government lost substantial sums of money to actual fraud in or by private health plans participating in the FEHBP or Medicare Advantage (although in some cases, discussed below, frauds aimed at all payers and affecting mainly original Medicare nonetheless imposed some small fraction of their costs on the FEHBP or MA). The only significant instance of FEHBP payment abuse by a private plan publicized by the U.S. Department of Justice (DOJ) involved the HMO PacifiCare Health Systems, covered eight years, and led to federal recovery of $87 million, or an average of about $10 million a year.[3] Yet it is well known and extensively documented that original Medicare is plagued by fraud levels that certainly reach billions of dollars a year, and may reach many tens of billions.

This is not to say that no consequential fraud exists in the FEHBP, Medicare Advantage, or the Medicare prescription drug program. To the contrary, a good deal of fraud certainly affects costs in these programs, roughly to the extent that such fraud is endemic in private health insurance and health care generally. Here is a simple example. Until recent years, almost all fee-for-service, indemnity, and PPO insurance in America (but not HMOs) specifically excluded from benefits preventive outpatient visits. Yet, whether in original Medicare, the Blue Cross FEHBP plan, or almost any private plan (other than HMOs), patients and physicians would routinely, with a wink and a nod, bill the payer for well-patient exams disguised as illness-related visits. This "fiddle" was reportedly roughly as common as traffic speeding violations, or exaggerations of charitable contributions on federal income tax returns. "Everyone" did it.[4]

Some categories of "abuse" exist almost exclusively in private rather than public insurance plans. Taking a well-known example from competitive Medicare, these include marketing violations through which unscrupulous agents seeking commissions try to enroll confused elderly beneficiaries in their plans. (This and other marketing abuses were addressed in the Medicare Improvements for Patients and Providers Act of 2008, or MIPPA, which essentially codified in law a set of HHS standards that were about to be codified as final rules through CMS administrative procedures described earlier in this chapter.) Other abusive practices that affect both public and private plans include remuneration to providers that is implicitly, if not explicitly, conditioned on the expectation that certain drugs or devices will

News Headlines Tell the Medicare Fraud Story

"The Looting of Medicare," *Parade Magazine*, April 20, 2008.

"Billings Used Dead Doctors' Names," *Washington Post*, July 9, 2008.

"Blatant Medicare Fraud Costs Taxpayers Billions," MSNBC.com, December 11, 2007.

"3 Hospitals Accused of Using Homeless for Fraud," *Los Angeles Times*, August 7, 2008

"Medicare Fraud Acute in South Florida," *National Public Radio*, October 11, 2007.

"South Florida Flagged in Medicare Fraud Report," *Miami Herald*, May 31, 2009.

"A High-School Drop-Out Pleaded Guilty to Conning Medicare Out of $105 Million," *Wall Street Journal*, August 23, 2008.

"Two Indicted in $179M Medicare Fraud," *South Florida Business Journal*, July 2, 2009.

"Once Again, Washington Pledges to Fight Medicare Fraud," *Wall Street Journal*, June 25, 2009.

From Google search on "medicare fraud"

be preferred over others. Congressman Pete Stark, a Democrat from California, has for decades been prominently associated with legislation seeking effectively to prevent ownership of ancillary medical services by providers who benefit directly from overutilization of those services because they own them or obtain some form of financial return from their use.

The issue at hand is not "soft" abuse of these kinds, but whether the kinds of robustly criminal health-care fraud that plague Medicare and Medicaid are remotely as common in the competitive programs, and if not, why not? Starting with public evidence, we know for certain that original Medicare suffers substantial fraud.

Recent headlines tell a great deal of the story. A Google search on "medicare fraud" generates over one million hits (as of June 30, 2009), which certainly shows that the matter is not being ignored. The sponsored advertisements on those same search results reveal a substantial and apparently profitable industry actively seeking whistleblowers for *qui tam* suits against those who commit fraud.

We know also that the problem is not new. A Google search including "1999" turns up a listing of then-recent Medicare fraud articles just as scary as those that appear today. Malcolm Sparrow's authoritative text on Medicare and other health-care fraud, *License to Steal*, assessed problems he identified as a researcher and analyst of fraud problems during the 1990s. Sparrow wrote in 1996, "Congress and the Clinton administration have paid unprecedented attention to the issue over the last six years" (Sparrow 2000, ix). Yet the problems continue.

We know that huge resources are devoted to fighting fraud, resulting in major accomplishments. A special budgetary account, called the Health Care Fraud and Abuse Control Account, will spend $1.5 billion in 2010 through the FBI and other components of the Department of Justice, the Office of the Inspector General at HHS, and the Centers for Medicare and Medicaid Services for these activities (U.S. Office of Management and Budget 2009). According to an article documenting all publicly available records of fraud recoveries through Department of Justice and/or *qui tam* cases, $9.3 billion had been recovered through 379 cases in recent years (Kesselheim and Studdert 2008). A recent annual report from the HHS and the DOJ includes impressive statistics as to workload, including 836 new criminal fraud investigations, 355 criminal charges, 547 defendants convicted of "health care fraud–related" crimes, and $2.2 billion won or negotiated in judgments and settlements (U.S. Department of Health and Human Services, Office of the Inspector General 2007b). The DOJ's website displays press releases for newsworthy fraud and abuse case settlements in which it has been involved since 1994,[5] a July 2009 search of which shows 428 involving "Medicare" (six months or so ago the total was 367), almost all involving fraud or some other criminal activity. A companion search shows about 75 items concerning the "FEHBP" or "federal employees," only a dozen or so of which involve fraud directed at the FEHBP either specifically or attendant to Medicare fraud. Of only three items concerning Medicare Advantage, none involves fraud. There are no mentions of fraud that appear to deal with the Medicare prescription drug program (but some deal with drugs paid for by original Medicare).[6]

A number of reports deal specifically with the possibilities of fraud and abuse in Medicare Advantage, prescription drug plans, and the FEHBP. Since these programs now spend in total almost $200 billion a year, one would suppose them to be fruitful targets of fraud and targets for investigations of possible fraud. A recent GAO report garnered headlines claiming that Part D plans had inadequate antifraud and abuse plans in place (U.S. Government Accountability Office 2008b). Pointedly stating on page 1 that "the size, nature, and complexity of the Part D program make it a particular risk for fraud, waste, and abuse," the report then went on to find no instances of fraud in Part D plans, no instance of a plan failing to have an effective antifraud program, and no more than five plans having four "missing" required and recommended elements out of a possible total of seventy—by usual bureaucratic standards, quite an impressive achievement. Demonstrating equal concern, the HHS made fraud and abuse in Part D its "Management Issue 1"—ahead of preventing fraud in original Medicare—in its 2007 financial report (U.S. Department of Health and Human Services 2007, section 3, page 1). In rationalizing this decision, the HHS presented information on a grand total of zero instances of known fraud in the Part D program.

With all this attention to potential fraud in Part D and Medicare Advantage over the last several years, one would expect these diligent efforts to produce some evidence. Yet the latest *Semiannual Report to Congress* fails to list a single instance of fraud in these programs, while listing dozens of fraud cases involving original Medicare or Medicaid (U.S. Department of Health and Human Services, Office of the Inspector General 2009b). The report finds a great deal to fuss about, such as the failure of many Part D sponsors to find even a single "potential" fraud and abuse incident through their own efforts (6), but no fraud.

The FEHBP is subject to the oversight of the OPM Office of the Inspector General (OIG). In semiannual reports to Congress covering the year ending March 31, 2008, the OPM OIG reported just two cases in which the FEHBP was the primary target of fraud (U.S. Office of Personnel Management, Office of the Inspector General 2007 and 2008). In both these cases, the fraud involved people falsely claiming to be married to get family coverage. The same reports mentioned nineteen other cases, almost all of which involved the Department of Justice and were presumably mentioned in its press releases[7] (though the FEHBP is not usually mentioned by the

DOJ when the effect of a particular fraud on the FEHBP is trivial). In none of these was the FEHBP consequentially involved as compared to original Medicare or Medicaid. For example, a cardiologist performed unnecessary surgery on hundreds of patients and agreed to a civil settlement of $1.9 million, of which the FEHBP share was $90,000; a biotechnology company illegally marketed a drug and agreed to a civil settlement of $42.5 million, of which the FEHBP share was $6 million; a pharmaceutical company failed to report discount-price information to the government and agreed to a $650 million civil settlement, of which the FEHBP share was $4 million; and a physician fraudulently billed for treatments to such an extent that total restitution and forfeitures totaled $22 million, of which the FEHBP share was $650,000. In none of these cases or any others described by the OPM OIG was the FEHBP other than an incidental target—its plans being merely among the many insurance companies affected, with original Medicare or Medicaid always by far the chief victim.

From the nature and types of cases reported by the OPM OIG, it can reasonably be assumed that some fraction of past and future fraud cases that heavily affect original Medicare or Medicaid will also affect to some far smaller extent private insurance firms, competitive Medicare, or the FEHBP. But nothing about any of the reported cases suggests any particular vulnerability of these programs to fraud or any consequential effects on their costs. Recall that these programs will spend almost $200 billion in 2009, and have spent perhaps $1 trillion over the past decade. If fraud consumed as much as 1 percent of total spending in these programs, it would have involved $10 billion over that period. Nothing in the DOJ or OPM case reports suggests a cumulative total even one-tenth that size.

The reasons original Medicare (along with most state Medicaid programs and TRICARE) is unusually vulnerable to fraud are fivefold.[8] First, size matters in many kinds of fraud. Original Medicare, a single plan, pays about $350 billion in medical bills a year. No one MA, Part D, or FEHBP plan pays more than about $20 billion through those programs, though several Blue Cross and other private insurance firms do business that is several times larger in total across all customers. Original Medicare, and Medicaid in states such as New York and California, is where the big dollars are.

Second, original Medicare's administration is designed to pay cheaply and quickly all bills presented by participating providers, using totally routinized and automated procedures that are inherently incapable of detecting fraud. Some 1.2 billion claims are paid a year. As Sparrow describes it,

> Control systems may work very well in pointing out billing errors to well-intentioned physicians and may even automatically correct errors, adjust claims, and limit code manipulation. But those same systems might offer no defense at all against determined, sophisticated thieves, who treat the need to bill "correctly" as the most minor of inconveniences. Most competent fraud perpetrators study the rule book carefully—probably more carefully than most honest providers—because they want to avoid scrutiny at any cost. (2000, 41)

The Medicare payment systems, therefore, have inherent vulnerabilities that are easily understood and, in some respects, almost impossible to guard against. Sophisticated statistical techniques can identify certain kinds of patterns that indicate potential fraud, but these take substantial resources to design and operate. Unfortunately, as we shall see, the Medicare problem is far more about stopping fraud than identifying it.

Third, private health plans can and do spend many times as much as Medicare on managerial oversight. A recent article points out that Medicare employs only about six dozen physicians, nurses, and other clinicians (most of them devoted to setting national safety standards for providers), whereas health plans employ thousands—Aetna over three thousand and Wellpoint about four thousand (Gottlieb 2008). A dozen of the most distinguished observers of American health care and health insurance wrote a pointed letter a decade ago pleading for substantial increases in the administrative budget for Medicare (Butler et al. 1999). No major increases have occurred since then, and the CMS has had to "eat" the expanded Medicare Advantage and the new Part D program with very few new staff resources. Congress routinely appropriates far less funding than even a parsimonious Office of Management and Budget (OMB) allows the HHS to request for program administration, with predictable effects on many CMS functions, not just antifraud efforts.

Fourth, private health plans have tools that are denied to original Medicare. Most important of these are the preferred provider panels on which most plans heavily rely. Patterns of billing and care are monitored carefully for all preferred providers. If any provider stands out statistically because billing is unusually high, he or she can be and probably is dropped without explanation, and without even spending staff resources to investigate the cause. Private plans don't have to detect fraud to fight many kinds of it successfully. Original Medicare, in contrast, has to meet burdensome "due process" standards to deny billing privileges to a provider (although Medicare can stop paying bills it believes are fraudulent until they are investigated).

Finally, private plans have major and far greater financial incentives to prevent fraud. Most fraud goes directly to the "bottom line." Particularly in competitive Medicare, most fraud losses can never be recouped, because payment is on a capitated basis determined in advance. Even where private plans are experience-rated, as in the FEHBP, each year's contractual amount is set in advance, and raising premiums in future years to recoup the loss suffered this year means a loss of business (as enrollees move to less expensive plans) and a disproportionate effect on profits. This creates huge incentives to deter and prevent fraud. No federal employee ever loses his job, or probably even a promotion, if he fails to detect a $10 million fraud that is later found by happenstance (most fraud, presumably, is never detected). In the private sector, in contrast, firing is "at will," and bonuses can be many times higher than in the federal government, so both firms and employees have far more directly at stake than government agencies and employees.[9]

Under competitive Medicare's capitated programs, the incidence of fraud falls directly and predominantly on the plans themselves. The same $10 million fraud that costs the taxpayer $10 million if perpetrated on original Medicare costs the taxpayer almost nothing if it falls on Aetna, Blue Cross, or United HealthCare plans in either MA or Part D. Hence, the repeated statements by bureaucracies involved in fraud detection and prevention that these programs pose exceptionally high risks to taxpayers border on the bizarre. Original Medicare belongs on a "high risk" list; MA and Part D do not even come close. Indeed, the failure of these bureaucracies to find any actual fraud specific to these programs is something of an embarrassment to them, and has led to proposals to require private health plans and their providers (for instance, individual doctors and hospitals) to report even suspicion of fraud as a condition of remaining in the competitive programs.[10]

Consider a masterful understatement in original Medicare. According to the OIG,

> In June 2003, the program safeguard contractor alerted the Centers for Medicare and Medicaid Services (CMS) that providers in three South Florida counties (Miami-Dade, Broward, and Palm Beach) were billing aberrantly for infusion therapy services for beneficiaries with HIV/AIDS. . . . In May 2004, CMS issued a National Medicare Fraud Alert describing the "infusion therapy scam." By 2005, the three South Florida counties accounted for 72 percent of submitted charges for beneficiaries with HIV/AIDS nationwide, though only 8 percent of such beneficiaries lived there. (U.S. Department of Health and Human Services, Office of the Inspector General 2007b, i)

The OIG concluded that "CMS has had limited success in controlling the aberrant billing practices of South Florida infusion therapy providers. CMS and its contractors have used multiple approaches, but none has proven effective over time" (ibid., ii). The OIG then explained that, in 2005, "providers in the three counties submitted bills totaling $2.5 billion to Medicare (of which Medicare paid $653 million) . . . more than twice the [amounts submitted and paid] by providers in all other areas of the country combined" (ibid., 1).

Obviously, success had been limited if, two years after the fraud was discovered, it was getting worse to the tune of more than a half-billion dollars lost in 2005 alone. Why wasn't the problem solved in June of 2003, in days, let alone weeks or months or years? How this fiasco could have occurred is entirely unclear in the report, as is the question of where the FBI, the Justice Department, and the OIG were in the intervening months and years. How could dedicated fraud-fighting funds in excess of a billion dollars a year not be effective in stopping such thievery in its tracks? Whatever the answers might be, it is apparent that whatever is going on in the world of original Medicare by way of fraud far exceeds anything conceivable in the world of competitive Medicare and the FEHBP.

In perhaps the most bizarre episode of all (leaving aside continuing sagas of billings by dead doctors and billings for dead patients), consider recent developments in the case of suppliers of fraudulent durable medical equipment in South Florida. It has been known for decades that fraud artists have been setting up phony businesses (with letterhead and physical addresses, but no actual employees or equipment for sale) by the hundreds in South Florida, and submitting hundreds of millions of dollars a year in false claims to Medicare.[11] Drawing a merciful veil over what happened— or, rather, what didn't happen—during the twenty years since regulatory standards were put into place to define fraudulent businesses that didn't qualify for Medicare payment, we will skip ahead to October 2006, when federal investigators made unannounced visits to more than 1,500 of these companies and found that about one-third did not operate real businesses (U.S. Department of Health and Human Services, Office of the Inspector General 2008). These scam enterprises were then denied Medicare billing privileges. Half of them appealed for reinstatement.

Unbelievably, the hearing officers employed by the HHS allowed 90 percent of the fraudulent companies that appealed to be reinstated because "there are no criteria regarding the types of evidence necessary to reinstate supplier billing privileges." These companies submitted various real or forged pieces of paper purporting to prove they were legitimate enterprises, and "hearing officers generally accept all documentation submitted as legitimate" (ibid., 8, 10). The OIG concluded by recommending that the CMS "develop clear criteria." The CMS responded that it would do so, but that "any guidance provided should not impinge on a hearing officer's ability to make an independent determination" as to the evidence (10). Again, without dwelling on the details (which do include such positive outcomes as criminal convictions of many of the fraud perpetrators, including some of those who ended up being reinstated, perhaps while serving hard time), what is important to understand about this case is that despite decades of effort by talented and hardworking civil servants, this known problem continues today and is likely to continue into the indefinite future.

This is the kind of problem that is inherent in the "any willing provider," "we pay all bills properly submitted," and "due process" principles written into Medicare law, regulations, and practices. It is not unique to original Medicare (Medicaid and TRICARE face similar constraints), but it is likely unique to health insurance programs that are operated by public agencies using such payment models and facing the due process, budgetary, and other governance constraints that are inherent, necessary, and proper in publicly run programs. It is hard to believe that any private payer would have taken twenty days, let alone twenty years, to stop paying blatant fraud artists for nonexistent medical equipment sales from nonexistent businesses. But in a nation of freedom under the law, the United States government cannot simply close down a business because a bureaucrat so decides.

In a fascinating piece of accidental evidence pointing up the difference between original Medicare and the FEHBP in this regard, the Government Accountability Office recently studied the effects of plan competition in the FEHBP and found, not surprisingly, that costs were lower in areas where there was more competition. In conducting the study, the GAO estimated FEHBP costs by metropolitan area. It determined that per-enrollee spending in Miami was only 92.8 percent of the national average (U.S. Government Accountability Office 2005, 69). This result is inconceivable if the FEHBP were as powerfully affected by fraud in South Florida as original Medicare.[12]

The examples used above, of course, merely reflect known cases and known situations. There is no reason to think they are more than the tip of the proverbial iceberg.

The importance of these issues is not merely one of law enforcement and justice. Large numbers of dollars are involved. A hypothetical calculation suggests the potential magnitudes. Total Medicare spending is now over $500 billion a year. If all of that were spent on original Medicare, and fraud losses were 7 percent of total spending in that program, $50 billion a year would be lost to fraud. This is not an outlandish estimate. "Law enforcement authorities estimate that health care fraud costs taxpayers more than $60 billion each year" according to the *Washington Post* (Johnson 2008). Between them, however, MA and prescription drug plans spend about $170 billion a year, about one-third of that $500 billion. Assume that fraud losses in competitive programs average 3.5 percent rather than 7 percent (these are the percentages used in the illustrative table on administrative costs presented earlier in this analysis, in the section on "Irrelevant Comparisons"). Then, simply by existing at present scale and reducing original Medicare spending by a roughly equal amount, competitive Medicare saves the taxpayer $5 billion a year compared to the same overall spending total in the publicly run program. Put another way, the "excess" costs of Medicare Advantage may be

8 or 9 percent a year rather than 12 or 14 percent a year, simply by virtue of its superior performance in preventing fraud.

Of course, we don't know the real numbers, and we probably never will. This hypothetical example is oversimplified. But based on the evidence of both documented cases and documented recoveries, something on this general order of magnitude seems likely. The fraud savings difference between original Medicare and competitive programs may even be larger.

Governance

Both original Medicare and the FEHBP are properly and necessarily subject to the oversight, and control, of the president and Congress. Both are subject to the will of the electorate through the normal vicissitudes of the American political process. There the similarities of governance end. The fundamental difference between original Medicare and the FEHBP is that the former was established as a command-and-control program whose myriad detailed choices were and are specified by government, and the latter was established as a voucher-like program whose detailed choices were and are determined by consumer decisions. It is as if the federal government were to provide needy families with government cartons of food, each item in the carton taken from a government warehouse according to a prescribed schedule for each family size from a predetermined inventory, rather than giving food stamps to be used by consumers in private grocery stores based on their selection of foods for their families. (In fact, the government once did provide millions of needy families food from government warehouses, exactly as described above, but the Lyndon Johnson administration had the wit to largely replace that surplus commodities program with food stamp vouchers.)

One fundamental problem in the governance of a program whose details are set in law by government fiat is that in any program whose design is based on Congress's exercising detailed management through legislation (either authorization or appropriations bills), the very existence of the legislative vehicle almost compels congressional decisions. If a health program pays doctors a set of rates that is set by Congress, it is essentially impossible and, arguably, irresponsible for Congress not to make "reasonable" adjustments to those rates in the annual reauthorization process. If the meat is on the table, it will be carved. In sharp contrast, if the health program operates on the basis of a design in which each of hundreds of health plans establishes its own payment rates, then "the rate" is not on the agenda (or table). Hence, simply as a part of inherent design, original Medicare almost compels congressional micromanagement of major classes of decisions, while competitive Medicare and the FEHBP make that all but impossible.

Another fundamental problem is that political responsiveness in a democracy virtually guarantees that issues before Congress will be framed and decided in terms of stakeholder interests. But many issues, including most health-care decisions, really don't belong in that institutional milieu; they are far better decided by private parties. For example, in the context of Medicare as a social insurance program, or the FEHBP as a fringe benefit program, it seems entirely appropriate for Congress to make such determinations as the level and type of subsidy, or whether or not means-testing should be involved. But it is far less evident that the questions surrounding how individuals spend their health insurance dollars should be subject to detailed congressional direction (as distinguished from systemic oversight).

To be sure, the Congress of the United States, in any endeavor in which it is involved, may well and properly decide to drill down into details. To continue the food subsidy example, Congress could decide that food subsidies be spent only on milk and not on soft drinks, on vegetables but not on fatty meats, on spinach rather than lettuce if the former were in surplus and the latter were not, or issue any other directive it chose in an attempt to dictate eating choices. When every consumer gets the same cartons of food from the same warehouse stocks, it would verge on the irresponsible for the Congress not to name the dozen or so foods to go into those warehouses and cartons. But when consumers are shopping for groceries in a store stocked with thousands of foods, specifying what can and cannot go into grocery carts would be a pointless exercise in micromanagement, enmeshing the government in a myriad of decisions which it has no practical or rational capacity to make. The fundamental design of any government program always dictates or precludes—favors or discourages—certain kinds of decisions in that program. Differences in original design decisions can and do lead to radically different governance regimes for federally funded health insurance programs.

Political Oversight. A staggering amount of attention is paid to original Medicare by the Office of Management and Budget, the Congressional Budget Office, Congress, the provider groups, the trade associations, the states, the medical schools, the unions, and any organized interest with a financial interest of any kind in the size, distribution, and allocation of health-care costs. While original Medicare is about nine times larger than the FEHBP in spending totals, with some $350 billion in spending estimated for 2009 (Medicare Advantage adds about $110 billion and Part D about $60 billion—some included in the MA total—for a complete total for all Medicare programs of about $500 billion), the FEHBP, at almost $40 billion in 2009, is hardly so small as to be ignored. But virtually ignored it is. In contrast, original Medicare is subject not only to the politics of what Bruce Vladeck called the "Medicare-industrial complex," but also to direct pork-barrel politics pertaining to "distributive" issues—the "allocation of financial benefits across regions and communities" (Vladeck 1999).

It is far beyond the scope of this study to discuss the extent and range of the influences brought to bear on Medicare payments through the political process. Suffice it to say they are immense, unrelenting, often successful, and often later reversed as another group prevails in another year's political decisions. As one of an almost endless list of possible examples, consider the success of the surgeons in gaming the "sustainable growth rate" (SGR) system to maximize their incomes compared to the payments to other physicians, as reported by Joseph Newhouse (2002, 46–48). The surgeons made a clever argument that because their volume of services was growing more slowly than the volume of other physician services, they should have a higher "conversion factor" in the zero-sum game of physician payments. When a multiyear averaging formula was about to pinch the resulting gains, they succeeded in getting the system changed. Ultimately, the system was reformed again to eliminate the bias in favor of surgeons, but meanwhile they enjoyed years of higher fees than would otherwise have been paid.

> Running a price control system, we found, was not a calm, orderly application of economic theories, but an eclectic mixture of economics, power, pressure, and politics.
>
> C. Jackson Grayson
> *Confessions of a Price Controller*

These problems are not, of course, unique to original Medicare. They necessarily arise in any system of government-administered allocation decisions.[13] There are innumerable other Medicare instances we might mention, but three recent ones will suffice.

First, the same SGR system under which the surgeons sought "economic rents" includes not only conversion factors but also an overall ceiling. The linchpin system enacted by Congress to control physician costs in Medicare Part B, the SGR is used to update annually the fees paid to physicians. If Medicare physician spending does not meet a spending target, then, the statute says, the annual increase in fees must be reduced; or, if that is insufficient to meet the target, the existing fees must be cut back (Dummit 2006). But spending never meets the target, because physicians are very adept at increasing volume to maintain income.

As a result, Congress is faced each year with deciding whether to accept the statutory cutback or write new legislation to restore the fees. At stake are not only the income and potential rage of a half-million or so MDs (living in every congressional district and quite prepared to punish their members of Congress if they do not deliver), but also access to physicians by beneficiaries. If fees are too low, more physicians will drop out of original Medicare, and the wrath felt by Congress will then include that of two groups of constituents—the other a group of enrollees in original Medicare some 35 million strong.

In 2008, as in every year since 2003, Congress made the politically wise decision to override existing law and provide a "temporary" halt to the physician fee decrease mandated by the SGR, as well as a small physician fee increase. This also enabled Congress to make a modest and beneficial reform tying a small portion of physician fees to "pay for performance." The cost of this budgetary increase in the MIPPA statute (the 2008 title for the annual set of amendments to the Medicare statute) was paid by an amendment to the conditions governing Medicare Advantage private fee-for-service plans, requiring most of them to establish preferred provider networks. This will likely have the effect, as estimated by the CBO, of decreasing total MA enrollment in 2013 from a previously projected 14.3 million persons to a newly projected 12 million (U.S. Congressional Budget Office 2008b).

The official scoring estimate does not take into account the likely cost increases, almost certainly exceeding projected savings, of the additional

2.3 million persons who, the CBO projects, will remain in original Medicare (presumably close to 90 percent of whom will enroll in Medigap plans or be forced into Medicaid). Interestingly, this particular approach to "reforming" the PFFS program was of special significance to physicians, who have chafed against the requirement that they accept Medicare payment rates from PFFS plans.

The second example lies in payment for durable medical equipment (DME). DME payment rates are notoriously complex, influenced not only by nominal rates but also by CMS decisions on classification of new types or models of equipment. Most of these price controls are based on 1986 and 1987 levels, adjusted for inflation (U.S. Medicare Payment Advisory Commission 2008b). These price levels therefore ignore the massive reductions in prices for most kinds of similar equipment generated by the revolution in global manufacturing and trade of consumer goods of comparable complexity over the past decade (such as the reduction in costs of tools, gas grills, bicycles, electronic equipment, and a host of consumer goods that are today far less expensive in real terms than they were a decade ago), and they lead to excessive payments of hundreds of millions of dollars a year (Leonhardt 2008).

Recognizing this problem, Congress enacted in the 2003 Medicare Modernization Act a new requirement that the CMS conduct competitive bidding to purchase DME in a relatively small number of categories, including some of the most expensive (in total cost) kinds. The new system was set to go into place in 2008, with winning suppliers selected in May, and projected to save, on average, about 26 percent compared to current fee schedule amounts (U.S. Department of Health and Human Services, Centers for Medicare and Medicaid Services 2008a). In the summer of 2008, bowing to pressure from DME suppliers and manufacturers, Congress overrode its own requirement. The bidding system was put on hold for at least a year, and more likely for a more extended period (U.S. Department of Health and Human Services, Centers for Medicare and Medicaid Services 2009c).

Ironically, this episode holds some FEHBP-related lessons. Because it was known that FEHBP plans had bargained effectively for DME rates, the MMA had included a temporary scheme for establishing rates for home oxygen equipment equal to FEHBP payment levels. Pursuant to the MMA, the Office of the Inspector General surveyed FEHBP plans and found that, on average, they paid 11–12 percent less than original Medicare in 2002 (U.S. Department of Health and Human Services, Office of the Inspector General 2005). This establishes the simple point that, even on as seemingly simple a price control issue as payment rates for equipment that can be purchased by private consumers in their local medical supply stores, the FEHBP plans sometimes do, and presumably often do, achieve lower prices than the huge price-setting Medicare system. At the same time, the ability of the CMS to generate savings even below the levels of the FEHBP plans illustrates that a price control system can almost always set payment levels lower than free-market levels, at least in the short run. (In economists' terms, short-run marginal costs are almost always well below the long-run marginal costs necessary to business survival over the long term.) Of course, the MIPPA outcome on both the SGR and competitive bidding suggests that in the real world of American politics, Congress is unlikely to have the fortitude to cut payments as low as might, in a technical sense, be feasible. Moreover, it is quite possible, and perhaps likely, that FEHBP plans have lowered these costs since 2002.

The third example arises from the American Recovery and Reinvestment Act of 2009, a massive spending bill ostensibly aimed at creating jobs by funding "shovel-ready" as well as infrastructure investment projects. One of its little known provisions, however, did something else entirely. The hospice industry (or, as it likes to call itself, the "hospice community") was faced with a CMS regulation, carrying out the relevant statutory directives from Congress, that would reduce its rates about 4 percent over a three-year period to eliminate what Congress had in 1997 determined were systematic overpayments. Faced with industry pressure, Congress created a one-year delay in letting the rate reduction take effect, conveniently included in the Recovery Act legislation.

Another inevitable product of the current design of original Medicare and the lobbying pressures to which it is subject is pure "pork-barrel" spending. Since Congress legislates in detail on virtually every aspect of the program, including payment rates and geographic adjustments to payments and classifications of providers, it is easy and natural for it to reward favored projects and entities.

Organizations that publicize earmarks and pork-barrel spending focus their attention on appropriations acts, not authorizations acts and not entitlement spending.[14] Although data on the extent of such earmarks in Medicare are apparently unavailable, pork-barrel spending is known to be common.

For example, an end-of-session Medicare bill passed in late 2006 contained hundreds of millions of dollars sought by such congressional luminaries as Democratic senator Harry Reid of Nevada, then Tennessee senator Bill Frist, a Republican, Democratic senator Daniel Inouye of Hawaii, and Illinois Republican and then Speaker of the House Dennis Hastert (Pear 2006). Likewise, the proposed 2007 expansion of the State Children's Health Insurance Program, vetoed successfully by President George W. Bush for unrelated reasons, contained hundreds of millions of dollars in earmarks for forty hospitals (Pear 2007). One of these would have increased payments to the Bay Area Medical Center complex in Green Bay, Wisconsin, to the levels it would get if it were located in Chicago, where Medicare payment rates (which are based in part on local labor market costs) are much higher.

> Granting relief to particular hospitals is sometimes a way for Congress to improve "the equity and fairness" of Medicare payments.
>
> House Ways and Means subcommittee chairman and political realist Pete Stark, commenting on forty hospital earmarks in SCHIP legislation
> In Robert Pear, "Select Hospitals Reap
> a Windfall Under Child Health Bill"

Sometimes the pressures on payment rates and systems are combined with pork-barrel exceptions from those reductions. Recently, Congress sought to enact legislation to prohibit the establishment of new doctor-owned specialty hospitals (Pear 2008b). But as the bills emerged from committee, they included special exceptions for favored hospitals. One of those was the Bay Area Medical Center.[15]

> Once you start making exceptions . . . everybody lines up and says "me too." Then you go hospital by hospital, and that's a political nightmare.
>
> House Ways and Means subcommittee chairman and "straight arrow" Pete Stark, commenting on legislation for doctor-owned hospitals
> In Robert Pear, "Concerned about Costs, Congress Pushes
> Curbs on Doctor-Owned Hospitals"

The FEHBP, on the other hand, leaves payment rate and benefit design decisions to private health plans, as does competitive Medicare. As a result, pork barrel is unknown in the FEHBP.[16] The number of successful political interventions into FEHBP plans' benefits and payment decisions have been so few as to be notable, and have usually come from above through administrative rather than legislative decisions, or as a byproduct of more broadly applicable mandates with spillover effects on FEHBP plans (see, for example, U.S. House of Representatives, Committee on Oversight and Government Reform 1997).

One of the few, and by far the most notable, congressional interventions came in 1994, when the Office of Personnel Management director acceded to the pressures brought in a congressional hearing and directed all FEHBP plans to pay for autologous bone marrow transplants for breast cancer in clinical trials, despite the fact that these treatments were still experimental and that most studies showed no benefit. Plans did not resist this administrative fiat as vigorously as they might have, because it brought them relief from lawsuits and large monetary judgments. As it later turned out, the few research projects purporting to show benefits from this treatment had been falsified, and the entire episode essentially amounted to subjecting cancer victims to expensive, painful, and completely worthless treatments that brought only *False Hope*, as Richard Rettig and colleagues entitled their 2007 book on the fiasco.[17]

Yet another issue arises for Medicare by virtue of its decisions being made in a politically charged environment where the penalties and rewards are essentially short-term, with the next election as the most relevant time horizon. In contrast, the bureaucrats who run the FEHBP are in their secure jobs for the long haul. They can afford to take a longer-term perspective and have incentives to do so because a mistake may well rebound on them in future years. A simple example illustrates the problem.

As shown in figure 6-1, Medicare and Medicaid spending, driven in largest part by increased per-capita health-care costs, will not only render Medicare insolvent, but will also lead to immense increases in taxes or premiums to finance costs that will rise from about 4 percent of the GDP today to about 20 percent some seven decades from now, almost doubling total federal spending (U.S. Senate, Committee on Finance 2008a). A provision of the MMA requires the Medicare Board of Trustees to issue determinations of

FIGURE 6-1

CBO's Best Estimate of Likely Fiscal Impact
of Current Medicare and Medicaid Programs

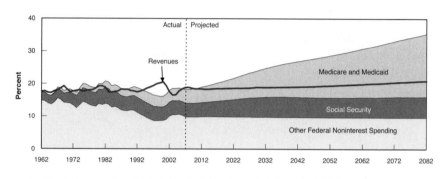

SOURCE: U.S. Senate, Committee on Finance 2008a, 4.
NOTE: Spending as a percentage of GDP compared to revenues under current tax rates.

"excess general revenue Medicare funding" as the finances of the program worsen. In 2008, these determinations, duly issued, led to a required "Medicare funding warning," requiring, in turn, a presidential legislative plan to respond to the warning, and Congress to act on that legislation on an expedited basis. Accordingly, President Bush transmitted his legislative proposals, and Congress promptly found a loophole by which it could ignore them.

Now it is certainly the case that all concerned might reasonably have been excused in a presidential election year from taking on any controversial issue that could possibly be avoided. It is also noteworthy that then president Bush's legislative proposals included nothing likely to solve the long-term shortfall problem, which totals some $86 trillion (Antos 2008). Regardless, Congress pulled the trigger on the trigger, and used a procedural maneuver to avoid debating, discussing, or considering any short- or long-term reform legislation. Interestingly, in the context of health reform Congress has requested and the Obama administration has proposed several models that might greatly reduce the congressional role in Medicare payment policy. One idea parallels the system that has been used several times for military base closings, allowing Congress only to vote up or down on an entire package of reforms crafted by an independent commission (Murray 2009). The entire purpose of such an approach is to restructure congressional oversight in a way that preserves ultimate congressional decision-making, but sheds the political micromanagement.

None of this analysis should be taken to suggest that either the OPM or private health plans are paragons of virtue or rationality, or that Congress and the CMS are any less rational or meritorious. It would not, however, be an overly severe criticism of the American political system to suggest that it strives to avoid hard decisions and, when it does make decisions, is vulnerable to a wide range of pressures—often driven by "rent-seeking" financial motives—that simply do not fall on market-driven systems, including competitive health insurance systems, with remotely the same force or frequency.

Nonetheless, the "hands-off" governance of the FEHBP and its location in an agency that focuses on other issues, and whose director has never been a health insurance expert, have contributed to management failures through policy neglect. Despite a handful of key policy and actuarial staff who have, through the years, rendered sensible policy advice as to needed changes, no OPM director has ever proposed (at least publicly) the kinds of design changes, such as risk adjustments and changes in the premium cost-sharing formula, that would improve the program's performance in "managed competition." Instead, the major premium-related initiative undertaken by the OPM—to create premium conversion—needlessly worsened an already weak set of incentives.

"Good Government" Procedural Protections and Delays. An entirely different set of restrictions affects original Medicare in ways that impinge to a far lesser extent on private plans. Like any public program, Medicare is subject to a host of legal, regulatory, budgetary, procedural, and practical constraints that radically limit its ability to operate in ways available to almost any private organization. Four examples should suffice.

First, most important administrative decisions concerning original Medicare must be made through the rulemaking process of a statute called the Administrative Procedure Act (APA). This means that any requirements that bind a health program's benefits and the procedures it uses are subject to what is called a "notice and comment" process, involving a publication of proposed rules, comments on that publication, a review of those comments, and a final publication announcing government decisions. Historically (and in the original APA statute to this day), the APA has exempted public benefit programs such as Medicare, in recognition of the need to make rapid and efficient government decisions in operating programs. In theory, benefit programs were allowed to promulgate their rules by fiat. After the requisite number of disasters, however, both the executive and legislative branches of the federal government decided that "enough was enough," and today the Medicare statute, as well as HHS and presidential policy, requires application of the APA process (subject to narrow exceptions) for almost all rules. This has many positive effects, not least of which is restraining the bureaucracy from its amazing capacity to conceive and impose bad ideas on the public.[18] But it also has a huge negative effect: Public programs like Medicare require years (not months, not weeks, not days) to make decisions that in the private sector can be and are often made in hours.

Second, original Medicare's implementation decisions are subject to a vast array of "due process" restrictions. These restrictions are important. In the real world, if a physician or hospital or even South Florida durable medical equipment supplier is banned from Medicare, he, she, or it is out of business. Medicare doesn't just control its own payments; it controls the livelihoods of millions of Americans. Likewise, some 45 million Medicare enrollees depend ultimately on the federal government to police the fairness by which their medical expenses are evaluated. The decisions by the hearing examiner that reinstated the South Florida scam artists[19] reflected the potential importance of such decisions; suppose, for example, that some of those accused suppliers were, in fact, legitimate businesses that for any number of important reasons were temporarily closed when the feds stopped by. In contrast, if a private plan were to drop a provider from its "preferred" or "participating" list, rarely would that provider's livelihood be affected. There are dozens of competing plans, and no one expects any provider to be in every plan.

So important are these kinds of issues, as well as the issue of beneficiary protection, that the budget of the HHS Office of the Secretary includes about $40 million for the salaries and expenses of administrative law judges whose primary function is to second-guess decisions to deny claims payments. The OPM, in contrast, maintains a strong beneficiary protection system, but it relies primarily on plans themselves, with the OPM as the "last resort." The plans are required to maintain responsive appeals processes. The FEHBP system has never been systematically compared to original Medicare, but one thing is certain: FEHBP appeals move to resolution light-years faster than Medicare appeals.

Third, most Medicare decisions are potentially subject to judicial review on a wide range of legal, rational, and due process grounds. An example of the challenges that may arise from judicial involvement is a recent ruling by the U.S. District Court for the District of Columbia regarding use of the "least costly alternative" principle as a basis for Medicare "coverage" decisions.

Resource constraints dictate that very few coverage decisions are made through an elegant and rational "evidence-based" process that applies to the most important issues. Instead, roughly 99 percent of all such decisions (in practice, primarily related to drugs and devices) are delegated to and made by contractors. One of the criteria contractors should use, according to CMS procedures and instructions, is a simple and sensible cost-effectiveness standard—that of the "least costly" alternative treatment.[20] In the classic formulation, it says that if there are two equally effective treatments, Medicare (or any other payer) will only pay for the least costly. The enrollee is free to pay the difference to get the higher-cost alternative, but at his or her own expense.

One of the most dramatic applications of this principle arose about twenty-five years ago. Late-night TV advertisements began to promote "seat-lift" chairs that would make it easy for obese Americans to sit up, get up, and visit the kitchen for refreshments, without effort, before returning to their televisions or other important pursuits. The advertised chairs were luxurious, with leather and fur and other desirable attributes, and would raise the largest couch potato effortlessly to his feet. They cost hundreds or thousands of dollars, but could be had for 20 percent of retail price (the Medicare coinsurance) with a physician signature on a prescription. The HHS spent years trying to quell the hemorrhage of payments for these chairs, and, ultimately, Congress had to enact a statute to dictate the simple solution: Medicare would pay for the least costly seat-lift chair on the market (an ugly $50 contraption sold in medical supply stores), and the enrollee would pay the difference if he wanted a $1,000 leather chair. Needless to say, this particular abuse stopped immediately, saving Medicare approximately $50 million a year. The several hundred million dollars already spent while the government struggled for years over how to handle this issue could not be recovered, however.

In 2008, despite the obvious necessity for such a policy in preventing wasteful spending, district court judge Henry H. Kennedy Jr. inconveniently cast doubt on the entire "least costly" scheme on which Medicare depends for a major portion of its cost containment efforts. The program had refused to pay extra for the more expensive of two medically identical drugs, one version dispensed in one inhalation dose and the other in two doses. In *Hays and Dey v. Leavitt*, Kennedy ruled that the Medicare statute's words "reasonable and necessary" did not authorize least costly decisions (Kennedy 2008). This ruling has been appealed. The key point, however, is that when Congress writes a complex and lengthy statute that makes simple business decisions legal decisions, it necessarily applies the entire legal system of the United States, at least potentially, to every one of those business decisions.[21]

The importance of this ruling is not the merit of the judicial decision per se, but what it tells us about the governance of Medicare. Any of hundreds of judges in the United States can parse any of thousands of sentences in the underlying statute or regulations and decide to change a major or minor feature of the program. In the FEHBP, in contrast, the statutory language consumes only a handful of pages, and the opportunities for judicial mischief (however otherwise meritorious) are immensely limited because health plans, not federal officials interpreting detailed statutory language, make virtually all decisions.[22]

These and many other managerial, legal, procedural, and other constraints have the effect of imposing restrictions on original Medicare that, while in part and in some aspects are applicable to competitive Medicare and the FEHBP, are far, far less burdensome in those programs. As we have noted above, any publicly run program faces these kinds of problems. In a relatively simple program, such as Social Security retirement benefits or the food stamp program, the procedural requirements create heavy but manageable burdens on program administrators. In a complex program like original Medicare or disability insurance, direct public operation sometimes prevents effective management, and often prevents timely management and timely corrective actions.

Conclusion: Lessons Learned and Recommendations

What can be made of the findings presented in this analysis? They lead to several conclusions and several prescriptions. As always with policy evaluations and policy prescriptions, "the devil is in the details," and I endeavor to present recommendations with enough details to be specific, but not so endlessly as to drown the reader in them. While many of these conclusions and recommendations have relevance to the debate over health reform, my principal and direct purpose is to focus on the half-trillion dollars of taxpayer money spent today on these programs. Medicare insolvency looms, and the FEHBP has lost its way. These problems need attention.

Relative Program Performance

The FEHBP has equaled or exceeded the performance of original Medicare in almost all respects, including benefit design, innovation over time, access, fraud control, manageable governance, and, above all, cost control, over nearly the entire history of both programs. What is most surprising about this performance is that the FEHBP has done so well despite multiple defects, including risk selection distortions that affect rational plan choices by consumers, a capped-premium design that was once strong but now provides only weak incentives to consumers to make frugal plan selections, the immense weakening of cost discipline by tax subsidies for both premiums and out-of-pocket costs, and restrictions on the entrance of new national plans. While the FEHBP has largely escaped benefit mandates, it has been lucky in little else. It has evidenced its superiority despite—or

193

perhaps because of—having to compete, with minimal policy supervision, against an original Medicare program that is subject to constant and detailed scrutiny by oversight bodies that generate an extensive number of annual "reforms," both large and small.

> In sum, the FEHBP has outperformed Medicare every which way—in containment of costs both to consumers and to the government, in benefit and product innovation and modernization, and in consumer satisfaction.
>
> Harry Cain II
> "Moving Medicare to the FEHBP Model,
> or How to Make an Elephant Fly"

As for competitive Medicare, the verdict is still out. The Medicare Advantage program still suffers from an overreliance on premiums based in large part on the costs of original Medicare in specific geographic areas. When fraud rises in South Florida, MA plans that are not the victims of fraud are actually paid more.[1] The first major reform of private plan participation in Medicare, in the Balanced Budget Act of 1997, was essentially aborted (unintentionally) by the BBA's sweeping reductions in the original Medicare costs on which plan premiums were based. As for the prescription drug program, it is a strange anomaly in the history of insurance. The robust performance of both Part D and MA since enactment of the Medicare Modernization Act, however, provides an early indication that Congress made sound design decisions in the MMA. The performance of Part D, in particular, has to date been extraordinary. In its first three years, it was able to improve its benefits and hold its costs almost level, and even the 2009 increases leave it cumulatively far below the originally projected costs. Any program that can attract a third of the veterans served by the Veterans Administration into paying for its benefits, despite having free prescription drugs provided to them by the VA, is doing something right.

Accumulating evidence, discussed below, indicates that both competitive Medicare programs are substantially reducing costs in original Medicare.

The successes of competitive Medicare in the last three years, and the record of the last half-dozen years in which even original Medicare has out-performed the FEHBP on cost control, suggest that the balance has now finally shifted. This should not be surprising. Congress copied many of the best features of the FEHBP, and improved on them, in enacting the MMA. We should certainly expect competitive Medicare to outperform the FEHBP in future years and be shocked if it does not. Moreover, competitive Medicare comprises an increasing share of the total Medicare program and will become, in time, an increasing factor in holding down costs even in original Medicare (with, for instance, medicines now part of the disease management arsenal). Meanwhile, the FEHBP suffers from the extraordinarily bad decision of a previous administration to curtail sharply its cost-constraining design features in the name of "modernizing" its premiums to obtain wasteful tax subsidies.

This prediction of future performance depends, of course, on the assumption that Congress does not once again—by accident or design—undercut the viability of MA or find a way to cripple Part D. For its entire history, the FEHBP has been a reliable customer and business partner for insurance plans. Medicare has not. The ill-considered assault on private fee-for-service plans enacted in MIPPA does not bode well. Moreover, the most recent changes in Medicare Advantage payment policy made by the incoming Obama administration (and threatened by Congress, as well), while certainly justified in part, appear more severe than is desirable. (For example, the MA premiums for 2010 rest on the artificial assumption that Medicare payments to doctors will be cut by 21 percent under the SGA formula, a patently unlikely event.)

To its credit, the administration has proposed reforming the Medicare Advantage premium-setting formula to decouple it from original Medicare and wed it to system-wide bids, similar to Part D and the FEHBP in concept, if not in all details. Unfortunately, the administration's proposed formula would severely reduce payments to MA plans, virtually end their ability to attract enrollment through supplemental benefits, and likely lead to a reduction in projected enrollment ten years from now from 14 million persons to about 7 million persons (U.S. Congressional Budget Office 2009b).[2] A reduction this drastic would, as we have shown, likely cost the Medicare program as much or more in wasteful spending as the nominal budgetary savings, as enrollees shifted to supplementation through Medicaid and Medigap plans with the attendant overutilization those options produce.

For the present, the performance records of both competitive Medicare and the FEHBP suggest reform lessons for each other as well as for both.[3]

Recent Evaluations

Medicare Advantage in its current form and the Medicare Part D program are both so new that is it unreasonable to expect any considered evaluative conclusions as to actual performance. Nonetheless, some studies are emerging.

With respect to Part D:

- "Providing Prescription Drug Coverage to the Elderly: America's Experiment with Medicare Part D" is a comprehensive evaluation that concludes, "The first two and a half years of operation for Medicare Part D [were] relatively successful overall, given the challenges involved" (Duggan et al. 2008, 90).

- "The Effect of Medicare Part D on Pharmaceutical Prices and Utilization" concludes that Part D "substantially lowered the average price and increased the total utilization of prescription drugs by Medicare recipients" (Duggan and Morton 2008, 1). This finding addresses the impact of Part D on overall prices for drugs, not the additional savings available to consumers who shopped prudently.

- "Comparing Pharmacy Reimbursement: Medicare Part D to Medicaid" concludes that "the average Part D and Medicaid pharmacy reimbursement amounts were similar" in 2006, and that the "Medicaid reimbursement amount was [only] .6 percent less than the Part D amount [for single source drugs and] 17 percent greater than the Part D amount for . . . multiple source drugs" (U.S. Department of Health and Human Services, Office of the Inspector General 2009a, ii and iii). In other words, schemes to return Medicare enrollees to Medicaid to save drug costs will cost more, not less.

- Numerous reports have shown that the use of generic drugs by seniors, relative to brand-name drugs, has greatly increased since

Part D was introduced. Part D plans also emphasize therapeutic substitution, such as using a less expensive off-patent statin rather than a higher-priced one. These efforts likely have spillover effects into prescribing under private insurance, as well.

- A recent study shows that in the first year over two-thirds of Part D enrollees were choosing wisely, if not perfectly, by enrolling in plans that saved them substantial amounts compared to more expensive plans (Gruber 2009).[4] Overall, more than three-fourths enrolled in the PDP plans with total costs to enrollees (premium and out of pocket) in the bottom 50 percent.

- One study (Thaler and Sunstein 2009) criticized the random assignment of low-income enrollees to PDP plans. The alternative of "intelligent assignment" to those plans in which the drugs they used were on the plan formularies could arguably have saved a good deal of confusion and complications. This study also found the Internet and other tools designed to assist seniors in choosing low-cost plans somewhat confusing.

- Yet another study found that enrollees' choices among plans were less than optimal, though nonetheless cost-saving, and that specially tailored and personalized information and assistance could improve plan choices (Kling et al. 2008).

- Medicare Part D, like Medicaid and SCHIP, has significant potential for "crowd-out" displacement of private insurance. While great pains were taken in the program design to minimize this effect, at least one study suggests that crowd-out has occurred on a substantial scale, perhaps as much as or even more than in those programs (Lichtenberg and Sun 2007).

With respect to Medicare Advantage, the evidence is even sketchier, though there are bits and pieces:

- *The Success of Medicare Advantage Plans: What Seniors Should Know* (Moffit 2008) reviews much of the literature and concludes that MA plans provide superior benefits, that they create savings for Medicaid, and that they may even improve health outcomes.

- On average, Medicare Advantage plans provide about $1,000 a year in additional benefits, such as catastrophic expense protection, compared to original Medicare (U.S. House of Representatives, Committee on Ways and Means 2007b).

- A study using older Medicare+Choice data is undoubtedly still accurate in its overall finding that Medicare Advantage keeps a large proportion of its enrollees, perhaps 20 percent or more, from enrolling in Medicaid (Atherly and Thorpe 2005). Medicaid enrollment eliminates cost-sharing incentives to reduce waste. This finding alone implies that MA saves federal and state governments more than is spent on excess premium support, with no net cost to original Medicare.

- A recent study shows that Medicare Advantage HMOs produce direct savings to original Medicare in the areas they serve in direct proportion to their market shares (Chernew et al. 2008; see also Baker 1996 for similar results). The magnitude of the effect is substantial, on the order of a 1 percent reduction in original Medicare spending per enrollee for every 1 percent increase in HMO penetration. The authors speculate that there may be a practice effect from greater HMO penetration in these markets. One mechanism for this may be that MA plans with cost-sharing attract enrollees who would otherwise be getting "free" care through Medigap plans or Medicaid, thereby inducing greater cost consciousness among both patients and local providers not only for these patients but for others as well. If so, this effect would arise from private fee-for-service as well as HMO enrollment, a question not yet studied. Regardless, the authors argue that their results "would imply greater payment to managed care plans than implied simply by the cost of serving beneficiaries in HMOs" (1460).

- "Medicare Private Plans: A Report Card on Medicare Advantage" (Gold 2008) provides a major update on MA data (reporting, for example, that 23 percent of Medicare enrollees are now in MA plans) and a robust, though apparently unintended, defense of PFFS plans as providing minimal paperwork and superior travel flexibility. Marsha Gold provides the best historical and current data on MA, bar none. But she fails to mention, let alone discuss or quantify, the major savings to enrollees from reduced Medigap premium payments, or to the government from reduced excess utilization and fraud.

- "Payment Policy and the Growth of Medicare Advantage" (Zaraboza and Harrison 2008) is highly detailed and competent in its assessment of MA, but, like Gold's study, it fails to discuss or quantify major savings from reduced Medigap premium payments, reduced excess utilization, or reduced fraud.

- "Medicare Advantage: Characteristics, Financial Risks, and Disenrollment Rates in Private Fee-for-Service Plans" (U.S. Government Accountability Office 2008a) hints that PFFS enrollees face unreasonable financial risks. The study fails to demonstrate, however, that any enrollees are exposed to, let alone subjected to, such risks. The report seems to criticize arrangements, long common in the FEHBP and private plans generally, whereby enrollees who fail to provide prenotification for elective hospitalizations face penalties. The GAO documents that this penalty facing PFFS enrollees is typically $100 to $150 or less (compared to $500 in all national plans in the FEHBP, a point unmentioned in the report).[5]

Some of these (and other studies) seem fixated on the premium subsidy advantage given to MA plans. They take a narrow budgetary accounting perspective and fail to deal with all benefits and all costs, to whomever accrued. The omitted benefits include reductions in unnecessary utilization, improved health care that reduces the need for other spending (drugs instead of hospitalizations), savings from reduced fraud and abuse, and savings to beneficiaries who drop expensive Medigap plans. All of these omitted savings together likely exceed, perhaps several times over, the 12 or 14 percent payment differential that obsesses many commentators. Yet another recent study makes this point most convincingly. Zhang et al. (2009) found that "The Effect of Medicare Part D on Drug and Medical Spending" in Medicare was to reduce substantially the amounts spent on medical care by enrollees in original Medicare. Part D enrollees who had previously had no or limited drug coverage spent more on drugs after enrolling in Part D, but their use of medical care (in original Medicare) decreased substantially enough to offset the increased spending on drugs.

Amazingly, there is almost no current evaluative literature on the FEHBP. The comparisons in this volume on cost control, risk selection, premiums and benefits, access, fraud control, and governance stand virtually alone. Previous studies exist, of course, in many but not all of these areas and are addressed throughout the text; but none is comprehensive, some are inaccurate, and few are contemporary. The only prior study remotely as comprehensive was published two decades ago (U.S. Congressional Research Service 1989).

Lessons for Both Programs

Both the FEHBP and the three Medicare programs compared here suffer from the extraordinarily counterproductive effects of the income tax system in distorting and subsidizing ever-increasing consumption of health-care services, not only at any point in time, but by encouraging overinvestment and overpayment for health-care services over time.

Despite Medicare's size, original Medicare does not have the tools to reverse the growth of bloat in health care. The ever-increasing share of GDP devoted to health care results in part from technological progress and in part from the rising wealth of our society, but in even larger part from government subsidies and their dynamic effects over time on health-care providers' incentives (Helms 1999). The cap on the value of the tax subsidy proposed in 2007 by President Bush (similar to a proposal advanced by President Ronald Reagan in the 1980s) was but one of many possible approaches to reducing that subsidy, and among the family of such reforms one of the mildest.

One of the best features of such proposals is the use of some or all of the savings from a cap to provide a tax subsidy for people currently without insurance (see Furman 2008 for an assessment of all these potential effects). The Senate Finance Committee is considering a tax cap as a major source of revenue for health reform (U.S. Senate, Committee on Finance 2009). A bigger reform would be to create a refundable tax credit. This would not only provide a major gain in horizontal equity, but would also reduce the number of uninsured.[6] There have been a number of proposals to substitute refundable tax credits or allowances to purchase health insurance for the current tax preference. Prominent among these is the "Healthy Americans Act" sponsored by senators Wyden and Bennett. This proposal has been estimated by the CBO and others as saving rather than increasing health care costs both to the economy and to the Federal budget, in marked contrast to other proposals under consideration by Congress (see Sheils and Haught 2008).

But, quite apart from revenues, almost any tax reform along these lines would eventually exert enormous pressure on profligate spending. Hence, the most important lesson to be learned—less from our analysis than from a large body of essentially unanimous economic literature—is that:

- The tax treatment of health insurance should be reformed to reduce one of the most damaging and least progressive features of the tax system and to reduce the rate of growth in both original Medicare and the FEHBP, as well as in other health-care spending.[7]

Other related ideas include these:

- Whether or not the tax treatment is reformed, the Internal Revenue Code should be amended to require that form W-2 include the dollar amounts for both employer and employee (or retiree) shares of health insurance that are not taxed as income. This would include Medicare beneficiaries, with the dollar amounts set at the average costs of taxpayer spending for the parts in which they enroll.

- The same disclosure should be strongly encouraged on all employee and retiree pay and pension statements, starting with all U.S. government employees, both civilian and military, and U.S. government retirees, and phasing in a requirement for all U.S. government contractors. These recommendations are in the spirit of Thaler and Sunstein's *Nudge* (2009), since they signal consumers through simple information that something about the spending patterns dictated by government policy and employer decision may not be their preference.

- In the event that the tax treatment is not reformed in the near future for the entire economy, the U.S. government should, at the very least, eliminate the tax preference for the federal employee share of all employer health insurance financed by the federal government, providing federal employees with an offsetting salary increase in the annual cost-of-living adjustment.

Both Medicare and the FEHBP also suffer from their own design features that encourage overinsurance and overspending through moral hazard. In the case of the FEHBP, the primary cause is direct interaction with Medicare. In the case of Medicare, the primary cause is Medigap and former employer supplementation of retiree health benefits, including that provided by the FEHBP.

There are effective but relatively draconian alternatives, such as the Rettenmaier and Saving (2007) proposal to make illegal supplementary plans that provide first-dollar coverage (including, presumably, the current FEHBP supplementation model). There are modest and timid options; for example, the MMA made illegal the sale of Medigap plans and the Medicaid program with drug coverage to new enrollees, but did not require existing enrollees to drop that coverage. Draconian or timid, a valuable long-run result of enrollment growth in MA plans is that they eliminate Medigap coverage by enrollees, who no longer face the large gaps in original Medicare.

In this context, MedPAC and the CBO have counterproductively proposed eliminating the approximate 12–14 percent "overpayment" of Medicare Advantage plans, arguing that "the Medicare program should be neutral as to whether the beneficiaries decide to enroll in private plans or remain" in original Medicare (U.S. Medicare Payment Advisory Commission 2007, chapter 4; U.S. House of Representatives, Committee on Ways and Means 2007c; U.S. Congressional Budget Office 2007a, 167). Actually, the Medicare program should not be neutral. These payments should not be identical. Not only do MA plans contain the promise of future cost control through disease management and benefit design innovations, but they also save money—big money—today. They reduce the use of Medigap plans and the Medicaid program as a source of moral hazard and, hence, wasteful spending in original Medicare. The welfare gains to enrollees in reduced premium costs (both Medigap and Medicare Part D), and to a lesser extent to taxpayers in reduced spending in original Medicare, undoubtedly dwarf the 12–14 percent payment differential. And those savings are just the beginning of proper accounting, since it appears that MA saves substantial sums both in original Medicare and in Medicaid.

Equally important from both a social welfare and budgetary perspective:

- Professional analyses of these programs from MedPAC, the CBO, the GAO, and other organizations should always address (even if they cannot estimate with precision) cross-program effects and all cost and benefit effects, not just direct spending effects.

If reductions were, however, to be made, the worst possible option would be to limit payments to the original Medicare level by geographic area, leaving wasteful utilization in areas such as Miami unscathed, and eliminating the feasibility of MA plan participation in the Midwest and other relatively low-cost areas. Reducing benchmarks below FFS levels in high-cost areas while preserving floors in low-cost areas, and moving gradually to benchmarks based on competing bids (as under Part D), would be far superior as a means of reducing payment differentials over time. Repeating the harmful effects the BBA created on MA plan participation and on enrollees is hardly a reasonable course of action to recommend, and would once again make Medigap plans and 100 percent coverage of all hospital and medical bills the only viable means of protection against the gaps in original Medicare for large areas of the country. In the longer run:

- Medicare Advantage premiums should be delinked from those of original Medicare, either completely through weighted bid averaging or through a weighted-average bid system that includes original Medicare as if it were a competing plan.

With respect to this recommendation, the Obama administration has proposed a competitive bidding system that would, indeed, delink MA bids from the cost of original Medicare in particular geographic areas (Jaffe 2009b). Instead, plans would submit bids as at present, but the "benchmark" would be set based on those bids without reference to original Medicare costs. A problem with this reform proposal lies not in its conceptual framework but in the implementation details—it would reduce payments to MA plans by $177 billion over ten years, a reduction so drastic as to threaten the viability of the program. Moreover, the pricing of this proposal ignores the many billions annually that MA plans save original Medicare, and the likely savings are correspondingly overstated and may even be nonexistent. A more radical proposal has been advanced, under which original Medicare would be one of the bidders (Coulam et al. 2009). This would generate far greater savings.

Any number of additional steps could be taken to reduce supplementation, singly or in combination. For example, a modestly subsidized benefit for catastrophic expense protection could be added to original Medicare. This could be done at a level and in an amount that would make it always a better buy than the equivalent protection in any Medigap plan, and made available only to those who did not have benefit supplementation for inpatient or outpatient costs.[8] (Alternatively, purchase of the new catastrophic-coverage Medigap policies K and L, created by the MMA, could be modestly subsidized. These policies eschew first-dollar coverage.)

As another example, coverage abroad on an indemnity basis could be added as a benefit in both original Medicare and MA, again available only to those without benefit supplementation.[9] This would eliminate a major incentive to purchase existing Medigap policies that provide first-dollar coverage. While the CMS itself does not have the capability to administer such a benefit directly, it could easily contract for it with, for example, any of the national plans under the FEHBP.

As a third example, a modest payment similar to the employer subsidy for prescription drug benefits could be made to those employers who provide "creditable coverage" benefits equivalent to or better than those of standard Part D if they also pay all or most of the Part B premium cost. This would be conditioned, however, on those employers' providing no benefit supplementation to original Medicare, but merely a subsidy to retain retirees in the same plan as active employees. Under such an arrangement, original Medicare would save on the order of $1,000 a year or more in reduced wasteful utilization. Since the beneficiary share of the Part B premium is of the same order of magnitude as savings to the program, numerous arrangements are possible to provide a "win-win" for all parties. The FEHBP would be a fine place to start, as proposed below.

As a fourth example, a "creditable coverage" exception could be created to the existing penalty for late enrollment in Medicare for persons enrolled in employer plans. Many employer programs—most notably the FEHBP but also many state and local plans—provide better benefits to retirees than original Medicare. Current law virtually forces retirees in those plans to join Part B at age sixty-five. Even with some risk selection (almost certainly negligible), postponing the late enrollment penalty by adopting the Part D "creditable coverage" standard would create large savings for Medicare.

Any of these options could be designed to save money, to add only modest costs to the program (by Medicare spending standards), or to be financed by small changes in original Medicare's cost-sharing. For example, a coinsurance requirement of several percent added to Part A benefits would finance almost any beneficiary-friendly reform. Regardless of which of these or other options is chosen, another lesson is:

- Reforms to original Medicare should attract enrollees away from, and strongly discourage provision of, supplemental benefits that reduce or eliminate first-dollar cost-sharing for inpatient or outpatient services.

The disastrously expensive (mis)coordination of premiums and benefits between original Medicare and the FEHBP requires additional tools. The prohibition on payment of Part B premiums by plans essentially forces them to reduce or eliminate cost-sharing, as doing so is their only remaining inducement for enrollees to join Part B. Since plans gain hugely whenever Medicare is primary payer, they naturally take this step. The prohibition also has the unfortunate side effect of attracting enrollees away from HMOs, since HMOs not only lose their benefit superiority for FEHBP enrollees with Part B, but also have distinctly inferior access. (Recall that with Part B an FEHBP enrollee gets not only free inpatient and outpatient care, but also elimination of network restrictions in almost all national plans.)

Replacing the prohibition on subsidizing the Part B premium with a requirement that plans pay the premium (to whatever degree they prefer) rather than supplement benefits would reverse these perverse results in an essentially budget-neutral and enrollee-neutral way. Plans' benefit supplements are worth on average about $600, a little over half of the Part B premium (Francis et al. 2008, 63). A national plan that eliminated benefit enrichment and paid half the Part B premium would roughly break even, as would the enrollee. This reform would likely increase the proportion of enrollees joining Part B, but, as we have seen, about 90 percent of those in Part A already do. Combined with the enrollment-reducing incentive of a "creditable coverage" exception to the Part B late enrollment penalty, the direct effects on Part B enrollment would likely be about even. However, both Medicare and the FEHBP, including these enrollees, would gain from the substantial reduction in utilization resulting from the elimination of first-dollar, 100 percent coverage. Hence, another lesson would be:

- FEHBP/Medicare coordination provisions should be reformed to benefit both programs, as well as age sixty-five enrollees, by substituting Part B premium subsidies for cost-sharing benefit subsidies in the FEHBP. [10]

Interestingly, the CBO has analyzed essentially this recommendation in its latest *Budget Options* publication (U.S. Congressional Budget Office 2008a). The CBO proposal (option 94, page 171) is aptly described by its title, "Require Federal Employees Health Benefits Plans to Subsidize Premiums for Medicare Part B and Reduce Coverage of Medicare Cost Sharing by an Equivalent Amount." The CBO estimates that this reform would reduce Medicare costs by about $11 billion over a ten-year period. Savings to the FEHBP would be much smaller, primarily because the program would be substituting one subsidy for another of roughly equal cost. Nothing says, however, that the new Part B premium subsidy has to equal fully the unreduced cost of current cost-sharing subsidies. Nor did the CBO estimate the potential savings to the FEHBP from putting older enrollees back into the fully competitive system they used before age sixty-five.

As previously described, the FEHBP contains a Medicare/FEHBP coordination option in the little known, and less used, statutory provision that allows FEHBP enrollees to suspend (not drop or lose) their FEHBP enrollment when receiving Medicare Part B benefits. Original Medicare, even with Part D to cover drugs, is not nearly as good as any FEHBP plan. But many Medicare Advantage plans are roughly comparable in benefit generosity for doctors and hospitals (though not prescription drugs) to the HMO plans used by FEHBP enrollees, and are, in most instances, available from the same companies. Some MA PPO and PFFS plans are not much inferior to the Blue Cross standard option in benefit generosity for doctors and hospitals (but again, not for drugs). Since the "suspend" option cuts total enrollee premium costs by roughly half and usually more (for example, in 2009 from $2,980 for both Part B and the Blue Cross standard option to about $1,160 for a "zero-premium" MA plan alone), this is a cost-effective option for age sixty-five retirees.

Neither program explains, let alone promotes, this alternative to federal retirees. The hundred-page *Medicare & You* handbook sent to all Medicare enrollees each year at a cost approaching $100 million simply says in its edition for 2009 that "in most cases it will be to your advantage" to keep FEHBP prescription drug coverage (U.S. Department of Health and Human Services, Centers for Medicare and Medicaid Services 2008c, 60). It completely fails to mention the FEHBP or the suspension option in its sections on Medicare Advantage. The OPM has several publications that should but do not mention this option prominently. *The Guide to Federal Benefits for Federal Retirees and Their Survivors* is printed only in token quantities and not routinely distributed to retirees (U.S. Office of Personnel Management 2008a). The OPM also publishes an FEHBP handbook, but it likewise fails to mention suspension of benefits when enrolling in Medicare, and cannot even be searched on this topic because it is presented on the website only as a series of discrete HTML documents rather than as a single PDF file (U.S. Office of Personnel Management n.d.). The OPM also mails almost two million retirees a flimsy, budget-constrained six-page *Open Season Health Benefits Guide* (U.S. Office of Personnel Management Office 2008c and prior years) that breathlessly covers such topics as, "What if my current health plan is not listed in the Guide?" (a rare event), but fails to mention the Medicare alternative that can save most retirees more than $2,000 a year in premium payments.

These agencies both sponsor among the very best consumer information programs of the federal government. Their websites offer superb information. But they are not profit-maximizing organizations with keen instincts for marketing. This leads to another lesson for both programs:

- Both the CMS and OPM should spend as much as it takes—perhaps as much as a penny per age sixty-five enrollee—to make sure that every single one receives in his or her annual open season advice a message saying in large, readable type, "If you are enrolled in both the FEHBP and Medicare, you should consider saving $1,000 or more by joining a Medicare Advantage plan and temporarily suspending your FEHBP enrollment, while retaining your right to enroll in any FEHBP plan without penalty in the next open season."

Through this reduction in moral hazard, these two programs would share savings reaching probably well in excess of $1,000 per person on average for each retired federal employee Part B enrollee whose overall coinsurance rate went from zero to 10 or 20 percent, whose deductibles went from zero to several hundred dollars, and whose utilization of health care dropped by 10 percent or more.[11] The FEHBP would save a few hundred dollars from its share of this reduced utilization. Based on this calculation, the messaging advice only has to persuade one enrollee in a hundred thousand to make this decision to pay for a penny-per-enrollee cost in the first year alone. Unfortunately, these myriad financial advantages to all concerned are likely to be vastly reduced if, as appears likely, Medicare Advantage plans are forced to reduce benefits drastically.

Not far behind the FEHBP in size as a Medicare supplement is TRICARE for Life, a program for military retirees ages sixty-five and over with a budgetary cost of approximately $8 billion a year. TRICARE cost-sharing is set by law at rates so low that it provides virtually free care and hence induces unnecessary utilization in Medicare. The Department of Defense (DOD) has "virtually no means to control the program's costs" (U.S. Congressional Budget Office 2007a, 29). TRICARE for Life's benefits for retirees with Medicare parts A and B are even richer than those in Blue Cross standard, since prescription drug copayments are lower. A DOD task force has been studying possible changes to increase cost-sharing in TRICARE, but the likely outcome of any such proposal is "dead on arrival" (Fales 2007). The CBO recently issued a report arguing strongly that modestly increasing cost-sharing in TRICARE could save billions of dollars annually (U.S. Congressional Budget Office 2009a). As an alternative to outright benefit reductions:

- Reforms to reduce moral hazard in Medicare through incentives against costly wraparound programs should focus not only on Medigap and the FEHBP, but also on TRICARE. Just as for the FEHBP, an effective reform that would introduce more appropriate cost-sharing would be to subsidize the Part B premium rather than Medicare copayments, and either eliminate TRICARE's Medicare supplementation benefits entirely or reduce them substantially.

A predictable and desirable result of this substitution would be to achieve a major reduction in moral hazard and generate a substantial reduction in overall costs to original Medicare and TRICARE—probably well over $1,000 per person, just like the same change in coordination of premiums and benefits between the FEHBP and Medicare. A related recommendation would be:

- Amend the Medicare statute to encourage or require that employer retiree plans in general fund Medicare Part B premiums before reducing cost-sharing.

Enacting such a proposal as a mandate might create unnecessary controversy and difficult transition problems, but there are ways to create modest incentives to this end that fall short of an absolute prohibition.

Lessons for the FEHBP from Medicare

Original Medicare has few lessons for the FEHBP other than, "Don't follow my example." It does, however, retain a useful feature that the FEHBP has lost—namely, cost-sharing in FFS payment. In recent years, the OPM has moved slightly in this direction by encouraging the creation of consumer-driven, high-deductible plans. OPM has refused to let those plans provide savings accounts higher than the enrollee share of premium costs, though, which is a severe and counterproductive constraint (as it is in the federal government's selfish interest as a premium payer to move as many employees and retirees as possible into low-cost plans like these). Recent research shows that these plans are achieving savings for private employers and employees, without adverse selection or other undesirable effects (American Academy of Actuaries 2009). Nominal savings to the government in premium payments average about $2,000 annually for every employee who switches from an expensive traditional plan to one of these plans, and real savings over time may be even greater through behavioral changes. Accordingly,

- The OPM should allow increased savings accounts to encourage enrollment in these plans.

Regardless, the movement of enrollees into these plans is almost certain to remain too slow to have consequential effects on the program as a whole. Therefore:

- The OPM, in its annual negotiations with FFS/PPO carriers, should halt or reverse the steady erosion of enrollee cost-sharing in traditional health plans. Benefit generosity has far passed the point at which cost-sharing effectively reduces unnecessary utilization.

In this respect, the OPM need not be a passive actor. A quarter of a century ago, the OPM's then director ordered a 10 percent cutback in all national plan benefit levels—effectively close to a 50 percent increase in enrollee cost-sharing—to avoid a major budgetary overrun. In subsequent litigation, his decision to increase cost-sharing was upheld.

Competitive Medicare, which is now a superior program, teaches the FEHBP many lessons. First and, arguably, foremost, the FEHBP premium design needs reform. A competitive program like the FEHBP depends critically on strong marginal cost incentives in choosing among plans. At present, taking into account a marginal tax rate generally around 33 percent, employee enrollees pay about two-thirds of the marginal cost of choosing a plan more expensive than average. They receive, however, only about 17 percent of the savings from choosing a plan whose premium is below the matching level (two-thirds of 25 percent). The government retains over 80 percent of the savings, which in practice means 80 percent of progressively smaller amounts as frugal plans lose share in the FEHBP market. In contrast, in Medicare Advantage, the enrollee retains 75 percent of the savings realized by a more frugal plan, through enhanced benefits or a reduced premium or both. The costs of paltry incentives (and huge subsidies) such as these are hard to overstate. One way to understand them is to imagine that employers paid for employee automobiles the way they pay for health plans—and why shouldn't they? For most occupations, an auto is an essential tool simply to get to work. Alain Enthoven (2002) came up with a superb metaphor using automobile subsidies as his counterfactual—showing the inability of a Honda to compete with a luxury car in such a scheme.

> Most employers that do offer choice of carrier pay the whole premium, or some flat, high percentage, like 80 percent, denying "Honda" the opportunity to pass the full savings to the would-be subscriber. It is very hard for "Honda" to compete on value for money in a market where employers systematically subsidize the competitor to the tune of 80 percent of the potential cost savings.
>
> Alain Enthoven
> "Where Are Health Care's 'Hondas'?"

In what follows I assume that reform of the tax subsidy is not changed. If it were, the same magnitude of incentive changes could be achieved with even fewer changes to the premium-support formula. Regardless, some simple changes to the capped-premium formula would considerably improve the FEHBP's incentive structure. Instead of paying only 75 percent of the premium up to the cap amount (set at 72 percent of the all-plan average premium), the government could pay 100 percent up to a somewhat lesser amount. That would have no effect on the premium cost-sharing for plans costing near average or above, but putting all the government payment below the cap would give the enrollees the entire savings (less tax preference) for plans whose premiums are slightly under the average, down to 72 percent of average. Since relatively few plans are significantly below the average, the short-run budgetary cost would be small.[12] This would, however, change the calculus of incentives to reward plans presenting lower-cost offerings. Over time, it would significantly restrain growth in program costs, probably restoring the FEHBP to historical levels of annual cost growth, or even lower. Accordingly:

- Congress should modify the premium formula for calculating the government contribution toward FEHBP plans to increase the return to employees who choose more frugal plans by allowing them to share meaningfully in the savings. The best way to do this is to increase the government contribution to 90 or 100 percent, up to a somewhat lower capped amount.

A separate recommendation would be served by the same reform. At present, perhaps as many as 200,000 federal employees believe they cannot afford health insurance and "go naked" without coverage. These persons could enroll in the program by paying in 2009 about $560 a year for a self enrollment or $1,330 a year for a family enrollment for the least expensive plan, but either do not know this or still do not believe they can afford this much. With a higher government contribution below a reduced capped amount, however, the enrollee premium could be substantially reduced or even eliminated for those choosing such a plan.

- Congress should use the same reform to reduce substantially or eliminate the employee share of premium for those employees enrolling in frugal plans, thereby eliminating the substantial risk faced by employees who cannot afford current premiums.

There is a corollary recommendation. If Congress were determined to provide retirees with additional premium help, perhaps to "make up" for their ineligibility to obtain "premium conversion," the worst possible reform would be to raise the government contribution from 75 to 80 percent.

That would essentially eliminate the ability of "Honda" plans to compete against costly plans, thereby eliminating competitive pressures on the latter, and accelerating the growth of costs in the program through both plan migration and costlier plans to which to migrate. Consumer-driven, high-deductible plans, to date unsuccessful in obtaining significant market share, would become ever more irrelevant in employee decision-making despite their cost advantage and superior incentives for consumer decisions. Unfortunately, U.S. House Majority Leader Steny Hoyer and an influential minority congressman, Frank R. Wolf of Virginia, introduced a bill in 2007 to raise the government cap to 80 percent of the average plan's cost.[13] The headline of the *Washington Post* article reporting on the bill read, "Hoyer Makes Good on Health-Care Promise" (Barr 2007a).

If Congress wishes to legislate a change in the contribution formula, and is determined to increase the contribution to more expensive as well as less expensive plans, there is a simple alternative to the one proposed in that bill. Congress could create equally generous savings that would improve rather than undermine the reward to frugal consumers choosing "Honda" plans. The cap could be raised from 72 percent to about 74.4 percent of the all-plan average premium, and the match rate for plan premiums increased to 100 percent until the cap were reached. This would reduce the enrollee premium for a self-only plan by about $180 on average, but would widen, rather than reduce, the enrollee share of the savings resulting from prudent plan choices.[14]

Table C-1 presents what would have been the static consequences of such a reform, had it been enacted for the 2007 plan year.

The differential effects of these formula alternatives are immense. In 2007, the enrollee share of premium cost was $1,490 in the Blue Cross standard option. That plan attracts about half of all enrollment in the FEHBP. Other plans above the threshold had enrollee premiums averaging about $1,600. The less expensive plans below the threshold typically have enrollee shares of premiums of about $1,000, a savings of $500 or $600. If the government matching rate were raised to 100 percent ("reform 1" in the table, to "raise match rate only"), the cost to the FEHBP and the corresponding savings to enrollees would be about $60 on average for self-only enrollees, a little above 1 percent of program cost. Taking into account family enrollments,

continued on page 216

TABLE C-1

ENROLLEE SAVINGS FROM FEHBP PREMIUM REFORM ALTERNATIVES
IN FIRST YEAR

| | | | Enrollee share of premium at alternative caps and matching percentages | |
| | | | Reform 1: Improve consumer incentives to choose lower cost plans | |
Plan	Total 2007 premium self-only	Current cap and matching rate 72/75	Raise match only 72/100	Savings from current cap and match
Blue Cross standard	$5,180	$1,490	$1,490	$0
Largest other plans above $4,920 match threshold				
GEHA high	$6,150	$2,460	$2,460	$0
Kaiser No CA	$5,490	$1,800	$1,800	$0
NALC	$5,370	$1,680	$1,680	$0
Kaiser DC high	$5,130	$1,440	$1,440	$0
MD IPA	$5,060	$1,370	$1,370	$0
APWU	$4,990	$1,300	$1,300	$0
Mail Handlers standard	$4,960	$1,270	$1,270	$0
Average for other plans above match	$5,310	$1,620	$1,620	$0
Large and small plans below $4,920 match threshold				
SAMBA standard	$4,780	$1,200	$1,090	$110
Kaiser So CA	$4,730	$1,180	$1,040	$140
PacifiCare CA	$4,300	$1,080	$610	$470
Blue Cross basic	$3,950	$990	$260	$730
Aetna HealthFund high-deductible	$3,790	$950	$100	$850
Aetna Standard DC	$3,630	$910	$0	$910
Mail Handlers high-deductible	$3,520	$880	$0	$880
GEHA standard	$3,460	$870	$0	$870
Average for other plans below match	$4,020	$1,010	$390	$620
Average for all plans	$5,120	$1,490	$1,430	$60
Dollar savings in switch to below cap plan		$550	$1,170	

SOURCE: Calculations by author using 2007 premiums for largest FEHBP plans.

	Enrollee share of premium at alternative caps and matching percentages		
	Reform 2: Raise government share and improve consumer incentives		Reform 3: Raise government share and eliminate consumer incentives
Raise cap and match 74.4/100	Savings from current cap and match	Raise cap only 80/75	Savings from current cap and match
$1,360	$130	$1,300	$190
$2,330	$130	$2,050	$410
$1,670	$130	$1,390	$410
$1,550	$130	$1,340	$340
$1,310	$130	$1,280	$160
$1,240	$130	$1,270	$100
$1,170	$130	$1,250	$50
$1,140	$130	$1,240	$30
$1,490	$130	$1,400	$210
$960	$240	$1,200	$0
$910	$270	$1,180	$0
$480	$600	$1,080	$0
$130	$860	$990	$0
$0	$950	$950	$0
$0	$910	$910	$0
$0	$880	$880	$0
$0	$870	$870	$0
$310	$700	$1,010	$0
$1,310	$180	$1,310	$180
$1,120		**$340**	

TABLE C-2

FEHBP PREMIUM REFORM ALTERNATIVES OVER TEN YEARS WITH 1 PERCENT PER YEAR CHANGE IN OVERALL PREMIUM GROWTH, PLUS OR MINUS

Average for all plans	Total 2007 premium self-only growing at 6%	Enrollee share of premium with alternative caps and matching percentages		
		Enrollee share with current cap and match below cap 72/75 growing at 6%	Reform 1: Improve consumer incentives to choose lower-cost plans	
			Raise match below cap 72/100 and slow growth to 5%	Savings from current cap and match
First year	$5,120	$1,490	$1,430	$60
Second year	$5,430	$1,580	$1,500	$80
Third year	$5,760	$1,680	$1,580	$100
Fourth year	$6,110	$1,780	$1,660	$120
Fifth year	$6,480	$1,890	$1,740	$150
Sixth year	$6,880	$2,010	$1,830	$180
Seventh year	$7,300	$2,130	$1,920	$210
Eighth year	$7,750	$2,260	$2,020	$240
Ninth year	$8,220	$2,400	$2,120	$280
Tenth year	$8,720	$2,550	$2,230	$320
Ten-year total	$67,770	$19,770	$18,030	$1,740

SOURCE: Calculations by author using 2007 general schedule premiums for all FEHBP plans.
NOTE: The 6 percent growth rate in premiums is conservative, slightly lower than in recent years.

continued from page 213

the total cost of this reform would be about $350 million dollars to the program as a whole. The average savings to enrollees choosing less expensive options would rise to almost $1,200 as the average enrollee premium share in these plans fell to about $200, and in some cases to zero. In contrast, the premium costs of the more expensive plans above the threshold would be unaffected, and their enrollees would have no savings.

An FEHBP reform that produced no direct benefit for those enrolled in the largest plan, and most other large plans, would suffer from an obvious

Enrollee share of premium with alternative caps and matching percentages

Reform 2: Raise government share and improve consumer incentives		Reform 3: Raise government share and eliminate consumer incentives	
Raise match and raise cap 74.4/100 and slow growth to 5%	Savings from current cap and match	Raise cap 80/75 and raise growth to 7%	Savings from current cap and match
$1,310	$180	$1,310	$180
$1,380	$200	$1,400	$180
$1,450	$230	$1,500	$180
$1,520	$260	$1,610	$170
$1,600	$290	$1,720	$170
$1,680	$330	$1,840	$170
$1,770	$360	$1,970	$160
$1,860	$400	$2,110	$150
$1,950	$450	$2,260	$140
$2,050	$500	$2,420	$130
$16,570	$3,200	$18,140	$1,630

political problem. The alternative of a reform raising the cap to 80 percent (reform 3 in the table) would, however, produce substantial savings for those enrolled in the more expensive plans while producing no benefit for those enrolled in the more frugal plans. (See the string of zeros in the right-hand column, showing no enrollee savings from joining a lower-cost plan.) Such a formula change would directly increase program costs by over 3 percent while essentially eliminating all incentives to choose lower-cost "Honda" plans. Other alternatives could, at the same cost, increase the incentives for choosing lower-cost plans (reform 2 in the table). In sum, there are relatively

A Parable for Insurance Design

Some beneficent employers subsidize employees' purchases of automobiles, a virtual necessity. The employers pay 75 percent of the purchase cost up to $16,000, imposing a $12,000 subsidy cap based on a percentage of average prices for all cars. Any employee who buys a car costing below $16,000 is throwing away seventy-five cents on the dollar, so most employees will buy cars costing $16,000 or more, whether they otherwise prefer them or not. Over time, makers of the least expensive cars find their market diminishing, and redesign their products to price them at the $16,000 level where the 75 percent subsidy ends. Because the $12,000 cap is tied to the average price of cars, the cap rises over time in response to these incentives.

Some frugal employers might increase their subsidy to 100 percent of the first $12,000 to reduce (but not eliminate) these incentives for waste. Inexpensive cars are now completely free. Putting hand-stitched leather seats and ten-speaker stereos into cars now costs employees their own money. While all car buyers get a $12,000 subsidy, they pay every dollar of cost over $12,000. There is no extra subsidy for cars costing between $12,000 and $16,000, and car manufacturers eliminate less desired frills. Paradoxically, the number of less expensive cars sold rises substantially, and over time the average subsidy payment decreases,

modest changes to the current FEHBP premium formula that would be budget-neutral and stakeholder-neutral, while reintroducing serious incentives for consumers to choose frugal plans and for plans to modify their offerings accordingly. Reform 2 in table C-1 is one such option, but there are others.

Note that all figures in table C-1 are in nominal dollars, unadjusted for the effects of premium conversion. Thus, the real value of the current reward for joining a lower-cost plan is not really $550, but under $400 for most employees, assuming a 33 percent marginal tax rate. Raising this amount to an average enrollee savings level of about $1,100 would produce a gain with a tax-preferred value of about $750 (again assuming a 33 percent marginal even though the matching rate was raised. The average price may still rise over time as technology, tastes, and affluence affect underlying preferences and costs, but the rate of increase is lower.

Alternatively, some affluent employers might raise the cap from $12,000 to $16,000, leaving the matching rate unchanged. A consumer who buys a $12,000 car is throwing away $3,000. And because the cost-sharing percentage stays the same, cars costing up to $20,000 are subsidized at 75 percent.

The most generous employers invent an alternative to subsidize employee auto purchases even more. They do away with the cap completely and pay 80 percent of the cost of any car, even a limousine or a large SUV.

The government, observing the pleasure employees take in their new purchases, and not wishing to be outdone in generosity by mere employers, has long since added a tax incentive to the entire scheme, and forgives payment of income and payroll taxes on the 75 or 80 percent subsidy. Taking yet another step, the government has recently decided to forgive tax payments even on the 20 or 25 percent employee share, so long as it is spent under a special "flexible car spending account." The last inexpensive car disappears from the market.

And some people wonder why cars are so expensive and cash wages rising so slowly![15]

tax rate), only slightly exceeding the weak incentive differential that lower-cost plans enjoyed before premium conversion.

A static one-year comparison like this barely hints at the cost implications over time. As shown in table C-2, very modest assumptions about returning to a seriously competitive system show that, over time, the benefits of an increase in the cap (reform 3 in tables C-1 and C-2) would be eroded for both enrollees and taxpayers, while the benefits of raising the match rate (reform 1 in both tables) would grow over time for both enrollees and taxpayers.

In table C-2, the key assumption is that restoring the FEHBP to an incentive structure slightly stronger than it enjoyed prior to premium conversion would bring it back roughly to historic levels of annual cost increases—about a percentage point lower than in recent years. Conversely, raising the cap level without raising the government matching rate would effectively end the competitive structure of the program and, arguably, raise the annual increase in program costs by a percentage point or more. Under these assumptions, over a ten-year period enrollees would, on average, save about $3,200 from improved matching of low-cost plans, compared to about $1,630 from raising the cap and leaving the match rate below the cap unchanged. Savings to enrollees would be doubled at the same first-year budgetary cost. (Not shown in the table, total costs to the government would rise substantially over time under the third reform.) These results are illustrative but suggest the magnitude of potential effects from changing FEHBP incentives to emulate more closely those of competitive Medicare. Indeed, as suggested in the parable that follows, the likely savings from such a reform are potentially far larger, such is the power of compound arithmetic. That is why the potential for greatly reducing the magnitude of the looming Medicare insolvency through reform of cost-sharing incentives is so important.

This metaphor is not inexact. It describes what is the usual practice among large employers in America, and the tax subsidies that compound the incentives problem. A premium cap, like that used in the FEHBP and competitive Medicare, is the only sensible premium contribution strategy for an employer wishing to restrain costs over time. So there is a modest reform, cost-neutral to employees, that any employer can consider today.

Another potential lesson from competitive Medicare lies in its use of risk adjustment methodologies that attempt to control for the differential costs that high-cost enrollees (with, for example, diabetes or congestive heart failure) bring to competing plans. Risk adjustment techniques have advanced over the years, and, with the use of substantially complete medical records on individuals, they can statistically predict a third or so of the variance among enrollees' future health costs. The relevance of these techniques to the FEHBP is low at this time, however, even assuming it had the medical records, which it does not (they are spread among the participating plans, in incompatible formats). The biggest drivers of risk selection among the FEHBP plans are age and Medicare status, and these should be attended to first.

It is neither conceptually nor computationally difficult to create formulas for varying the government match rate by such risk factors, while keeping the overall fraction of premiums paid by the government the same. Unfortunately, some of the swings in plan reimbursements and resulting premiums could be very substantial. For example, while the Blue Cross standard option has about half of all enrollees, it has a far lower fraction of younger employees and a substantial majority of all retirees with Medicare parts A and B. It would be difficult in both a political and practical sense to introduce differential payments in this situation without at the same time addressing the entire issue of Medicare/FEHBP interaction, and perhaps increasing the government share of enrollee costs. The same political incentives that originally led to the "grandfathering" of existing health plans into the FEHBP are likely to weigh even more heavily on any reforms that substantially disrupt premium shares and current plan choices of enrollees. This said:

- Any legislation aimed at improving the performance of the FEHBP as a competitive program should include risk adjustment for age and Medicare status as an adjustment to an unchanged overall government share of premiums, while seeking to minimize disruption to settled enrollee expectations and current premium payments by enrollees. To achieve this, these risk adjustments should be phased in over time.

Another reform that may require Congressional action would be to allow the FEHBP to admit more national or regional plans. Both Medicare Advantage and Medicare Part D allow essentially unlimited plan entry, and in most areas of the country there are about four dozen plan choices in each program. Most of these are effectively national but charge different rates in different areas. As previously discussed, OPM has had to act ingeniously to admit new plans that depart from the traditional HMO model and are available in most of the nation, under a statute that allows unlimited local "comprehensive" plan entrants but no new "government-wide" plans or national union or employee association plans. There is no reason to be parsimonious. Instead, the FEHBP should follow the free entry policy used in Medicare (also adopting the recent CMS reform discouraging any one company from introducing multiple near-identical products in any one market area).

- OPM should openly solicit new national, regional, or local plans to participate in the FEHBP. Free entry is essential to the best functioning consumer choice health insurance markets. If necessary, the statute should be amended to allow this.

There are two steps that OPM can arguably take within existing law to reduce the number of uninsured federal employees. Automatic enrollment has been used on a large scale for Medicare Part D, with some administrative problems, but would be far easier in the FEHBP. Automatic enrollment has proven very effective in obtaining increased participation in 401(k) savings plans (Thaler and Sunstein 2009, 109-111).

- All newly hired federal employees should be "auto enrolled" into the FEHBP absent a positive decision to opt out. For those who do not actively choose a plan, a simple random assignment to a low premium plan can be made (for example, one of the four lowest premium plans could be assigned, depending on whether the first day of employment is odd or even, and on whether the employee's last name starts in the first or second half of the alphabet).

- For existing employees, the OPM should initiate an enrollment campaign emphasizing some of the lowest cost plans, including consumer-driven and high deductible plans whose savings account is as large or larger than the employee share of premium. Employees without FEHBP insurance could be electronically identified and encouraged to enroll in an inexpensive plan if they are not covered by a spousal plan.

Brochure boilerplate relating to Part D is misleading, by failing to point out that enrollees can save a good deal of money in many cases by signing up for Part D despite having a good prescription drug benefit in their FEHBP plan. Both in plan brochures and in open season information the OPM could make Medicare Part D coordination and choices both better and far clearer to enrollees. Encouragement of Part D enrollment is particularly important to contain cost growth in the FEHBP because when Part D is primary it covers roughly one third of FEHBP costs. Accordingly:

- OPM publications should make it clear that Part D enrollment can benefit enrollees in many plans, in some cases (e.g., GEHA standard option) quite substantially. Relatedly, inadequate and misleading language like "you do not need to enroll in Part D and pay extra for prescription drug benefit coverage" (inside front cover page of all brochures) and weasel wording like "[if you enroll in Part D] we will review claims … and consider them for payment under the FEHBP plan" (in most brochures) should disappear.

As a final recommendation on consumer information, budgetary resources should made available to provide an annual open season guide to annuitants, as Medicare does for its enrollees. The OPM has a 100 page long *Guide to Federal Benefits For Federal Retirees and Their Survivors* (U.S. Office of Personnel Management 2008d) roughly comparable to *Medicare & You* (U.S. Department of Health and Human Services, Centers for Medicare and Medicaid Services 2008c) that it prints in small quantities. The OPM hierarchy, the Office of Management and Budget, and the Congress keep the FEHBP program on a starvation ration of "salaries and expenses" funding—pennies on the dollar compared even to the under-funded Medicare administrative cost budget. As a result, only a relative handful of annuitants ever see the document in print. Those with Internet access can review it but often do not know it exists. Hence:

- The administrative budget for the FEHBP should be substantially increased, including not only increased analytic resources (see Afterword below) but also resources for improving information dissemination to retirees in open season. (Hint: by mandating that the plans mail the *Guide to Federal Benefits* to their annuitant enrollees, such mailings can be subsumed in plan costs rather than visible salaries and expenses appropriations.)

There is a final lesson to be learned from Medicare. The intellectual resources devoted to analyzing potential improvements to the Medicare program have been formidable. Congress has substantial staff and member expertise in the entire range of Medicare issues. The CMS has a team of competent and experienced actuaries to augment its otherwise substantial research and analysis staffs. The OMB has an expert staff specializing in Medicare and Medicaid. Congressional staff offices, notably the CBO and GAO, have substantial Medicare analytical assets. Finally, the independent MedPAC is an expert voice on most Medicare issues, especially payment issues. These resources, however, have focused overwhelmingly on improving payment policies in original Medicare.

In contrast, the congressional committees overseeing the FEHBP have historically devoted neither time nor attention nor serious resources to analyzing FEHBP reform options. The location of the FEHBP in the OPM provides some benefits to the program's governance, but expert and sustained top-down attention to insurance design issues is not among them. The policy and actuarial staffs supporting the FEHBP are competent but small and isolated. A handful of persons is not enough. The intellectual resources available to TRICARE are also small. Therefore, to bring to bear a reasonable level of resources and attention to the immense and interrelated problems of coordination between and among these programs:

- MedPAC or the CBO or both should be charged with developing and refining periodically a coherent set of policy proposals that would discourage excessive cost-sharing by supplementary insurance, reduce moral-hazard costs to these programs, and otherwise improve the programs' long-term functioning. These proposals should be applied to reforms not only directly in the Medicare statute, but also in the statutes of the FEHBP and TRICARE programs, and potentially to the tax system or other levers, to influence Medicare supplements paid by either enrollees or former employers. These agencies should be directed to take into account behavioral incentives and system effects in future recommendations on such topics as Medicare Advantage benchmark premium levels.

Any such effort would ultimately run into complex committee jurisdiction problems in Congress, but these are not insurmountable if a coherent set of sensible reforms is proposed. The House Ways and Means Committee and the Senate Finance Committee have influence on and competence in issues such as these. The impending insolvency of Medicare makes the importance of such an effort all the greater. Note also that most of the important FEHBP reforms, such as requiring employers to pay Part B premiums before subsidizing cost-sharing, do not necessarily require the action of other committees.

Lessons for Medicare from the FEHBP

Before enactment of the Medicare Modernization Act, the FEHBP had many lessons for Medicare. While the MMA stopped short of fully converting Medicare to a premium-support program, the reforms it set in place show promise, over time, of rendering that final reform either unnecessary or readily achievable, to the benefit of enrollees as well as the taxpayer. For now, the FEHBP has taught Medicare better than it has taught itself.

The FEHBP does, however, have two important lessons left for Medicare. First, for unknown reasons CMS has never adopted the simple lesson from the FEHBP of requiring plans to create brochures in a standard format that makes it easy and convenient for enrollees to compare plans and to be assured that there are few or no "gotcha" omissions or descriptions. Insurance policies in the private sector are usually almost indecipherable to lay persons. But the FEHBP brochures used to be models of clarity and brevity, and still remain models of clarity on most subjects. As succinctly stated by the GAO, it has been (and remains) difficult to compare plans in what is now the Medicare Advantage program because each company "independently chose the format and terms it used to describe its plan's benefit package. In contrast [FEHBP] plans are required to provide prospective enrollees with a single comprehensive and comparable brochure to facilitate informed enrollment choices" (U.S. GAO 1999, 2–3).

- CMS should establish a system of plan-financed brochures presented in common format and language, similar to that used by the FEHBP but shorter, for all Medicare Advantage and Part D prescription drug plans.

Second, and of massive import given the effects of the Balanced Budget Act, the continuing emphasis of MedPAC on accounting dollars and cramped formulations of "fairness" rather than real world effects, the Obama administration's budgetary proposals, and the Congressional search to find revenue sources for health reform:

- Medicare should be a good business partner to private health plans.

Being a good partner means, above all, not creating sudden, drastic changes in payment and program terms. The Balanced Budget Act lost Medicare more health plans and harmed more enrollees indirectly than through its direct (though unintended) payment reductions, because it demonstrated, as nothing else could have, the volatility of doing business with a federal government that could adversely and unilaterally change major terms of participation virtually overnight. Quite apart from the fact that, until this year, MedPAC recommendations to reduce Medicare Advantage payments would have left untouched plans in the Lexus areas of the country (like Miami) and severely penalized plans in the Honda areas (like Minneapolis), those recommendations would, if enacted, have yet again demonstrated the unreliability of the federal government as a business partner. It is one thing to modestly reduce Medicare Advantage capitation payments (which are already scheduled to be reduced from 14 percent higher than original Medicare to 10 percent higher over the next three years). It is quite another to make drastic reductions that will halt or reverse the savings MA brings, not only to its enrollees but also to original Medicare. The temptation to make unnecessarily adverse reductions will be even stronger as Congress searches for budgetary savings to finance health reform. That temptation should be resisted.

Lessons from Each to the Other

The three competitive programs demonstrate that there are many workable designs for plan competition. Even continuing the implicit competition between original Medicare (that is, as supplemented by Part D and Medigap plans) with Medicare Advantage plans is not an impossible model. In fact, as current Medigap enrollees die off over time and more employers drop coverage for persons ages sixty-five and over, and if new beneficiaries find themselves with viable PFFS and other plan options, original Medicare may slowly fade away, much as happened to the old Blue Cross high option in the FEHBP. That is not the best model. But, as analyzed by Mark Pauly, several workable and potentially politically feasible competition designs would preserve something like original Medicare (but better), and likely prove far better than the status quo at producing short-run savings to enrollees and long-run savings to the program (Pauly 2008).

It would be remiss not to mention yet another alternative. Henry Aaron and Jeanne Lambrew devote a chapter of their book to "Strengthening Medicare as a Social Insurance Program" (Aaron and Lambrew 2008). If it is possible, they write, for private plans to use cost-effectiveness criteria in setting benefit levels, it might also be possible for original Medicare to do the same. As an example, Aaron and Lambrew suggest "reference pricing," where the government would, in effect, pay for the most cost-effective alternative, with the enrollee allowed to spend more, but entirely from his or her own resources (an option not all that different from Feldman's 2008 proposal, or from the "least costly alternative" approach used by the contractors who administer original Medicare for some drugs and devices).

Aaron and Lambrew posit in this example the elimination of private-plan alternatives to a reformed original Medicare (the Part D benefit would become government administered). Recognizing the formidable problems presented by such a model in terms of congressional governance, they argue that success would require delegating a great deal more "hands-off" decision-making to neutral experts than at present.[16] Congress is unlikely to be capable of such forbearance in a "one-plan-fits-all" system, where a decision that affects only a fraction of a percent of spending nonetheless results in billion-dollar consequences to potent interests, not least of which are the patients who would be deprived of their favored treatments. There are, however, modest improvements to original Medicare (some suggested above) that could renew its viability as an alternative program, reduce its cost growth, and enable Medicare to serve as a platform for the care management reforms that will be an essential component of rescuing the program from insolvency.

Aaron and Lambrew seem rightly pessimistic as to the prospects for introducing such radical payment reforms into original Medicare. Original Medicare will, however, be with us for a long time under any reasonably foreseeable scenario. Of the cost-saving reforms available to the health-care financing system at large and to Medicare in particular, "least costly" and related pricing approaches, used judiciously depending on the medical condition and menu of treatment alternatives, are clearly among those with the most potential.

> If you think health care is expensive now, wait until you see what it costs when it's free.
>
> P.J. O'Rourke
> "The Liberty Manifesto"

"Lessons" such as those enumerated here present difficult problems of design and achievement. However, two factors make them potentially viable. First, with the addition of prescription drug coverage to Medicare, that program finally provides a substantially complete, though still badly flawed, system of health insurance. The last missing piece is in place to allow plans and providers to use drug benefits to secure savings in hospitalization and other high-cost services and to enable capitation levels that cover all necessary services. Second, in all three programs—the FEHBP, Medicare, and TRICARE—it is conceptually easy to adjust the government and enrollee shares of premiums (and, in original Medicare's case, to rationalize the benefit structure) to improve benefits to enrollees while reducing costs. Such adjustment is needed both to improve incentives for sensible choices and to substitute premium cost-sharing improvements for cost-sharing reductions that "hold harmless" enrollees while reducing overall costs. Systems that depart so far from optimum economic performance provide major opportunities for reform, while saving money for all stakeholders. In the FEHBP, increases in government matching for premiums in less costly plans can actually reduce overall government costs. Comparable opportunities to spend more to save far more exist in both Medicare and TRICARE.

The extent to which a rationally designed system of capitated health plans competing for consumer enrollment under the supervision of watchful but mostly "hands-off" management can reduce unnecessary Medicare and FEHBP spending in future years remains unclear and will not be answered soon. As a matter of actuarial arithmetic, even substantially reduced rates of growth in per-capita spending through disease management, benefit incentives, and other techniques will not be enough to preclude the sizable tax and premium increases needed to prevent future Medicare insolvency.

They can, however, contribute substantially to reducing the size of the time bomb. At present, about 90 percent of all original Medicare enrollees pay almost nothing for medical or hospital care through their participation in Medigap or employer plans or, for low-income enrollees, Medicaid. Reducing that proportion rapidly to reduce the wasteful spending created by "free" care should be a high public policy priority. It is no coincidence that the Dartmouth estimates of the locations of most wasteful spending in Medicare—about one-third of all costs are estimated to be for unnecessary utilization—coincide geographically with the areas of highest overall spending in that program (Fisher et al. 2003 and 2009).

Cost-saving techniques vary in their acceptability to consumers and to the political system. The American political system appears to be even less tolerant than consumers of certain kinds of controls. Consequently, the only politically painless way to allow unpopular coverage, cost-effectiveness, or cost-sharing decisions is, apparently, to decentralize them to local plans, subject to that minimal oversight necessary to guarantee, for example, that no plan would be allowed to refuse to pay for a drug that is necessary to prevent blindness or any other disabling condition.

Drugs to Prevent Blindness: Teaching NICE to See

In 2007, the expert body that makes national coverage decisions for English health care, the National Institute for Clinical Excellence (NICE), decided not to allow the use of the drug Lucentis in the treatment of certain types of age-related macular degeneration. This decision provoked the following headlines: "Cruel Watchdog Is Condemning 20,000 People to Blindness" (*Daily Telegraph*, June 14, 2007) and "Couple May Have to Sell Their Home to Save Their Sight" (*Daily Mail*, June 18, 2007).

Meanwhile, the equivalent Scottish expert body had allowed use of the drug, provoking the headline, "Eye Drug Only for Scottish Patients" (*Daily Telegraph*, June 12, 2007). The head of NICE said, on national television, that NICE would consider allowing the drug after the patient went blind in one eye, defending this as a reasonable compromise since most patients didn't present until it was too late to save the first eye.

This is not an anecdote about national health insurance, since the Scots and English both use the National Health Service. But it seems inconceivable that the American political system would allow any such result, or allow any expert body to try to produce such a result. The story has a partially happy ending: In its August 27, 2008 issue, the *Daily Telegraph* reported,

> In a decision that marks a climbdown for the National Institute for Health and Clinical Excellence (NICE). . . . the sight-saving drug Lucentis will be paid for by the NHS . . . The ruling overturns previous draft guidance that patients would have to go blind in one eye before receiving treatment with Lucentis, which costs more than £10,000 per eye, on the second. . . . NICE has taken over two and a half years to issue its final guidance on the drug in which time many thousands of people have already gone blind as a result of the condition. The drug has no effect on the condition once the patient has gone blind.

Of arguably far greater importance is reform of the income tax system to remove the excessive wasteful spending and moral hazard that it produces, victimizing both Medicare and the FEHBP in the process, to say nothing of working private-sector employees and the overwhelming majority of Americans. Neither set of reforms, however, can produce important advances without the other. Nothing need delay consideration of ways to rescue the FEHBP from the follies of its recently weakened incentive structure, and to rescue the FEHBP, TRICARE, and Medicare from unlimited subsidization of "free" medical care.

Quite apart from these larger issues of reform, these programs could take some smaller steps that would benefit both taxpayers and enrollees.

Several have been suggested above, and one problem is common to two of the three competitive programs: Of all the benefit design decisions that a manager of competition among insurance plans should insist upon, surely none is more important that that each plan actually provide an insurance guarantee. Too many plans in both Medicare Advantage and the FEHBP have no limit on out-of-pocket spending, or a limit that contains major loopholes, or a limit that is misleadingly described to sound lower than it is. The CMS has taken an excellent step in its call letter for 2010 plan designs in calling attention to this problem (2009a). But the CMS did not focus on all plans, including HMOs. To address this critical omission:

- Both programs should, over the next several years, seek to achieve improvements in catastrophic limits. Uniformity of levels is not essential or even desirable (the temptation is to set them too low, which impedes plan innovations in cost-sharing), but at the very least these limits should be established in all plans, loopholes eliminated or minimized, and limits clearly described in comparable detail in all plan descriptions.

It is a great irony that the FEHBP was rapidly declining in performance through the unanticipated effects of well-intentioned decisions, even as Medicare reform set out to emulate the FEHBP model as it once had performed. The failures as well as the successes of the FEHBP demonstrate, however, the value of competitive Medicare and ways in which Medicare Advantage and even original Medicare can be improved over time.

Afterword: Improving Information for Policy Analysis and Consumer Decisions

This analysis has benefited from a wide and diverse array of information sources, documented in footnotes, bibliography, table notes, and other references. A good deal of information is available on the four programs I have analyzed most extensively: original Medicare, Medicare Advantage, Medicare prescription drug plans, and the Federal Employees Health Benefits Program. The available information is, however, grossly inadequate in the light of the magnitude of these programs and the many fundamental evaluative issues on which any analyst, myself included, has no choice but to speculate rather than report robust findings. Together, these programs involve spending which in 2009 will total over one-half trillion dollars, almost one-fifth of total federal spending. Our knowledge base on them is pathetically inadequate to guide that spending.

Take a simple set of questions. What is the federal government spending on each of these programs, for each of the years 2000 through 2009? What is the total number of enrollees in each of those years? What are those enrollees spending in premiums for those years? What is per-enrollee spending for premium costs in each program, including both government and enrollee share? What proportion of total health-care spending does each program cover, in total and per enrollee (that is, what is the out-of-pocket spending in each program)? How much is spent on supplementary health insurance (such as Medigap) in each program, in total and per enrollee, for each of those years? These are simple and obvious questions. Bits and pieces of the answers to them exist in the appendix to the annual U.S. Budget, in the trustees report, in MedPAC documents, in a plethora of tables scattered throughout the CMS website, in spreadsheets available from the OPM Office of the Actuary, and in foundation-funded research cited in this volume. *However, a complete or near-complete set of accessible answers to these simple data questions does not exist for any one of these programs!*

For none of the programs involved is there a comprehensive set of the simplest kinds of obvious spending and workload data that are oriented toward policy decisions (which is not to say that there are not massive investments in useful data for other important purposes). This shows up in all sorts of strange ways. For example, MedPAC publishes careful and thorough descriptions of Medicare programs in its annual *Data Book* (U.S. Medicare Payment Advisory Commission 2008a and prior years), but the chapter on Medicare Advantage includes no data on total spending on that program, presumably because no such data have been compiled for this purpose (it is hard to imagine an alternative explanation for such a gap in such a comprehensive data source). The Budget Appendix includes data on FEHBP spending and enrollment, but no data on either spending or enrollment for any of the three Medicare programs. How could the federal budget omit basic program statistics and unit cost data on three of its largest programs, while presenting in mind-numbing detail information on the number of federal employees devoted to counting beans?

As another example, there are informed judgments, and soft data, to the effect that about one in ten federal employees fails to join the FEHBP, about half of these because of spousal coverage and about half because they find the premiums unaffordable. Demographic and other data on these issues could readily be developed from existing payroll records, and obtaining additional information (for instance, as to spousal insurance) through sample surveys of uninsured employees would be easy and inexpensive. With respect to Medicare, data files already exist, for example, that could be used to estimate Medigap coverage and its effects on Medicare spending, but the research efforts on this topic have not only been sparse but led by other organizations, and are still inconclusive in some respects (Lemieux et al. 2008, Chandra et al. 2009).

Many potential research and evaluative efforts would be of value to both organizations. For example, despite the availability of Medicare, OPM, and plan data files that could be merged to allow detailed analysis of the effects of dual FEHBP and Medicare enrollment on health-care spending, neither the CMS nor the OPM has created such an analysis. As another example, both the CMS and OPM rely heavily on results of the Consumer Assessment of Healthcare Providers and Systems (CAHPS) survey as a source of consumer satisfaction information on health plans in their online and print resources for enrollees. CAHPS data contain known biases, however, most notably that older enrollees give substantially higher ratings to plans than do younger ones, as discussed earlier in this analysis (see also Francis et al. 2008, 99). Since many plans attract very different age mixes of enrollees, this means that currently published ratings are misleading. Adjusting for age and other biases would be quite simple, and very important to improving information on plan quality. Neither agency (nor the sponsoring body, the NCQA) has made that investment.

Throughout this analysis I have commented on the vast cognitive gap between accounting data and data that reflect real world realities. Data that are not developed through federal government accounting systems are often, and perhaps usually, more accurate and valuable than those that are routinely counted. None of the cognizant agencies, excepting the CBO, has routinely attempted to create or use data that accurately depict actual program performance without regard to federal ledgers. This is indefensible.

> Everything that can be counted does not necessarily count; everything that counts cannot necessarily be counted.
>
> Albert Einstein

Most importantly, a great deal more research should be devoted to the huge voids on issues that affect "big dollar" policy decisions on these programs and others, such as SCHIP and Medicaid. How large are substitution (crowd-out) effects? What premium design and premium contribution levels could best reduce crowd-out or increase prudent shopping? How much do 100 percent wraparound policies (such as Medigap and the FEHBP plans operating like Medigap) cost in increased utilization? How much does cost vary by type of health plan (for example, FFS versus HMO) when benefits are rich, and what design details work best in each type of plan to reduce wasteful overuse of care? Does HMO penetration really reduce costs in original Medicare as much as research studies suggest, and for the reasons they cite (Chernew et al. 2008)? Does the same effect result from private fee-for-service penetration? Does enrollment in Medicare Advantage save as much in Medicaid spending as research suggests (Atherly and Thorpe 2005), and, if so, what other interventions are available that will reduce the Medicaid time bomb by discouraging enrollment in that program where alternatives exist? Does Medicare Part D really reduce medical spending costs almost as much as it increases drug spending, and what does this mean for cost control in original Medicare (Zhang et al. 2009)? What kinds of benefit designs can, in a practical way, encourage spending on high-payoff health-care interventions while preserving incentives to reduce spending on unnecessary care (and how well do existing and potential variants on high deductible plans with savings accounts and free preventive care or even maintenance drugs meet these tests)? How can some of the promising alternative service-delivery designs, such as "medical homes" and accountability for overall cost, be integrated into these programs, and do these reforms work? What payment incentives—bundling? least costly alternative?—could best replicate the kinds of cost-saving results achieved by Kaiser and some other HMOs, while providing broad provider access? How much does consumer information of the right kinds (CHECKBOOK's Guide to Health Plans for Federal Employees and Medicare Planfinder) save these programs, and how can money-saving consumer information best be improved or expanded upon?

To emphasize just one of these important unknowns, what is the effect of price controls in original Medicare on prices and payments by private health plans? Standard economic theory says, in effect, that cost shifting is all but impossible (Morrisey 1994 and 2003). Yet there is a substantial and apparently largely accepted literature (though rarely published in peer-reviewed journals), that not only takes cost shifting for granted but that also estimates its effects in multiple tens of billions of dollars. This divergence has profound implications for comparing the effectiveness of Medicare and the FEHBP in controlling costs, as well as for health reform. To the extent that cost shifting is real, then the "scoring" estimates for health reform are fictions that estimate effects on federal budget accounts as if they were actual savings to the American economy. To the extent that cost shifting is incorrectly believed to occur, the case for tougher price controls to reduce spending in original Medicare and the case for the "public plan" option is buttressed. As the health reform debate unfolds, the failure of researchers to nail down robust theoretical and empirical results on this issue leaves all conclusions adrift. These and other questions carry some ideological baggage, but they are vital to making sensible decisions about the $2.5 trillion spent annually on American health care, regardless of which reforms are enacted or not enacted in the near term.

More broadly, the research and evaluation resources devoted to these four programs (and one might as well add TRICARE, Medicaid, and SCHIP) are trivial in relationship to their fiscal and programmatic importance. The Department of Health and Human Services has a legislative authority commonly called the "1 percent evaluation set-aside authority" that says the secretary may earmark up to 1 percent of the funds appropriated for Public Health Service Act programs for evaluations of those programs. In decades past, that money was almost all spent on evaluations or returned to the programs. In more recent years it has been spent in more eclectic ways, but there is still a robust evaluation program at the HHS for all programs except those administered by the CMS. In the FEHBP, a program whose scanty appropriation will not even finance the mailing to federal retirees of its annual guidebook on choosing health plans, evaluative research grants and contracts are nonexistent, and in-house evaluation nearly so.

Many other important kinds of missing data could be produced and published for consumers, or for researchers who advise consumers, at minimal cost. One example is the disenrollment or "quit rate" for each plan during open season. Information on the loss by one plan of 20 percent of its enrollees in the previous year while another lost only 2 percent would be very significant to prospective enrollees. The OPM used to collect such data, providing an essential measure of customer service that was published annually in *CHECKBOOK's Guide* after multivariate statistical adjustments were made to control for variables such as changes in plan costs (Francis 1986). Despite the ready availability of computer files that would allow creation of these data, however, neither the CMS nor the OPM has taken the obvious step of creating them for competing plans and either publishing them directly or making them available to others.[1]

Another important resource are data the CMS has on the cost of medical procedures in its own payment schedules. At present, these are available online in formats that are useful to provider business offices but essentially unusable by consumers. Surely consumer-friendly data on (say) the cost of child-bearing or of an appendectomy (hospital, physician, and other) could be presented on the Medicare.gov website so consumers might judge the reasonableness of charges they face in Medicare Advantage, the FEHBP, and other private plans, or simply in their capacity as consumers sharing in these costs. (See U.S. Congress, Joint Economic Committee 2006 for these and other examples.)

Consumers' CHECKBOOK has engaged in litigation with the federal government over obtaining information on the number of medical procedures performed on Medicare patients by Medicare-participating providers. For many kinds of procedures, strong research evidence indicates that physician experience bears a substantial relationship to performance. The data would also be invaluable as a tool to detect fraud in cases where patients are in a position to know that a particular physician could not or did not perform the number of procedures paid for by Medicare (in the simplest case, because he has died). These data do not identify patients; however, the government's view, which has so far prevailed in court, is that because they could be used to determine roughly how much income individual physicians receive from Medicare, such a release would be a violation of personal privacy under existing law (Henderson 2009). (The courts ignored the routine publication of government data on payment to individual consultants and to farmers for crop supports, which even more directly disclose income than would the Medicare procedure data.) Surely, then, the proper response is for the government to seek an amendment to the Freedom of Information Act clearly establishing that such data can and should be released for use by consumers in choosing physicians.

As a final example of new and valuable consumer information, a pilot program organized by CHECKBOOK and involving a consortium of health plans, healthcare coalitions, local medical societies, and philanthropic organizations has developed and reported patients' ratings of doctors in three metropolitan areas (see press release at http://www.checkbook.org/press/patients_ratings_of_doctors.cfm). Statistically valid numbers of patient experiences are used to rate physicians on such variables as how well their doctors listen and explain, and make themselves available for appointments when needed. This project could be easily and relatively inexpensively expanded to cover many more areas and physicians if OPM and CMS encouraged private plans participating in Medicare and the FEHBP to join in the collaboration. The initial findings and an explanation of purposes and methods are available at www.checkbook.org/patientcentral.

The best sources of real-world data on the competitive insurance programs for both researchers and consumers exist on the websites at www.medicare.gov, www.opm.gov/insure, and www.guidetohealthplans.org. Most evaluative reports on these health insurance programs have relied heavily on one of these websites. Meanwhile, private philanthropies, most notably the Henry J. Kaiser Family Foundation and the Robert Woods Johnson Foundation, have funded virtually all the nitty-gritty data assemblage for evaluative research on these programs.

Despite these philanthropic efforts, the information and policy gap is huge. It brings us to two final lessons emerging from this analysis:

- The OPM and CMS should be tasked and enabled by the administration and Congress and funded to invest in both short- and long-term efforts to improve substantially the knowledge base for making future policy decisions on these programs.

- These agencies should likewise be tasked and enabled to provide substantially more information to consumers, either directly or by making it available to organizations that could use it for that purpose.

To its credit, the Obama administration has proposed a significant increase in spending on health insurance–related research in the 2010 budget, which should help a great deal with these and associated research issues. Whether or not these increases will be granted by the Congress, or be sufficient, is unclear. None of the increase is proposed for the OPM, however, which needs such resources the most.

There is a coda to the rebuttal of low administrative costs as a measure of efficiency. The core CMS computer systems are extremely old and written in computer languages that are antediluvian, such as COBOL. The CMS cannot efficiently use its systems to analyze its own data for research, fraud detection, and decision support, or easily and inexpensively provide such data to others. During the implementation of Part D startup, the computer systems were almost always the root cause of the early errors and missteps in plan enrollment, premium payments, and coordination among plans. Yet by comparison to the FEHBP, CMS resources for analytical and decision support capabilities are huge. With national health-care spending of $2.5 trillion annually, and the Medicare and FEHBP programs at the forefront of potential reforms, systemic underinvestment in administration of these programs as information and data tools and resources is indefensible.

Notes

Introduction: The FEHBP as a Model for Reform

1. "Rent-seeking" is a term used by economists to describe the activities of individuals and organizations that seek to make money by manipulating the political system to their advantage rather than by earning it fairly in free and open markets in response to consumer choices.

2. In the interest of transparency, readers should know that the author of this book has been a procompetition advocate in the political and scholarly debate over consumer choices among health plans—through testimony before the U.S. Congress, articles published by "conservative" think tanks, and private advice given to members of Congress and politicians of both parties. I played a small role in the enactment of the Medicare Modernization Act in 2003 and have served as a consultant to the Centers for Medicaid and Medicare (CMS) administrator on initial implementation of the Part D prescription drug program and the Medicare Advantage program.

3. "Original Medicare" is a term used by the Centers for Medicare and Medicaid Services to refer to parts A (covering mainly hospital services) and B (covering mainly physician services) of the program. Originally the only parts of the program, they have remained largely unchanged for almost a half-century. Thus, in explaining Medicare basics, the *Medicare & You* handbook refers to the "Original Medicare Plan" (U.S. Department of Health and Human Services, Centers for Medicare and Medicaid Services 2008c). In contrast, "competitive Medicare" is used here to refer to parts C (Medicare Advantage) and D (covering prescription drugs), the former extensively modified and the latter added in the 2003 Medicare Modernization Act. The design of parts C and D is built around competition among competing private plans, in sharp contrast to the original program's monolithic structure.

4. "Moral hazard" is an economists' term used to describe the simple truth that if the purchase of anything—medical care or food or housing—is subsidized, more of it will be consumed. If health care is subsidized to the point where additional consumption in any amount is essentially free, as is the case for many private employees, the great majority of Medicare enrollees, and the great majority of federal retirees, "more of it" can be a great deal more, and wasteful consumption can be immensely costly.

5. Enthoven then and since has criticized the FEHBP for some of its design features, especially for allowing benefit differences among plans and for lacking risk adjustment, but his core proposal for consumer choice among competing plans was and remains essentially identical to the FEHBP model. See Enthoven 1989 for a telling critique of the FEHBP's failures to live up to its promise.

6. As my own modest contribution to the literature on using the FEHBP not just as a model, but as an actual program for the uninsured, I have a possible solution to the vexing issue that lower income persons might find it difficult or impossible to cope with even the modest copays and other cost-sharing features in most FEHBP plans. In some states Medicaid enrollees pay nothing for health care and in states where they face cost-sharing it is usually just a few dollars for prescription drugs or physician visits. In the FEHBP, most plans have much larger cost-sharing. Furthermore, as discussed in the section on *Future Benefit Design Decisions*, there is growing evidence that even modest copayments can inhibit obtaining needed medicines. There is a straightforward solution to these problems. Low-income enrollees could be given a special Health Savings Account of (say) $1,000 for a single person and $2,000 for a family. (The account could vary by income level, and an enrollee choosing a high deductible plan would simply have this amount added to that plan's HSA.) This account could only used on health care and would be used, just like an HSA, to pay for deductibles, copays, and coinsurance. As an example of how it would work, suppose someone joins Blue Cross standard option. The account would handily pay the $300 deductible, a half dozen $20 visit fees, four $65 payments for a three month supply of a name brand drug and, if needed, the $200 for a hospital stay. The enrollee obtains the service, the HSA card is debited for the cost-sharing, and Blue Cross pays the rest. Unused funds would carry over from year to year, and earn interest, just like an HSA in a high-deductible plan. But this account could be used in all FEHBP plans, most of which have low deductibles and copays, so it would stretch much further. Like an HSA, it would provide first dollar coverage, but create incentives to shop wisely and frugally. Combining an HSA account with premium subsidies would enable FEHBP plans to enroll low-income families without changing their cost-sharing or other benefit features.

7. A fascinating discussion of the internal dynamics of the commission deliberations (for example, the battle for the Stuart Altman vote) appears in a 2003 study by Jonathan Oberlander. The commission would probably have reached a necessary supermajority had a prescription drug plan been included in its proposal. In the event, the Medicare Modernization Act (MMA; see below) included a seemingly bizarre prescription drug plan that has created a competitive market which, in its first three years, appears as strong and successful as any government health insurance program ever created.

8. Throughout this analysis we refer to various laws. In no case do we quote, or does the reader need to read, the text of these. Should an adventurous reader wish to

see the text, however, the best locations are at gpoaccess.gov, and thomas.loc.gov, searchable websites operated by the U.S. Government Printing Office (which prints and displays almost all official government documents) and the Library of Congress (which displays all proposed and enacted public laws), respectively. The Medicare statute as amended can be found in the United States Code, a compilation of all federal laws currently in force, at gpoaccess.gov. It comprises Subchapter XVIII within Chapter 7 of Title 42 of the code. It is also sometimes referred to as Title XVIII of the Social Security Act. The Medicare statute comprises 768 typeset pages of the code and has been amended many times by laws referred to in this analysis, such as the Medicare Modernization Act of 2003 (Public Law 108-173), the Medicare Improvements for Patients and Providers Act of 2008 (Public Law 110-275), the American Recovery and Reinvestment Act of 2009 (Public Law 111-5), and the Medicare Catastrophic Coverage Act of 1988 (Public Law 100-360), all at thomas.loc.gov. Most of these laws contain hundreds of pages. The first digits of public law numbers refer to the Congress in which they are enacted. For example, the Congress in office from 2008–9 is the 111th since the founding of the Republic. The FEHBP program and Administrative Procedure Act (APA) have been amended far more rarely. Both are found in their current form in Title 5 of the United States Code, the FEHBP in Chapter 89 (39 pages) and the APA in Chapter 5 (59 pages), also accessible at gpoaccess.gov. There are additional sources of text, including committee reports. For example, the conference report on the Medicare Modernization Act (MMA) containing both the legal text and explanations can be found at http://frwebgate.access.gpo.gov/cgi-bin/getdoc.cgi?dbname=108_cong_reports&docid=f:hr391.108.pdf (850 pages of text).

9. In the FEHBP, consumers receive at most only 25 percent of the savings if they select plans with below-average premium costs, which greatly attenuates cost-saving incentives. In contrast, under Medicare Advantage, consumers receive, in either reduced premiums or improved benefits, 75 percent of the savings for plans with below-average costs.

10. Most of Reischauer's suggestions were good ones (competitive bidding for premiums), but others were not well reasoned (forcing all plans to offer identical benefits).

11. "Adverse selection" is a term used by economists to describe the incentive for high-risk consumers to enroll in health plans with better coverage than the plans selected by low-risk consumers. Adverse selection occurs not only in health insurance, but also in other markets involving asymmetries in information between buyer and seller, such as life insurance, car insurance, and the buying or selling of used cars. We address adverse selection extensively in chapter 3.

12. Adverse selection can have other effects, good or bad. The recently enacted Genetic Information Nondiscrimination Act prohibits the use of genetic information by health insurers and will therefore worsen adverse selection in the market for

individual health insurance policies. In this case the government has made a decision that reducing potential discrimination by reducing the information available to insurance underwriters has social benefits that outweigh its costs, including payment of higher premiums by purchasers who do not have a genetic predisposition to conditions that are expensive to treat.

PART I: A TALE OF TWO HEALTH INSURANCE PROGRAMS

Chapter 1: Medicare

1. It would not be unfair to say that Medicare payment policy has been brilliantly modified over time from abysmal to functional, subject to the fundamental criticism that original Medicare remains almost entirely a piece-rate system similar to the classic Soviet nail factory, in which providers are rewarded for volume of production crudely measured, not for valued outcomes. In a sensible world, a physician who botches an operation would not be paid either for the original work or the repair. In Medicare, he is paid twice as much as the physician who gets it right the first time (this is now changing, slowly, for a few procedures in hospitals, but not for physicians). As in all fee-for-service systems in medicine, all Medicare providers with a license are equal, and all are paid equally. "Pay-for-performance" is a valiant attempt to change this model, but, as of 2008, it had achieved only baby steps (see Wennberg, Fisher, et al. 2007 and Wennberg, O'Connor, et al. 2007 on extending the pay-for-performance model).

2. "Social insurance" programs, enacted during the New Deal and using the term "insurance" broadly and ideologically rather than in a technical sense, included not only Social Security but also Railroad Retirement, Unemployment Insurance, and Aid to Families with Dependent Children.

3. The imminence of insolvency depends on how one cares to view it. For example, the Part A hospital trust fund already raises less money in payroll taxes annually than it spends and is only nominally in surplus because of the accounting fiction whereby it is credited with interest earnings from other funds in the U.S. Treasury (U.S. Boards of Trustees 2008, 5, table II B1). Looking ahead, and ignoring parts B and D, Medicare Part A's trust fund will be exhausted in 2017, according to the 2009 trustees' report, and the necessary tax increases to finance Part A will rise from about 3 percent of taxable payroll today to about 12 percent in 2083 (ibid., 3). Overall, Medicare expenditures for parts A, B, and D are forecast to rise from 3 percent of gross domestic product (GDP) to 11 percent in 2083. This long-run forecast is somewhat more favorable than at the turn of the century because the trustees now assume that something—they know not what—will hold down health-care costs in future decades. Meanwhile, since total federal tax revenues are historically less than 20 percent of GDP, the trustees' forecast implies a likely 50 percent increase in federal taxes

to finance Medicare alone, quite apart from the rapidly increasing fiscal burden of Medicaid and Social Security.

4. In this description, I deliberately skip numerous qualifying points and technical details that are irrelevant to the issues this study addresses and analyzes. For example, Medicare Part B does pay for a few prescription drugs, notably some expensive chemotherapies that must be injected under the direct supervision of physicians, and for immunosuppressive drugs taken by transplant recipients, if the transplant took place after age sixty-five. Such details provide only a disservice to readers. In addition, I will use the term "insurance" to refer to original Medicare, following usual practice, even though original Medicare is not technically an insurance program as such. I will use the terms "beneficiaries" and "enrollees" more or less interchangeably.

5. http://www.cms.hhs.gov and http://medicare.gov.

6. Perhaps the best explanation of these byzantine fraud and abuse requirements, which go far beyond fraud as conventionally understood, is found in Hyman 2006, 32–35.

7. In contrast, policies supplementing the FEHBP, other than for dental and vision coverage, are virtually nonexistent.

8. Two recent comparisons of benefit values in original Medicare, the FEHBP Blue Cross standard option, and a typical employer-sponsored preferred provider organization (PPO) reached similar conclusions, using similar, but not identical, calculations (Yamamoto et al. 2008 and U.S. Congressional Research Service 2009b).

9. Now that the annual payroll taxes to the Part A trust fund are lower than annual spending, Part A is also funded in part from income taxes.

10. This includes costs paid by other programs, other insurance, and the enrollee.

11. Unlike Medicare Part A, Social Security and Disability Insurance financing is subject to a limit on taxable earnings, set at $107,000 in 2009. In neither case is income from interest, dividends, capital gains, or other nonpayroll earnings subject to tax.

12. Strangely, many states impose taxes on health-care services to finance health-care programs, such as risk pools. States also impose taxes on providers as a way of "gaming" the federal rules on matching payments to finance Medicaid by reimbursing these taxes to providers after claiming them as state matching funds. For a brief recent analysis of this issue and a proposed reform, see U.S. Congressional Budget Office 2007a, 154.

13. There have also been some shifts on the margin between allocating services to parts A and B when the former, but not the latter, was on the verge of exhausting its trust fund. Home health care is now financed by Part A following a hospital stay, and by Part B otherwise.

14. When the 1988 Medicare Catastrophic Coverage Act was largely repealed a year later, certain provisions were retained. One of these provided that for Medicare beneficiaries with incomes below the poverty level, Medicaid would pay both the Part B premium and parts A and B cost-sharing.

15. "Qualified Medicare beneficiaries." There are lesser subsidies for a slightly less impoverished low-income group called SLMBs (special low-income Medicare beneficiaries).

16. There are similar proposals in U.S. Congressional Budget Office 2007a, 184–85. Pauly (2008) demonstrates that means-testing can very substantially reduce the future fiscal burden of Medicare (see also Pauly 2004).

17. Economists call this a loss of utility. "Utility" is an economists' term that means, essentially, value to the person. A gallon of fresh water has a great deal more utility than a gallon of diamonds to a person expiring of thirst in a desert.

18. HMO premiums in the FEHBP reflect local rather than national costs but, as discussed below, do not vary significantly by geographic area.

19. A useful discussion of this problem and its effects can be found in the chapter "Medicare Supplementary Insurance Must Go," in Roger Feldman's *How to Fix Medicare: Let's Pay Patients, Not Physicians* (2008), and of the potentially massive savings from this reform in the chapter, "Scoring Medicare Reform III: Controlling First-Dollar Coverage," in Rettenmaier and Saving (2007).

20. This is not to imply that the Medicare statute has not been amended many times in important ways. See the timeline provided by the Kaiser Family Foundation (2009).

21. A confession. In 1987, as one of the more senior career bureaucrats available during the summer lull, and because no political appointee was willing to interrupt his vacation to oppose medicines for seniors in an irrelevant hearing, I was dragooned into testifying on behalf of the Department of Health and Human Services against including prescription drug coverage in MECCA before a nonlegislative committee of the United States Senate. I was told that if I delivered the officially prepared negative testimony, the chairman of the committee would not pillory me. Accordingly, I testified against such coverage. The chairman glared, but the promise was kept. Almost two decades later I spoke informally to key members of the Senate in favor of such coverage. For the record, the only testimony I have ever delivered that does not represent my own views can be found in U.S. Senate, Special Committee on Aging (1987). Ironically, had the administration position been accepted by Congress, and MECCA stripped of prescription drug coverage, the future history of Medicare reform, including the MMA, would have been far, far different.

22. As discussed later in this analysis, recent CMS and pending congressional actions will significantly change this pattern.

23. www.medicare.gov. Use "Medicare Health Plan Data," and then either "Find and Compare Medicare Health Plans" or "Learn More About Health Plans and Medigap Policies in Your Area." Under either option follow directions until offered the option to "Review Plan Details." Out-of-pocket limits are shown at "Premium and Other Important Information."

24. Although all national plans and many HMOs in the FEHBP have explicit catastrophic limit guarantees, as in Medicare Advantage many HMOs do not. Even so,

with copays commonly in the vicinity of $10 for primary care visits and $20 for specialist visits, prescription drug copays that rarely exceed $20, and no other consequential cost-sharing for ordinary hospital, medical, or drug expenses, it is virtually impossible for out-of-pocket costs to reach (say) $10,000 in FEHBP HMO plans when using plan providers. Catastrophic protections in Medicare Advantage are, in general, inferior to those in the FEHBP because they almost always impose the prescription drug coverage gap of $4,350 in 2009, and sometimes exclude all prescription drug coverage.

25. The FEHBP uses the same practice, though generally with far less content. Call letters are a management tool that avoid the many disadvantages of rulemaking. Especially importantly, they allow for strong encouragement rather than prescriptive rules.

26. "Churning," a term derived from the use of churns to make butter, refers to turning enrollments over to increase commissions to agents.

27. Original Medicare's various prospective payment systems all make geographic adjustments based on Bureau of Labor Statistics and other data on salaries of relevant professions in different areas, and other, similar information. These adjustments are crude and take little account of behavioral factors (for instance, the likelihood that a physician in a high-rent area will invest in a smaller office than a physician in a low-rent area). Most of these systems are updated annually, and these figures are frequently adjusted to the advantage and disadvantage of local providers. Dividing lines have to be drawn more or less arbitrarily, and great political efforts are made by providers either to have their counties in the higher-paid areas or to be reassigned from lower- to higher-paid areas.

28. A brief explanation of the complex calculations involved can be found in Biles et al. 2008, and a far more detailed explanation in Merlis 2007.

29. In the FEHBP, most HMO plans are paid a capitated rate based in part on the best rate they charge other plan sponsors in the area in which they operate. Most other plans' rates are based in part on their estimated costs. But every plan's payment rate, as will be explained later, is based in large part on a benchmark derived from the average rates of all participating plans.

30. As it happens, most of this evidence comes from the FEHBP. Francis 1993, Schmid 1995, and U.S. Government Accountability Office 2005 show that cost variation among local plans was driven more by competition than by provider prices or other factors. In them, Miami and South Florida turned out to be relatively low-cost areas over an extended period of time. For example, the GAO study (65–71) showed Miami as ranking 154th in average per-enrollee cost among 232 metropolitan areas in 2001. The Francis and Schmid studies also showed the Miami area as below average in costs in 1993. These results may also reflect Medicare's unusually high vulnerability to fraud, with particular cities such as Miami notoriously at risk, as discussed later in the analysis.

31. For a detailed history, see Merlis 2007.

32. PFFS plans are not allowed to or able to use certain kinds of utilization control more suited to HMOs, but, in fact, have tools at their disposal to restrain spending. For example, they can and do give preference to generic drugs.

33. The availability of Kaiser may have been a quirk of fate. That plan was one of the minority of private plans in Medicare+Choice that was paid on the basis of its own costs rather than on per-capita costs in original Medicare. Hence, Kaiser had a cushion unavailable to most other HMOs.

34. These figures are from U.S. Boards of Trustees 2006, 34. They differ somewhat from figures in later reports, and in other sources, but all versions of these data show an enrollment reduction of over one million persons. There are a number of categories of what are now called MA plans that reports have summarized differently over the years.

35. A brief description of the functioning of Part D can be found in U.S. Medicare Payment Advisory Commission 2008d. An extended description can be found in U.S. Congressional Research Service 2008. Apparently, no in-depth summary of the extraordinary efforts made in launching the program has been written, although numerous press accounts relate the various glitches encountered along the way.

36. One of the major sources of those estimates was the utilization experience of elderly FEHBP enrollees in the Blue Cross standard option plan, which already used both aggressive bargaining and sophisticated cost-sharing features to reduce drug costs. The planners vastly underestimated the power of the Part D design to restrain spending through its even more potent cost-sharing features, the ability of Part D plans to encourage switching to generic drugs as well as therapeutically equivalent drugs, and the willingness of Part D plans to sacrifice short-term profits to gain market share in both Part D and Medicare Advantage.

37. Data are from U.S. Department of Health and Human Services, Centers for Medicare and Medicaid Services 2006, 2007, and 2008b.

38. Not surprisingly, research has shown that most enrollees in original Medicare do not understand many of its most important features. By the criterion of avoiding confusion, even one plan is apparently too many.

Chapter 2: The FEHBP

1. Interestingly, this plan offers a particularly useful extra benefit for enrollees' children turning age twenty-two, and hence ineligible for regular FEHBP coverage under the current statute, to obtain insurance without underwriting for preexisting conditions. This is an example, common in the FEHBP, of benefit design planned to increase plan enrollment and revenues. This particular benefit enrichment would almost exclusively attract employees ages forty-five and over, not a low-risk group. No system locking all plans into government-set benefit packages would allow such

an innovation, despite its obvious benefits for young adults who would otherwise be uninsured, and the parents who might otherwise have to foot their bills.

2. TRICARE for Life, a plan for military personnel, offers several constrained choices. The Veterans Administration and the Indian Health Service offer one choice.

3. Calculations by the author from unpublished OPM data; see Francis 1986 for details of earlier years.

4. Calculations by the author, using total premiums for each plan and the OPM's spring Headcount data, pre– and post–open season, to compute enrollment-weighted premium costs. Headcount data are available upon request from the Office of Actuaries at the OPM.

5. The federal tax code does not allow any retirees, public or private, to obtain the same tax advantages given to employees covered by employer-financed health insurance.

6. Postal and Federal Deposit Insurance Corporation (FDIC) employees receive somewhat higher government contributions but still pay full marginal cost for plans more expensive than average, less tax savings.

7. Enrollees can also switch among plans at other times of the year in prescribed circumstances such as marriage, birth of a child, enrollment in Medicare or, for enrollees in local plans, geographic transfer.

8. A major statutory exception is included in both programs. In Medicare Advantage, physicians who participate in original Medicare (about 95 percent of physicians) may not charge PFFS plans more than the Medicare fee for the same procedures. The same is true in the FEHBP for enrollees ages sixty-five and over, whether or not they are enrolled in Medicare. These provisions present major policy issues, not least of which is extending the fee schedules of original Medicare to many more transactions than these price-controlled fees were originally intended to cover.

9. Any given HMO is likely to offer local employers a menu of hundreds of possible benefit variations, such as whether the copayment for physician visits will be zero, $5, $10, or $20, whether that copayment will be the same for primary care physicians and specialists, whether that copayment will apply to preventive visits, and so on, almost ad infinitum. The employer and the HMO bargain over these and the premium tradeoffs they require. When the employer contracts with only one or two plans, this underlying complexity of offerings is hidden. In the FEHBP (and in competitive Medicare) it becomes highly visible.

10. For example, the OPM had long frowned on several plans' substantial prescription drug deductibles. These deductibles were gradually reduced over a period of years, and only one is left. Removing them necessarily raised plan costs and premiums, and neither the OPM nor the plans wanted a precipitous premium increase. As another example, the OPM has long had a moratorium on new or improved dental benefits to help hold premiums down. But plans with dental benefits in place were not forced to remove them. The OPM uses an annual "call

letter" to inform all plans of directions it wants to encourage or discourage, but it does not insist on uniformity. The CMS has adopted a similar approach, but it issues many, many times more instructions to MA and PDP plans. For a description of the CMS guidance approach, which annually includes many dozens of issuances through the "Health Plan Management System" (HPMS), see U.S. Senate, Committee on Finance 2007.

11. They may be too "radical" for federal employees, who famously refused, by a 96 percent to 4 percent margin, enrollment in a superior and safer, but seemingly riskier, Federal Employees Retirement System (FERS) when offered that choice in the 1980s. Since then, all new hires have been FERS enrollees, but the old Civil Service Retirement System (CSRS) lingers on. See Thaler and Sunstein 2009, 34–37, for a discussion of "status quo bias" in retirement planning decisions.

12. When one of the "big six" plans left the program, the formula was modified by Congress to be calculated using a "phantom" plan, as if that plan had never left.

13. For an enrollee with Medicare parts A and B, Medicare would pay over 90 percent of hospital costs and about 80 percent of physician costs, but little prescription drug cost. Since prescription drug costs encompass only about one-seventh of total spending, the Medicare cost is over two-thirds of total spending. This pattern had the additional effect of making FEHBP premium costs unusually sensitive to changes in prescription drug costs, which is part of the reason FEHBP cost-control performance relative to Medicare worsened in the first decade of the twenty-first century.

14. It is far beyond the scope of this analysis to explore the vagaries of the federal procurement system, in which the government issues a "request for proposals" and private entities bid on which can meet the written contract specifications at lowest cost. Suffice it to say that no independent analysis or appraisal has ever concluded that this system, whatever its occasional successes, succeeds overall in achieving either effective or efficient outcomes. It is particularly weak where, as in the case of health insurance, such vital outcomes as costs avoided are not directly measurable, and where there are multiple objectives that are necessarily given more or less arbitrary weights in evaluation of bids. For example, "service" may be defined as processing claims timely (but not necessarily either accurately or to the satisfaction of either providers or enrollees) and given X percent of the weight in comparing bids.

15. The U.S. Postal Service provided this de facto wage increase to its employees several years before other civil service employees received it.

16. Interestingly, very few employees understand they have this tax savings on their share of premiums, let alone on the employer share. Requiring W-2 forms to show the dollar value of these tax-free benefits would provide a major advance in transparency of wage information.

17. "Consumer-driven" is used here as the generic term. Not all consumer-driven plans qualify under Internal Revenue Service rules as high-deductible plans. The biggest

practical difference is that the savings account under a qualified high-deductible plan becomes the property of the enrollee, whether employed or retired, and remains so when he changes plans or becomes ineligible to qualify for a high-deductible plan through coverage by Medicare or other insurance.

18. Part B is automatically available at ages sixty-five and over without regard to prior Social Security coverage.

19. These data are from pooled MEPS tabulations for 2002–4, with an inflation adjustment to 2006.

20. The RAND Health Insurance Experiment (HIE) is perhaps the most famous social experiment ever conducted. Sponsored by the U.S. Office of Economic Opportunity and later managed by the Office of the Secretary at HHS, it set out to determine, through a true randomized experiment, the extent to which enrollee cost-sharing could reduce utilization of health care and the effects of such reductions on health status. The HIE found massive reductions in health-care costs and minimal effects on health status from even very substantial cost-sharing. One of the best summaries of the HIE and its results is found in Manning et al. 1987. See also Gruber 2006.

PART II: DIMENSIONS OF FEHBP AND MEDICARE PERFORMANCE

The Natural Experiment: The FEHBP versus Medicare

1. Quite apart from the tax status of Medicare revenues from the currently employed, the insurance value of the government's payments from these revenues on behalf of Medicare beneficiaries is not counted as taxable income to those beneficiaries. The untaxed Medicare benefit payments are approaching the value of the average Social Security benefit payment and will soon exceed it. The untaxed FEHBP retiree subsidy is a much smaller proportion of the average federal pension—on the order of one-third the proportion of Medicare.

2. See note 4 in the introduction to the book.

3. In the debate over whether or not health reform should include a "public plan," a similar argument is sometimes made that the public plan will guarantee certain rights, such as the ability to enroll with preexisting conditions, better than private plans. Yet the FEHBP and Medicare Advantage plans, despite their foibles, have never turned away a single person who was legally eligible, administrative errors aside. How can such a record be bested?

4. Both programs ultimately allow appeal to the courts.

5. Medicare refuses even to consider claims that fall below a threshold of several hundred dollars, varying by the type of service.

6. These references all address the role of a so-called "public plan" in health reform. Unfortunately, this same fallacious comparison is ubiquitous in the debate

over health reform. Whatever the other merits of a public plan (Francis 2009 says they are few), lower administrative costs in Medicare are a minus, not a plus, in citing Medicare as a model.

7. Uncharacteristically and remarkably courageously for a government contractor, Blue Cross had the gumption to say that the draft GAO report "ignores the much larger and more critical issue of FEHBP's total costs," and that its conclusions were "simplistic," "weak," and "unsubstantiated." The GAO final report summarized these comments as saying that Blue Cross "agreed that FEHBP's costs are probably higher than necessary and could be reduced without harm to the program" (14).

8. For various reasons, including lack of education or mental disability, the fraction of the elderly who cannot read or understand complex information is large and increases with advancing age. Of course, younger persons suffer similar deficits, but in lower proportions. See the U.S. National Center for Educational Statistics, National Assessment of Adult Literacy, 2003.

9. See the enrollee assistance websites at www.medicare.gov and www.opm.gov/insure.

10. The National Committee for Quality Assurance (NCQA) administers the major national system that publishes comparative data on enrollee satisfaction with health plans. The NCQA promulgates only summary data, however, not stratified by or controlling for age. This creates substantial bias in the ratings that misleads consumers.

11. All NCQA data that follow are from Francis et al. 2008, 100–102.

12. Blue Cross basic does not cover any services from out-of-network providers—that is, it has no fee-for-service benefit—but almost all enrollees know this before joining, and in both plans almost all enrollees get almost all services from the same large group of network providers.

Chapter 3: Risk Selection

1. In what follows I will use fairly standard terminology (see Pauly 2007, Feldman and Dowd 2000, and Jones 1989). "Risk selection" refers to the process whereby enrollees with varying levels of health risk (and expense) decide which health plan to join, based on their health status and concerns. "Favorable" risk selection for a plan means that it gets a disproportionate share of lower-risk enrollees. "Adverse" risk selection (or the shorthand "adverse selection") means a disproportionate share of higher-risk enrollees select a plan. "Risk segmentation" means a pattern resulting from risk selection in which some plans wind up on average with higher-risk and other plans with lower-risk enrollees. Obviously, use of the term "adverse selection" necessarily implies "favorable selection" as well. (In theory, and in the real world, risk selection could have different kinds of higher- and lower-risk enrollees joining the same plans, with a resulting distribution that, on average, shows neither risk selection nor risk segmentation.)

2. If all plans were identical in all dimensions except cost, there would still be adverse selection, because enrollees with higher expected costs would be more likely to choose the higher-cost plan in the expectation that it was squeezing providers less tightly. Lower-risk individuals would be likely to opt out of joining any plan. The closest approach to preventing adverse selection fully is to allow only one plan, and to enforce effectively everyone's enrollment in that plan.

3. Alternatively, many, and perhaps most, of these may be enrolled but not captured in the official statistics, which may therefore substantially overstate the number of uninsured. All existing estimates are fraught with peril. See the summary of an AEI conference on this issue in American Enterprise Institute 2005.

4. The OIG did find that twenty-six confused individuals had enrolled multiple times in multiple HMOs over a ten-year period. The CMS, of course, pays only one premium at a time for an enrollee, and the latest enrollment decision was the one that counted. Signing up people who obviously want extra coverage is hardly a way to lower a plan's risks. Considering the number of retirees in South Florida, and the proportion of these likely to be confused, this paltry duplicate enrollment total is astoundingly low. Regardless, the answer to such problems (which can arise in any consumer market) is not to deny market choices to the rest of us.

5. The doughnut hole refers to the coverage gap that Congress created into the Part D program to make it possible to provide some benefits to most enrollees, provide a catastrophic protection, and stay within a ten-year budget projection that would meet budget scoring targets. In the "standard" benefit for 2009, the enrollee pays a $295 deductible and 25 percent coinsurance up to $2,700 in total drug spending. Thereafter, in this doughnut hole the enrollee pays 100 percent of costs until his out-of-pocket spending reaches $4,350. At that point the doughnut hole closes, as catastrophic coverage kicks in. We later show that the doughnut hole is, arguably, a desirable insurance design feature, quite apart from reducing the costs to the plan sponsor (in this case, the taxpayer).

6. Nor does the FEHBP. This is foolish policy in both programs, and a relic of their antique origins. They should allow penalty-free enrollment if the enrollee has been continuously covered by a health insurance plan as good as or better than Medicare or the average FEHBP policy, respectively. This would reduce program costs and improve retiree choices, with minimal risk selection effects. In contrast, the Part D program sensibly allows "creditable coverage" that continues after retirement to eliminate its late enrollment penalty precisely because Congress wanted to minimize migration to the program. Part D also pays a subsidy to employers who maintain creditable coverage, a bargain to the government and taxpayer since the subsidy costs less than Part D enrollment.

7. Employee health plans that can be kept indefinitely after retirement are not rare. Many state and local governments, for example, have such plans. The best financial deal for original Medicare would be to follow the Part D model by reforming its penalty

provision to allow for "creditable coverage" and by adding a subsidy for those employers willing to retain regular employee coverage (but not Medigap) for their retirees.

8. Several plans limited to special groups, such as SAMBA and Foreign Service, had an even better mental health benefit.

9. In my own volunteer counseling of hundreds of individual Medicare beneficiaries making Part D decisions, I found that many cared deeply about their preferred drugstore and were willing to pay higher premiums to obtain that access.

10. Interestingly, every one of these studies uses some type of data, usually out-of-pocket-cost data, from *CHECKBOOK's Guide* (Francis et al. 2008 and prior years).

11. The key feature of FEHBP premium design that most of these studies emphasized is that the premium contribution by the plan sponsor is both generous and capped. That is, an employee may purchase an inexpensive but comprehensive plan at low premium cost, but will pay all the additional premium for joining a more expensive plan. This design was copied by (and improved in) competitive Medicare. Ways to improve it further in the FEHBP are discussed extensively in later chapters.

12. The interested reader could turn to a Google search on "airline deregulation kennedy" for sources providing history, information on benefits (and costs), and references.

13. See Cutler and Zeckhauser 2000, 625, for an overall analysis of risk adjustment alternatives, and Newhouse 2002 for a detailed analysis of risk adjustment techniques and their strengths and weaknesses.

14. Note, however, that the California Public Employees Retirement System (CalPERS), which is operated much more according to the managed competition "ideal," has failed to control costs as well as the FEHBP has done (U.S. Congress, Joint Economic Committee 2003).

15. See the congressional testimony of Francis in U.S. House of Representatives, Committee on Government Reform 2002 and U.S. House of Representatives, Committee on Oversight and Government Reform 2008 for specific diagnoses and proposed remedies.

16. This comparison abstracts from the role of the FEHBP itself as a source of de facto Medigap plans (plans that are nonetheless far superior in both costs and benefits to actual Medigap plans). Implicitly, I am comparing the situation of someone (say) age sixty-four in the FEHBP with someone (say) age sixty-five in Medicare. The former pays far less in a "pay-more-to-protect-better-against-sickness" penalty than the latter.

Chapter 4: Cost Control

1. This issue is common in assessments of the economy, where partisans of either party habitually select the trough or duration of comparison that best supports their case. So long as there are booms and recessions, such games are easy to play.

2. The decision was motivated almost entirely by short-run budgetary motives, since the federal government retained its 72 percent share of the rebates.

3. Recent GAO testimony provides a perfect example of peak-to-trough comparisons (U.S. Senate, Committee on Homeland Security and Government Affairs 2007, 2–3). "Growth in FEHBP premiums recently slowed, from a peak of 12.9 percent for 2002 to 1.8 percent for 2007. Starting in 2003, FEHBP premium growth was generally slower than for other purchasers," said the GAO. In fact, the last decade had seen the worst performance in the history of the program, and, as indicated by the GAO, the 2006 and 2007 premiums were held artificially low by drawing on reserves.

4. One study was published a month after the enactment of the MMA, but the research and analytical work obviously preceded the publication date by months.

5. In fact, it may be White who is dangerously confused, as the sources he quotes (for example, U.S. Medicare Payment Advisory Commission 2008a, 9) largely fail to deal with changes in benefit generosity in insurance programs over time, while studies controlling for this have found the opposite (U.S. Senate, Special Committee on Aging 2003). To his credit, he admits that the issue is still open.

6. In that analysis, and those that follow, I calculate average Medicare costs by adding the average cost of those with Part B to the average cost of those with Part A. This is a simple approach to avoiding the complexities of dealing with the relatively small proportions of enrollees with A but not B, or vice versa.

7. Illustrating the volatility of these calculations, the average ten-year rate of increase in the FEHBP would have been 8.9 percent, and in Medicare 8.6 percent, had the Francis analysis ended in 1992.

8. As we show later, this often quoted study made several significant errors that rendered its conclusions as to the cost control performance of private plans versus Medicare suspect and most likely erroneous, quite apart from its failure to present any FEHBP-specific calculations. It was not alone. Every other study analyzed below (including mine) made at least one error that erroneously favored Medicare.

9. The various studies apparently used data sources and measures sufficiently different from one another to affect their conclusions, even when they appeared, and claimed, to be measuring the same thing. As an illustration, consider three years using three different data sources but the same measurement approach—growth in average premium costs—for assessing performance of the FEHBP. The Levit study used data obtained from the OPM actuaries. It said that in 2000, 2001, and 2002, FEHBP premium costs increased by 8.1, 10.7, and 13.4 percent, respectively, for an arithmetic total of 32.2 percent (not compounded) for the three years. The Merlis premium-cost estimates showed increases of 8.9, 10.8, and 13.3 percent, 33.0 percent in total, for these same years. My own (previously unpublished) estimates of premium-cost increases for these years were 9.0, 10.2, and 13.1 percent, or a total of 32.3 percent. These are seemingly small differences, but it is not clear why any should have existed. In a cryptic footnote, the Levit study said its FEHBP data excluded unspecified

"certain benefits." Why any health benefits should have been excluded, or left unnamed, is not obvious. The Merlis estimates were taken in part from OPM press releases announcing projected premium increases using weights based on current enrollment. These press releases always slightly overstate actual cost growth, because during open season enrollees move to less expensive plans, on average.

10. The increase in the catastrophic protection limit from $4,000 in 2007 to $5,000 in 2009 is still a reduction in real terms from the level in 2005 and all prior years.

11. The effects of Medicare on these costs are discussed separately below.

12. For purposes of this benefits analysis, total premium costs for each calendar year are assumed to equal health-care costs, including administrative costs, financed under each plan. This is a close but not perfect approximation, because in particular years reserves can be under- or over-financed.

13. With the exception of inflation erosion of the Part B deductible prior to the indexing added in the 2003 MMA, Medicare benefit changes have been negligible in relation to total spending. Over the last two decades, Medicare has added some preventive health benefits, such as influenza immunizations, and a few service benefits, such as the hospice benefit. On the other side, the hospital deductible and hospital coinsurance payments have risen faster in most years than the CPI, because they are linked to rapidly increasing hospital payments. That said, without benefit adjustments, original Medicare is slightly disadvantaged in this comparison.

14. As a matter of arithmetic, the largest cost to the FEHBP for enrollees ages sixty-five and over with original Medicare is prescription drugs, since Medicare is the primary insurer for inpatient and outpatient medical costs but pays very little for drugs under parts A and B. This skews the FEHBP's overall cost structure heavily toward drugs. At present, very few federal retirees have joined Part D, since drug coverage in FEHBP plans is always superior, and usually markedly so. There are, however, some situations in which federal retiree enrollment in Part D makes sense, as addressed in CHECKBOOK's Guide (Francis et al. 2008 and prior years).

15. There are other ways to characterize MSP. One is to view it as a tax on work for the elderly (Goda et al. 2007). It could be cast in the "crowd-out" context analyzed later in this chapter. Certainly, one way to characterize the purpose of MSP is as seeking to reduce displacement of private insurance spending by Medicare (Glied and Stabile 2001). But this could have been done by postponing Medicare eligibility until retirement. In that case, age-sixty-five workers would not be counted as Medicare enrollees. Regardless of how the program and the legal status of those affected are characterized, conventional Medicare accounting and other statistics count as enrollees persons who are not, in fact, being paid under Medicare, and thereby understate the average per-enrollee costs of those who are paid through the program.

16. Retirees have to sign up for Part B at age sixty-five or pay a penalty of 10 percent of premium for every year above that age in which they are not enrolled. There

is no discretion as to Part A, which is nominally free. Under longstanding HHS legal interpretation of a paragraph in the Social Security Act, as probably unintentionally misdrafted, a worker who is merely "eligible" for Part A must take Part A at age sixty-five or lose his Social Security benefit. Virtually all Americans are "eligible" for Part A. The CMS and SSA take the position that it would cost hundreds of millions of dollars in administrative costs to change enrollment procedures to allow an election, were the law to be changed.

17. The Boccuti and Moon 2003 analysis does use total covered lives rather than enrollees. This means that as the proportion of children (at roughly $1,000 per-capita cost in 2007) decreases, while the proportion of young and middle-aged adults (at roughly $5,000 per capita in 2007) rises, their estimates necessarily show a substantial increase in FEHBP costs, even if there is no "real" change in per-capita costs for each group. Hence, that analysis is clearly biased against the FEHBP through its failure to use the enrollment contract as the unit of analysis.

18. Technically, Medicare is primary, and the FEHBP plan is the supplement. In the minds of virtually all federal retirees, however, the FEHBP is the mainstay program, and Medicare an option to consider adding. In counseling thousands of future federal retirees, I have often been asked, "Should I enroll in Medicare to supplement the FEHBP?" and have never been asked whether the FEHBP should be kept so it can be added to Medicare.

19. As shown previously, there are federal retirees without any Medicare coverage. These are mostly persons who retired before 1984 without any substantial private employment history. Since federal employee retirement at age fifty-five is common, especially for workers whose entire career was with the government, many of these people are still alive, age eighty or more.

20. At present, the Office of Management and Budget's official "program assessment rating tool" (PART) program neglects even to include displacement as a potential aspect of program performance for any federal program. This is ironic because one of the earliest studies of displacement, an unpublished paper by then-OMB employee Bill Robinson, showed decades ago that displacement effects in the interstate highway program were likely a fourth or more of the total amount spent by the federal government. That is, spending $100 in grants to states for highway construction resulted in a net increase in total highway construction of only about $75. A substantial literature on displacement effects of numerous federal programs can readily be located by searching Google Scholar.

21. Food stamps also create substantial displacement of state spending, because the food stamp program reduces the amounts states would otherwise need to spend to provide desired levels of overall income support for poor people.

22. This is not to suggest that the taxpayer subsidy dollar does not wind up costing the taxpayer more than a dollar. It surely does, if the perverse incentive effects of the tax subsidy on the health insurance and health-care markets are taken into effect.

But in terms of individual purchasing decisions, the pure displacement of spending is surely considerably less than the subsidy cost.

23. It is not entirely a transfer effect because of the "deadweight" losses caused by taxation. Another adjustment to government costs almost always neglected by estimates focused only on costs recorded in ledgers is that using taxes to finance government programs costs the economy perhaps 10 percent of the amounts raised by taxes, through reduced economic activity. A brief introduction to "deadweight" loss from taxation can be found in Wikipedia, at http://en.wikipedia.org/wiki/Excess_burden_of_taxation.

24. Recent proposals by the George W. Bush and Barack Obama administrations to "income test" Medicare would, taken together, greatly reduce displacement. With means-testing imposed on both parts B and D and not indexed to inflation, over a period of decades the proportion of these costs paid by average and higher-income enrollees would rise to about three-fourths of part B and D costs and about half of all Medicare costs. These proposals, if enacted, would very substantially reduce the budgetary insolvency faced by the Medicare program. Implicit in their rationale is the undoubtedly correct assumption that very few elderly would drop Medicare even if they were no longer able to rely on subsidies from others to pay for almost all of their insurance costs. The affluent elderly would simply pay for Medicare from their own funds. Such a reform could be implemented far more rapidly if the political system allowed. It will not, because a rapid change would unfairly harm existing beneficiaries who quite reasonably planned their retirement finances on the implicit guarantee that their Medicare premiums would be heavily subsidized by others. Younger workers who will age into Medicare do not have the same settled expectation.

25. Sustainable growth rate (SGR) is a statutory formula that ties allowable growth in physician fees inversely to the overall growth in physician payments, with a ceiling on total payments. Since volume continues to go up, and is indeed likely to go up even faster as fees get lower, SGR provides an annual opportunity for Congress, after intense physician lobbying, to decide the extent to which it will provide partial relief to physicians by overriding or delaying the effects of the statutory formula. Congress has postponed implementing SGR reductions since 2003, and the cumulative reduction in physician payments needed to meet the SGR formula is now 21 percent. The system is perverse in that it rewards every physician for increasing his volume in order to overcome its effects on his income. But since all physicians face this same calculus, they all have an incentive to increase volume as much as possible—the very opposite of the behavior the SGR was supposed to reward. SGR and most other Medicare price controls create, to some degree, the same kinds of incentives facing the apocryphal Soviet nail factory that produced many small nails when paid piece-rate for its output, and a few heavy nails when paid by weight.

Chapter 5: Premiums and Benefits

1. See the introduction to part 1.

2. This kind of problem explains why in states like New York, which impose "community rating" that does not allow setting premiums by age for policies sold to individuals, large proportions of younger and healthier adults deliberately choose not to buy health insurance. This in turn raises the costs of the insured pool, and premium costs to those in that pool, which leads even more people (including those who are older and less healthy) to choose not to purchase such bad deals. Note that even compulsory purchase, if it were attempted, would not solve the problem that when younger and older adults are pooled, the young are forced to purchase policies whose insurance value to them is worth far less than their cost. Also, when employers subsidize the insurance to the point where young enrollees are presented with a reasonable value, older workers receive bargains—policies worth far more than the premium they pay. Using the numbers above, for the same $1,000 the younger worker gets a policy worth $1,000, and the older worker a policy worth $7,000. Thus, typical employer group insurance in which all workers pay the same share of premium provides substantial additional compensation to older workers, but not to younger workers. In the United States, younger workers almost always pay most of the cost, not only for their own insurance, but also for the insurance of their older workplace colleagues, as well as the (Medicare) insurance of the retired. The cumulative effect of these penalties on the income of young workers lends new meaning and potency to the term "ageism," since it is not the elderly who lose in the political sweepstakes of age discrimination.

3. Amazingly, no government study appears to be available on any official website that analyzes and critiques this deeply flawed insurance design. The OMB's official "program assessment rating tool" evaluation of FEGLI fails even to hint at this issue, focusing instead on such mundane matters as whether or not claims are paid in a timely manner after employees die (U.S. Office of Management and Budget 2008). Since some younger employees sign up for this program without realizing it is a "bad buy," the risk pool is not as distorted as it might otherwise be and is actually a "good deal" for older employees in their forties or fifties, most of whom enroll in FEGLI in one of its rare open seasons. For a journalist's assessment, see Yoder 2000.

4. Recall that low-income enrollees pay nothing for Medicare and receive Medicaid for free as well. Under the so-called "income-testing" for the Part B premium enacted in the Medicare Modernization Act, the highest upper-income enrollees will pay 80 percent of the Medicare Part B premium, or about a third of the cost of original Medicare.

5. One doubts the authors share a similar concern over Medicare's progressivity in taxes paid, or in its means-testing at lower income levels.

6. See U.S. Medicare Payment Advisory Commission 2008c and 2008d for a summary explanation of these features in MA and Part D, respectively, and U.S.

House of Representatives, Committee on Ways and Means 2007c and Merlis 2007 for far more detailed explanations. Jaffe 2009a provides a brief overview, as well.

7. The flawed formula by which the government pays MA plans in each county an amount substantially determined by costs in original Medicare in that county does not interfere with the competitive incentives within each county, since all local plans there get essentially the same payment. Regional PPO plans face complex problems, however, since the rate they get for the region—an average across higher- and lower-cost counties—will often be too low in urban areas to compete effectively with plans located solely in those counties that get a higher rate. National plans in the FEHBP face what could be a similar problem, except that with local plan rates being set by the market, geographic variations are far, far smaller than those created by the use of local payment levels from original Medicare in the Medicare Advantage formula.

8. Even political causes doomed to perpetual defeat have their own virtues in generating membership and publicity. Rectifying the claimed injustice to the "notch babies" of Social Security was a perennial issue until it largely died of old age because it affected only those reaching age sixty-five between 1979 and 1989. Few of these people are still alive.

9. See the syntheses in Gruber 2006 and Morrisey 2005.

10. I say "arguably" only because the tax treatment of health insurance benefits is probably worse. As these two spectacular failures of public policy compete for the title of "worst," there is no serious contender for third place. Note that the issue has nothing to do with progressive politics. The tax subsidies for retirement benefits create no serious moral hazard.

11. As mentioned in chapter 1, above, Medicare has covered those few drugs that can only be delivered in a physician's office, notably chemotherapy drugs delivered intravenously. In recent years it has also covered immunosuppressive drugs for organ transplant recipients. These are important benefits for the small proportion of enrollees needing them.

12. As long ago as the mid-1970s, federal and state governments knew that published drug average wholesale prices, termed AWPs, were creations of drug manufacturers who had numerous discounts from list prices for each drug, tailored to the demand curves of different purchasers, and therefore had to choose which discounted prices to make public. Obviously, manufacturers had numerous business reasons not to publish the lowest price obtained by any buyer, and did not do so. Federal and state employees in charge of drug purchasing decisions knew this. Nevertheless, primary reliance on published AWPs lasted for another two decades. Even today, a number of states are suing drug companies over the states' past decisions to rely on published AWPs that the states knew were not the lowest wholesale prices (The states had other options for setting payment levels but elected not to use them, in part as a conscious decision in recognition that state-set dispensing fees were unreasonably low, and that using AWPs provided some offsetting relief to hard-pressed pharmacies.) Problems

and issues such as these would undoubtedly have been presented by any federal prescription drug program enacted as a single, congressionally designed plan.

13. These matters are not documented, so far as I know, in any published source. However, I was there when the staff in HHS tried to figure out ways pharmacies could communicate with HHS and realized there was no money in any budget to cover the multi-hundred-million-dollar annual cost of those telephone calls.

14. In 2007 HHS published a rule establishing, for Medicaid, how "upper-limit" drug prices would be calculated, the latest of as many as a dozen rule changes over the prior three decades. Affected pharmacy chains promptly and successfully challenged this rule in court. Congress also imposed a statutory delay in the Medicare Improvements for Patients and Providers Act (MIPPA) of 2008.

15. Because most pharmacy dispensing costs are what economists call "joint costs," and because there are many equally reasonable (and always arbitrary) methods of allocating joint costs among programs, it would be impossible to arrive at a widely agreed-upon allocation methodology and resulting dispensing fee. This problem has existed for decades in Medicaid, generating countless conflicts in all states, and it will persist for as long as states choose such drug payment methods.

16. See U.S. Boards of Trustees 2009, 114, which shows that 2007 benefit payments were 27 percent below the amount predicted in 2006. Even a year after the program began (three years after the original estimates), the actuaries were still underestimating how far costs would fall below projections.

17. How many readers of this book annually seek to find a better house insurance rate by comparing all firms that offer such insurance, or try to compare every automobile repair shop to find the best one in town, and revisit that question every year? Most consumers "satisfice" rather than maximize, and markets are driven by the relative handful of consumers who are canny shoppers. This usually provides enough market discipline to drive out bad offerings sooner rather than later.

18. Fox et al. 1999 describes that process. In essence, it was conducted by a committee of distinguished experts who reached a consensus after considerable internal debate.

19. Two such Medigap options were finally added by statute in the MMA.

20. After age sixty-five, however, PPO plans offer such good Medicare coordination that they attract most HMO enrollees away from their plans. This is one of the unnecessary and counterproductive effects of Congress's failure to sort out Medicare/FEHBP interaction sensibly.

21. Congress enacted a national parity law in the financial "bailout" legislation enacted in October 2008. Under this statute, most private insurance in the United States will have to undertake reforms similar to those already taken in the FEHBP. Because private plans have the same kinds of flexibility to manage benefits and costs as already available to the FEHBP, the likely cost impacts will be relatively minimal (see Pear 2008a).

22. Congress almost every year enacts a multi-hundred-page law that amends the Medicare statute (Title 18 of the Social Security Act). To implement the statutory

changes in such a law, the CMS issues proposed implementing directives and details, through what is called a "proposed rule." Proposed rules are subject to a variety of legal and presidential requirements, including what is usually a months-long period of internal reviews and a period of public comment that is usually sixty days long. These comments must be reviewed and addressed, and another round of internal review conducted, before the "final rule" is issued. The final rule is published in a set of government books called the Code of Federal Regulations. That is not the end of the matter, as even more detailed implementing instructions will be devised for health-care providers and the contractors who pay Medicare benefits. Many CMS rules are not driven by annual statutory changes, but rather by existing statutory requirements to update certain rules annually to reflect changes in technology or costs. The entire body of rules for Medicare comprises approximately 2,400 typeset pages, virtually all of which are devoted either to original Medicare or to the safety and other regulations that the Medicare statute imposes on health-care providers. The *Federal Register* documents by which these rules are amended involve several thousand pages a year of issuances. Both codified rules and the *Federal Register* documents can be found at www.gpoaccess.gov and www.cms.hhs.gov. Most of the comments on proposed rules can be found at www.regulations.gov. Most of the tens of thousands of pages of manuals and implementing instructions can be found at www.cms.hhs.gov.

23. A recent study (Hsu et al. 2006) found statistically significant drug noncompliance and adverse health effects from a natural experiment in which some Kaiser Health Plan enrollees were subject to a prescription drug cap of $1,000 in a Kaiser Medicare+Choice plan, while others had unlimited drug benefits. The magnitude of the effects was small, however; and Part D not only has no cap but also does not start the doughnut hole until spending reaches $2,700 (in 2009), a level far higher than in the capped Kaiser plan. Also, the study did not control robustly for socioeconomic status, and both study data and the circumstance of M+C enrollment make it quite likely that the capped enrollees were disproportionately less educated and with lower incomes than those with the unlimited drug benefits, factors not unrelated either to drug compliance or to health outcomes. In Medicare Advantage, deductibles and all but nominal cost-sharing is waived for lower-income enrollees.

24. It is likely this approach has not worked, or it would already have emerged in many plans. It does, however, illustrate the kinds of innovations that private plans can undertake. A variation of this idea is found in the much-touted and much-condemned use of "medical tourism" to hospitals abroad (or in distant parts of the United States) to obtain, at far lower cost, treatments that would otherwise be obtained in the United States near the enrollee's home.

25. Gawande, apparently innocent of knowledge of the RAND Health Insurance Experiment results and what they mean in the real world, seems to equate cost-sharing with haggling over price, and dismissively equates price signals as relying on "the sheep to negotiate with the wolves" (44). I pass on the following

example, which shows that even negotiating with the wolves can work wonders. When asked recently what could help a woman with breast cancer who had no insurance and was to have a mastectomy in the next week, my advice was simple: "Immediately call both the surgeon and the hospital, explain your situation, and ask to be given the Medicare rate." She did so, halved her surgical fee, and wound up with hospital assistance that got her far below even the Medicare rate.

26. The CMS does have an alternative, routinely used in the vast majority of situations in which it has not made a formal coverage decision. It can leave the medical necessity decision to its bill-paying contractors, who are given discretion to make such judgments. Not uncommonly, different contractors, covering different areas of the country, make inconsistent decisions. In this case the CMS decided to make a nationally binding coverage decision, likely because of such inconsistencies as well as the importance of the issue.

27. An obvious example of a more life-threatening alternative is prostate cancer, where the least-cost alternative treatment is "watchful waiting" at a cost of a few hundred dollars a year for laboratory tests, and the higher-cost alternatives can reach $50,000 or more.

Chapter 6: Access, Fraud Control, and Governance

1. Considerable press attention has turned in 2009 to the allegation that reasonable and customary free-market charges, as calculated by the dominant firm, Ingenix, are actually lower than those typically charged, to the considerable profit of insurance firms offering out-of-network benefits. These alleged differences, however, are only a few percent, and are dwarfed by the usual differences between preferred provider payments and fee-for-service payments, however calculated. Moreover, insurance firms can achieve any result they desire by varying the percentage at which fee-for-service rates are paid, for example, whether at 70 percent or 75 percent.

2. Unfortunately, the CMS has not put into place a standardized system of describing MA plan benefits comparable in scope and detail to the FEHBP brochures. Hence, it is impossible to be certain, beyond the most obvious categories of benefits, whether a particular Medicare Advantage plan offers some service that is not among the relative handful of plan features described on the CMS website. It is possible, and perhaps likely, that a few MA plans offer a benefit that I have described as unavailable.

3. See U.S. Department of Justice 2002. This may be, however, an example of a plan trying to stretch reimbursement rules as far as possible and having its wrist slapped, rather than actual fraud. It is impossible to tell from the cryptic summary public documents.

4. I am unaware of any documentation of this practice, but have heard it discussed in dozens of conversations.

5. See http://www.usdoj.gov/03press/03_1_1.html.

6. Many, and perhaps most, fraud cases inevitably have some effect on competitive Medicare or the FEHBP. For example, in January 2009, in what was apparently the largest fine ever imposed on a drug company, Eli Lilly agreed to pay $1.4 billion to resolve allegations of off-label promotion of Zyprexa, an antipsychotic drug. This drug had been promoted in nursing homes for treatment of dementia, an indication never approved by the FDA or, apparently, otherwise proved effective (U.S. Department of Justice 2009). While this case only covered the period 1999–2003, it would undoubtedly have affected Part D had the program then existed, as Part D has taken over from Medicaid as the primary payer of drugs for nursing home residents ages sixty-five and over. Doubtless, some FEHBP-covered nursing home residents were part of the affected group.

7. See above.

8. Most of these reasons apply to Medicaid as well, though obviously its size in any one state is far smaller than Medicare's, and the existence of separate payment systems in every state greatly reduce the potential return compared to the "cracking" of one national system. Medicaid suffers from an additional problem, however. Because the federal government pays at least half the cost in every state, and far more in many states, the return to states from investing in fraud control is greatly diminished (Helms 2007).

9. The failure of the Securities Exchange Commission (SEC) either to detect or deter the multibillion-dollar Bernie Madoff ponzi scheme, even after outside whistle-blowers provided the necessary information for an easy catch, suggests that the federal government's ability to prevent and find fraud is weak in many contexts, and apparently far weaker in some than for Medicare.

10. See the request for comments on "mandatory self-reporting" of suspicions in the final rule with comment period in U.S. Department of Health and Human Services 2007. Apparently, the regulatory drafters were unaware of what happened when the government imposed a similar requirement on banks to report any suspicious transactions to the U.S. Treasury Department. Rather than undertake the immense time and effort needed to make informed judgments on vast numbers of transactions, the banks simply settled for the expedient solution of submitting "suspicious activity reports" on one million "suspicious" transactions of $10,000 or more to the Treasury every year. Now the Treasury's Financial Crimes Enforcement Network agency drowns in useless information on perfectly normal transactions. (For more details, see Brown 2007.) All is not wasted, however, as this is the program that led to the discovery of the peccadilloes of former New York governor Eliot Spitzer.

11. During my tenure as "regulatory cop" at HHS I reviewed early rulemaking attempts to prevent such fraud. Regulations aimed at such operations (requiring, for example, a physical address, regular hours of business, a visible sign, employees on site) were first promulgated two decades ago and have since been repeatedly revised.

12. This same study provides additional evidence that paying Medicare Advantage plans on the basis of locality-spending under original Medicare is far removed from a sensible or defensible policy.

13. The congressional micromanagement of Department of Defense weapons systems procurements is a notorious example. Recently, the Obama administration prevailed in a Senate vote on ending a multi-billion-dollar investment in producing unneeded numbers of a fighter aircraft, the F-22, only by the narrowest of margins (the interested reader could find an up-to-date account at http://en.wikipedia.org/wiki/F-22_Raptor).

14. See the "Pig Book" at Citizens Against Government Waste at http://www.cagw.org/, and a newer site called Earmark Watch, at www.earmarkwatch.org.

15. Amazingly, one of the 2008 appropriations bill earmarks noted at Earmark Watch was, once again, for the Bay Area Medical Center. This institution clearly has exceptional lobbyists, effectively reaching across both chambers and to different committees in each.

16. While pork-barrel legislation has been rare in Medicare Advantage and Part D, these programs operate in the original Medicare congressional environment, and the risks there are ever present. There has been at least one instance involving a company seeking more opportunities and time to sign up Part D beneficiaries (Pear 2006).

17. The Centers for Medicare and Medicaid Services have robust protections against this particular kind of interference in coverage decisions.

18. These are not merely issues of the past. Recently, Medicare officials, desperate to control fraud by durable medical equipment suppliers, considered imposing an incredibly burdensome set of prescriptive rules on these businesses, including specific requirements as to the exact recordkeeping and accounting systems they would use, their methods of strategic planning, written standards of conduct, lengthy advance notice before they could change their hours of business (no allowance was made for emergencies), and a host of other red tape and operational requirements never before imposed on any American business by any regulatory agency (Abt Associates 2005). Among other impositions extraneous to quality of care, they would have required compliance with all existing federal, state, and local laws (such as immigration laws, tax laws, minimum wage laws, zoning laws, parking laws, and Sabbath laws), as determined by the CMS or its contractors (without due process or any official deference to the decisions of the agencies officially delegated to enforce those laws under the governing statutes, and without regard to whether any given federal, state, or local law authorized such a livelihood-terminating penalty), as a condition of being allowed to provide health care services. These requirements would have applied equally to large drugstore chains and to solo physician and therapist practitioners who provided splints or braces to their patients. Only at the last minute were the more onerous and irrelevant standards derailed through a sensible reappraisal by the officials involved, albeit after external prodding. There have been times, in the past,

when some of the more unreasonable standards would have been imposed. In fact, two decades ago almost all regulations governing providers that were issued by the Health Care Financing Administration (HCFA, the predecessor agency to the CMS) did require compliance with all federal, state, and local laws. Only through diligent and arduous internal HHS reviews, and sensible CMS decisions, were all these finally repealed. Until final Medicare Advantage regulations were issued in 2005, such grotesque overreach even applied to private plans participating in the predecessor program.

19. See the section on fraud control, above.

20. There is a long history of Medicare attempts to deal with cost-effectiveness criteria in making payment decisions. The underlying principles of cost-effectiveness analysis and decisions are fundamental to all proposals to use "evidence-based" medicine to dictate payment decisions (see Aaron and Lambrew 2008, Daschle et al. 2008, and Feldman 2008, for example).

21. As an utterly bizarre example, consider that lawsuits are now being brought to apply Medicare Secondary Payer rules to tobacco-related illnesses. The MMA created a definition of "self-insured insurance plan" to clarify certain MSP provisions. That definition created a presumably unintended opportunity for advocacy groups to sue tobacco companies on the grounds that they, not Medicare, should be the primary payer for the costs of treating smoking-created illnesses. So far the federal courts have rejected the claim that tobacco companies are now legally categorized as "self-insured" plans, the key to these lawsuits (U.S. Congressional Research Service 2009c, 12). But the mere fact that such claims could be given credence in a court of law tells us much about Medicare in the modern era.

22. Sometimes both the political process and the judicial process come into play. For example, a number of California health-care and professional organizations are involved in both lawsuits and political maneuvering to amend Medicare payment methods to pay more to physicians located in urban areas in that state. According to news accounts, the Speaker of the House, Nancy Pelosi, is involved in this effort (Brown 2009).

Conclusion: Lessons Learned and Recommendations

1. Incredibly, if the federal government were able to reduce fraud levels substantially in South Florida, under current law the current payment level would be "grandfathered," and MA plans in that area would continue to be paid an inflated amount for phantom rather than real fraud.

2. There are a number of different ways to reform Medicare Advantage premium benchmarks and the administration proposal is at the draconian end of the spectrum. Some of the other alternatives that would rectify geographic imbalances without slashing overall payment levels so drastically are shown in a CBO letter to the Senate Finance Committee (U.S. Congressional Budget Office 2009b). Quite apart from the issue of where benchmark and spending levels should ultimately be set is the issue

of how rapidly the adjustment should be made. A reduction of 14 percent in average payments to plans, made in one year, would require wrenching changes in benefit generosity, and likely force millions of enrollees to drop or switch MA plans in open season, effects even greater than those of the Balanced Budget Act. As this is written, the press accounts addressing the health reform debate have scarcely hinted, and none have stated, that some of the pending bills would immediately and substantially reduce health benefits in existing insurance plans for over 10 million Medicare beneficiaries.

3. Some but not all of the FEHBP recommendations that follow can be found in my recent testimony to the cognizant subcommittee of the House Committee on Oversight and Government Reform (U.S. House of Representatives, Committee on Oversight and Government Reform 2008).

4. Incredibly, this study faults enrollees for not making perfect choices because fewer than 10 percent enrolled in the very lowest cost PDP in their area, as measured by the drugs they wound up consuming. Nobody can predict future drug consumption with certainty, and important plan characteristics other than cost (for instance, provider network) can influence enrollment decisions. What the study demonstrates, but does not calculate, is that a competitive system of plan choices saves enrollees many hundreds of dollars a year on average compared to what they would have spent had they been allowed to enroll only in the "average" plan. The study also demonstrates that, directly or with help, senior citizens can make wise choices among all those confusing plans. This study used 2006 data from the first year of the program, and we can hope that updates will both find and present even greater success.

5. Even an innocuous report such as this one, with unimportant findings such as these, can generate fireworks. In a December 15, 2008, press release of the House Energy and Commerce Committee, California representative Henry Waxman, then a committee member and now Democratic chairman, characterized these GAO findings as demonstrating "egregious behavior" by the plans. Another member claimed the report painted "a troubling picture of how much of a rip-off PFFS plans are for Medicare beneficiaries" (U.S. House of Representatives, Committee on Energy and Commerce 2008). Interestingly, a Google search on "egregious medicare waxman" turns up about 11,700 references, many them, of course, press reports responding to his statements. Nonetheless, a quick scan of results shows that the word "egregious" is very prominent in the congressman's daily vocabulary.

6. There has been a lively but inconclusive debate as to the likely magnitude of the effect a tax credit would have in reducing the number of uninsured. The outcome depends not only on the generosity of the proposal, but also on unknown behavioral changes. The only way to find out is to "get on with it." Unlike many other proposed reforms, this one would cost less money the less successful it was. Hence, it would not drive out the available resources for alternative reforms if it proved disappointing.

7. I have deliberately refrained from an extensive discussion of the literature and evidence on reforming the tax treatment of health insurance. For four recent, brief analyses that focus on implementation issues as well as rationale, see Burman 2009, Butler 2009, Dorn 2009, and Helms 2009. These otherwise divergent authors, read together, should convince readers of any political persuasion that a tax cap or other reform of the current subsidy is desirable not only as a method of controlling health-care costs, but also for tax equity and (perhaps) revenue purposes.

8. Part D implicitly used a similar strategy. The CMS calculated that, on average, and virtually without exception, everyone who dropped Medigap H, I, or J drug coverage and joined a standard Part D plan would save approximately $1,000 a year in reduced premiums and get better coverage of routine expenses, without even taking into account the catastrophic coverage protection. This is obvious from the fact that the enrollee pays only one-fourth of the Part D benefit but all of the Medigap benefit. The standard Part D benefit is also better than the Medigap plans' drug benefits in almost all circumstances. Unfortunately, this conclusion was not conveyed to beneficiaries as clearly as it should have been, and many did not drop their inferior Medigap plans. To change now they would face the 12 percent a year delayed enrollment penalty. There could, of course, be a one-time "penalty mora-torium" to give these persons a chance to reconsider, now that the Part D program has proved so valuable to their friends and neighbors and the uncertainty has been removed. As discussed in recent Part D evaluations (Thaler and Sunstein 2009, Kling et al. 2009), despite massive efforts by the CMS, almost 10 percent of those eligible for Part D, and likely to save under the program, failed to enroll during the original penalty-free period.

9. For the program to be administrable, no original Medicare rules regarding provider agreements, conditions of participation, ownership of services, and so forth could apply. Such a program could be run by any major insurance firm or by multi-ple competing firms. The benefit should become common in MA plans, as well.

10. This reform was first proposed by Francis, to the Committee on Government Reform of the U.S. House of Representatives (2002), with no effect whatsoever.

11. This is a very conservative estimate of likely savings. See U.S. Congressional Budget Office 2006a for a discussion of the severe difficulties in extrapolating from the RAND price elasticity findings to current health plan designs. As discussed earlier in this analysis, however, the CBO feels comfortable using a 25 percent sav-ings estimate for older enrollees in modern health plans.

12. An additional benefit of this reform is that it would significantly reduce the cost to low-income employees who now go "naked" by allowing them to join a low-cost plan without paying any premium. If the reform were coupled with a presumptive enrollment in the lowest premium plan for those employees who do not positively "opt out," over one hundred thousand, and perhaps almost two hundred thousand, federal employees would join the ranks of the insured.

13. The bill as introduced (H.R. 1256) would change the formula in several ways, and would both hurt and help the ability of lower-cost plans to compete by producing two opposite effects on relative prices. The savings from choosing a lower-cost plan would, however, still decrease on average. With apologies to the sponsors, I model below the bill as reported in the press, not as actually introduced, to sharpen the comparisons.

14. An even better option would be to let employees retain any premium savings below the cap through a refund.

15. When I first drafted this parable, little did I know that there was a government program very similar to the most generous one I describe (Hernandez 2008). It turns out that members of the U.S. House of Representatives (but not the Senate) are fully subsidized not only for the cost of any car they choose, but also for gasoline and other expenses. Of the dozen or so New York–area members profiled as to their choices, not one chose a Honda. Choices ran almost entirely to luxury cars (Cadillac, Lexus, BMW), or to large SUVs. One member chose a Nissan Altima, but as a second car to his BMW, and one member made the relatively frugal choice of a Chevrolet Impala.

The "Cash for Clunkers" program provides a wonderful contrast to the bloated results of the unlimited Congressional subsidy. The $4,500 government payment creates incentives similar to a capped premium subsidy. News reports indicate that the cars being purchased are overwhelmingly high mileage small cars (on average far above the government's required gas mileage) such as the Honda Civic, Ford Focus, and Toyota Corolla.

16. As I write this, it appears the Aaron/Lambrew model may well be adopted by Congress, by designating MedPAC as the neutral arbiter of medical-care prices and salaries under health reform legislation (Meckler 2009). This is an amazing development. It will work best if MedPAC learns to eschew the concept of premium "fairness" and instead focuses on actual performance in reducing waste in health care.

Afterword: Improving Information
for Policy Analysis and Consumer Decisions

1. In the case of the CMS, the GAO has repeatedly urged creating and providing enrollees with such data. Why the CMS has resisted is unclear (U.S. Government Accountability Office 2008b).

References

Aaron, Henry J., and Jeanne M. Lambrew. 2008. *Reforming Medicare: Options, Trade-offs, and Opportunities.* Washington D.C.: Brookings Institution Press.

Abt Associates. 2005. *Quality Standards for Suppliers of Durable Medical Equipment, Prosthetics, Orthotics, Supplies (DMEPOS) and Other Items and Services: Draft of Proposed Recommendations.* September 26. http://www.cms.hhs.gov/DMEPOSCompetitiveBid/downloads/9-22-2005_Draft_QS_PAOCv3.pdf (accessed June 30, 2009).

Akerlof, George. 1970. The Market for Lemons: Quality Uncertainty and the Market Mechanism. *Quarterly Journal of Economics* 84 (3): 488–500.

American Academy of Actuaries. 2009. *Emerging Data on Consumer-Driven Health Plans.* May. http://www.actuary.org/pdf/health/cdhp_may09.pdf (accessed June 30, 2009).

American Enterprise Institute. 2005. 9 Million Fewer Insured? Agenda and other documents from a conference held at the American Enterprise Institute, Washington, D.C., April 8. www.aei.org/events/filter.ecoomic,eventID.1042/summary.asp (accessed June 30, 2009).

American Federation of Government Employees. 2009. Federal Employees Health Benefits Program (FEHBP). AFGE 2009 Conference Issue Papers. February 9. http://www.afge.org/index.cfm?page=2009ConferenceIssuePapers&Fuse=Content&ContentID=1742 (accessed June 30, 2009).

Anderson, Odin, and Joel May. 1971. The Federal Employees Health Benefits Program, 1961–1968: A Model for National Health Insurance? In *Perspectives.* Chicago: Center for Health Administration Studies, University of Chicago.

———. 2008. Medicare's Bad News: Is Anyone Listening? *Health Policy Outlook.* American Enterprise Institute. April 16. http://www.aei.org/outlook/27825 (accessed June 30, 2009).

Antos, Joseph R. 2008. Medicare's Bad News: Is Anyone Listening? *Health Policy Outlook.* American Enterprise Institute. April 16. http//www.aei.org/publications/pubID.27825/Pub_detail.asp (accessed June 30, 2009).

———, and Consensus Group Signatories. 2007. The Facts: Medicare Advantage. Heritage Foundation. March 21. http://www.heritage.org/Research/HealthCare/upload/Medicare_Advantage_factsheet.pdf (accessed June 30, 2009).

Atherly, Adam, and Kenneth E. Thorpe. 2005. *Value of Medicare Advantage to Low-Income and Minority Medicare Beneficiaries.* Report prepared for the Blue Cross and Blue Shield Association. Rollins School of Public Health, Emory University. September 20. http://www.bcbs.com/issues/medicaid/research/Value-of-Medicare-Advantage-to-Low-Income-and-Minority-Medicare-Beneficiaries.pdf (accessed June 30, 2009).

Avalere Health. 2008. Average Medicare Prescription Drug Premiums to Rise 24%. Avalalere Health press release. September 26. http://www.avalerehealth.net/wm/show.php?c=1&rid=790 (accessed June 30, 2009).

Baker, Laurence C. 1996. The Effect of HMOs on Fee-for-Service Health Care Expenditures: Evidence from Medicare. *Journal of Health Economics* 16 (1997): 453–81.

Ball, Robert M. 1995. What Medicare's Architects Had in Mind. *Health Affairs* 14 (4): 62–72.

———. 1998. Reflections on How Medicare Came About. In *Medicare: Preparing for the Challenges of the 21st Century*, ed. Robert D. Reischauer, Stuart Butler, and Judith R. Lave. Washington, D.C.: Brookings Institution Press.

Barr, Stephen. 2007a. Hoyer Makes Good on Health-Care Promise. *Washington Post.* March 2.

———. 2007b. Retiree Health Care Back on Hill Agenda. *Washington Post.* February 22.

Beavers, Sarah, and Jim Mays. 2005. Growth in Premiums in the FEHBP from Mental Health Parity. Memorandum to the Office of the Assistant Secretary for Planning and Evaluation. May 20. http://aspe.hhs.gov/health/reports/05/mhsamemo.htm (accessed June 30, 2009).

Bennett, Johanna. 2002. Insurers Push Higher Co-Payments for Treatment at Pricey Hospitals. *Wall Street Journal.* June 6.

Biles, Brian, Lauren Hersch Nicholas, Barbara S. Cooper, Emily Adrion, and Stuart Guterman. 2006. *The Cost of Privatization: Extra Payments to Medicare Advantage Plans—Updated and Revised.* The Commonwealth Fund. November 30. http://www.cmwf.org/publications/publications_show.htm?doc_id=428546 (accessed June 30, 2009).

———. 2008. *The Continuing Cost of Privatization: Extra Payments to Medicare Advantage Plans in 2008.* The Commonwealth Fund. September 5. http://www.commonwealthfund.org/Content/Publications/Issue-Briefs/2008/Sep/The-Continuing-Cost-of-Privatization—Extra-Payments-to-Medicare-Advantage.aspx (accessed June 30, 2009).

Blum, Jonathan, Ruth Brown, and Miryam Frieder. 2007. *An Examination of Medicare Private Fee-for-Service Plans.* Henry J. Kaiser Family Foundation. March. http://www.kff.org/medicare/upload/7621.pdf (accessed June 30, 2009).

Boccuti, Cristina, and Marilyn Moon. 2003. Comparing Medicare and Private Insurers: Growth Rates in Spending over Three Decades. *Health Affairs* 22 (2): 230–37.

Book, Robert. 2009. *Illusions of Cost Control in Public Health Plans.* July 24. Heritage

Foundation Backgrounder. Washington, D.C.: Heritage Foundation. http://www.heritage.org/research/healthcare/bg2301.cfm (accessed July 30, 2009).

Bovbjerg, Randall R. 2009. Lessons for Health Reform from the Federal Employees Health Benefits Program. Urban Institute. August 12. http://www.rwjf.org/grantees/connect/product.jsp?id=47148 (accessed August 15, 2009).

Brown, J. M. 2009. Farr to Introduce Medicare Bill to Fix Underpayments to Doctors. *Mercury News*. April 17. http://www.mercurynews.com/centralcoast/ci_12162095 (accessed June 30, 2009).

Brown, Paul. 2007. Shortsighted Management. *New York Times*. November 24.

Brown, Ruth, Miryam Frieder, Jonathon Blum, and Penny Mills. 2008. *The Emerging Role of Group Medicare Private Fee-for-Service Plans*. Henry J. Kaiser Family Foundation. December. http://www.kff.org/medicare/upload/7841.pdf (accessed June 30, 2009).

Buchmueller, Thomas C. 2000. The Health Plan Choices of Retirees under Managed Competition. *Health Services Research* 35 (5, pt. 1): 949–76. www.pubmedcentral.nih.gov/articlerender.fcgi?artid=1089178 (accessed June 30, 2009).

Burman, Leonard E. 2009. Give Up a Benefit, Gain Jobs. *Washington Post*. July 8.

Butler, Stuart M. 2009. How to Design a Tax Cap in Health Care Reform. Heritage Foundation WebMemo. July 1. http://www.heritage.org/Research/healthcare/wm2517.cfm (accessed June 30, 2009).

———, and Robert Moffit. 1995. The FEHBP as a Model for a New Medicare Program. *Health Affairs* 14 (4): 47–61.

———, Patricia Danzon, Bill Gradison, Robert Helms, Marilyn Moon, Joseph P. Newhouse, Mark V. Pauly, Martha Phillips, Uwe E. Reinhardt, Robert D. Reishchauer, William L. Roper, John Rother, Leonard D. Schaeffer, and Gail R. Wilensky. 1999. Open Letter to Congress and the Executive: Crisis Facing HCFA and Millions of Americans. *Health Affairs* 18 (1): 8–10.

Cain, Harry. 1999. Moving Medicare to the FEHBP Model, or How to Make an Elephant Fly. *Health Affairs* 18 (4): 25–39.

Caplan, Craig, and Lisa Foley. 2000. *Structuring Health Care Benefits: A Comparison of Medicare and the FEHBP*. AARP Public Policy Institute. http://assets.aarp.org/rgcenter/health/2000_05_benefits.pdf (accessed June 30, 2009).

Chandra, Amitabh, Jonathon Gruber, and Robin McKnight. 2009. Patient Cost-Sharing, Hospitalization Offsets, and the Design of Optimal Health Insurance. NBER Working Paper No. 12972. June. http://www.nber.org/papers/w12972 (accessed June 30, 2009).

Chernew, Michael E., Philip DeCicca, and Robert Town. 2008. Managed Care and Medical Expenditures of Medicare Beneficiaries. *Journal of Health Economics* 27: 1451–61.

———, Allison B. Rosen, and A. Mark Fendrick. 2007. Value-Based Insurance Design. *Health Affairs* 26 (2): 103–12.

Coulam, Robert, Roger Feldman, and Bryan Dowd. 2009. *Bring Market Prices to Medicare! Essential Reform at a Time of Fiscal Crisis*. Washington, D.C.: AEI Press.

Cutler, David M., and Richard Zeckhauser. 2000. The Anatomy of Health Insurance. In *Handbook of Health Economics*, ed. Anthony Y. Culyer and Joseph P. Newhouse, 563–643. Amsterdam: Elsevier North Holland.

Daschle, Tom, Jeanne M. Lambrew, and Scott S. Greenberger. 2008. *Critical: What We Can Do About the Health Care Crisis*. New York: St. Martins Press.

Davis, Karen, Barbara S. Cooper, and Rose Capasso. 2003. *The Federal Employee Health Benefits Program: A Model for Workers, Not Medicare*. The Commonwealth Fund. At http://www.cmwf.org/usr_doc/davis_fehbp_677.pdf (accessed June 30, 2009).

————, and Cathy Schoen. 2003. Creating Consensus on Coverage Choices. *Health Affairs* Web Exclusive. April 23. http://content.healthaffairs.org/cgi/reprint/hlthaff.w3.199v1 (accessed June 10, 2009).

————, Cathy Schoen, Michelle Doty, and Katie Tenney. 2002. Medicare versus Private Insurance: Rhetoric and Reality. *Health Affairs* Web Exclusive. October 9. http://content.healthaffairs.org/cgi/reprint/hlthaff.w2.311v1 (accessed June 10, 2009).

Dobson, Allen, Joan DaVanzo, and Namrata Sen. 2006. The Cost-Shift Payment "Hydraulic": Foundation, History, and Implications. *Health Affairs* 25 (1): 23–33.

Dorn, Stan. 2009. *Capping the Tax Exclusion of Employer-Sponsored Health Insurance: Is Equity Feasible?* Urban Institute. June. http://www.urban.org/uploadedpdf/411894_cappingthetaxexclusion.pdf (accessed June 30, 2009).

Dorn, Stan, and Jack A. Meyer. 2002. *Nine Billion Dollars a Year to Cover the Uninsured: Possible Common Ground for Significant, Incremental Progress*. Economic and Social Research Institute. http://www.esresearch.org/newsletter/october/cpolicy4.pdf (accessed June 30, 2009)

Dorschner, John. 2007. Cuban-Style Clinics May Be a Model for U.S. *Miami Herald*. March 12. http://www.miamiherald.com/154/v-print/story/38715.html (accessed June 30, 2009).

Dowd, Bryan E., Robert F. Coulam, Roger Feldman, and Steven D. Pizer. 2005. Fee-for-Service Medicare in a Competitive Market Environment. *Health Care Financing Review* 27 (2): 113–25. http://www.cms.hhs.gov/HealthCareFinancingReview/downloads/05-06Winpg113.pdf (accessed June 30, 2009).

Dubay, Lisa, John Holahan, and Allison Cook. 2006. The Uninsured and the Affordability of Health Insurance Coverage. *Health Affairs* Web Exclusive. November 30. http://content.healthaffairs.org/webexclusives/index.dtl?year=2006 (accessed June 30, 2009).

Duggan, Mark, Patrick Healy, and Fiona Scott Morton. 2008. Providing Prescription Drug Coverage to the Elderly: America's Experiment with Medicare Part D. *Journal of Economic Perspectives* 22 (4): 69–92.

————, and Fiona Scott Morton. 2008. The Effect of Medicare Part D on Pharma-

ceutical Prices and Utilization. NBER Working Paper 13917. April. http://www.
nber.org/papers/w13917 (accessed June 30, 2009).

Dummit, Laura. 2006. *Updating Medicare's Physician Fees: The Sustainable Growth Rate
Methodology.* National Health Policy Forum Issue Brief No. 818. November 10.
http://www.nhpf.org/library/issue-briefs/IB818_SGR_11-10-06.pdf (accessed
June 30, 2009).

Enthoven, Alain. 1980. *Health Plan: The Only Practical Solution to the Soaring Cost of
Medical Care.* Reading, Mass.: Addison-Wesley.

———. 1989. Effective Management of Competition in the FEHBP. *Health Affairs* 8
(3): 33–50.

———. 2002. Where Are Health Care's "Hondas"? *Wall Street Journal.* October 24.

———. 2008. Health Care with a Few Bucks Left Over. *New York Times.* December 28.

Fales, John. 2007. Veterans Gird for New Fight of Sharp Health Care Fee Rises. *Washington Times.* March 12.

Feldman, Roger. 2008. *How to Fix Medicare: Let's Pay Patients, Not Physicians.* Washington, D.C.: AEI Press.

———, and Bryan Dowd. 2000. Risk Segmentation: Goal or Problem? *Journal of
Health Economics* 19 (4): 499–512.

———, Kenneth E. Thorpe, and Bradley Gray. 2002. The Federal Employees Health
Benefits Plan. *Journal of Economic Perspectives* 16 (2): 207–17.

Finkelstein, Amy. 2005. The Aggregate Effects of Health Insurance: Evidence from the
Introduction of Medicare. NBER Working Paper 11619. http://www.nber.org/
papers/w11619 (accessed September 30, 2008).

Fisher, Elliot S., Julie P. Bynum, and Jonathon S. Skinner. 2009. Slowing the Growth
of Health Care Costs—Lessons from Regional Variation. *New England Journal of
Medicine* 360 (9): 849–52.

———, David E. Wennberg, Therese A. Stukel, Daniel J. Gottlieb, F. L. Lucas, and
Etiole L. Pinder. 2003. The Implications of Regional Variations in Medicare Spending. Part 1: The Content, Quality, and Accessibility of Care. *Annals of Internal Medicine* 138 (4): 273–311.

Florence, Curtis, Adam Atherly, and Kenneth E. Thorpe. 2006. Will Choice-Based
Reform Work for Medicare? Evidence from the Federal Employees Health Benefits
Program. *Health Services Research* 41 (5): 1741–61.

———, and Kenneth E. Thorpe. 2003. How Does the Employer Contribution for
the Federal Employees Health Benefits Program Influence Plan Selection? *Health
Affairs* 522 (2): 211–18.

Fox, Peter, Rani Snyder, Geraldine Dallek, and Thomas Rice. 1999. Should Medicare
HMO Benefits Be Standardized? *Health Affairs* 18 (4): 40–52.

Fox, Will, and John Pickering. 2008. Payment Level Comparison of Medicare, Medicaid, and Commercial Payers. Milliman. Press release. December. http://www.ahip.
org/content/pressrelease.aspx?docid=25218 (accessed December 30, 2008).

Francis, Walton. 1986. HMO Customer Service. *Health Affairs* 5 (1): 173–82.

———. 1988 (slightly revised in 1991). How to Reform, and How Not to Reform, the Federal Employees Health Benefits Program. Testimony presented to the U.S. Office of Personnel Management, July 26, 1988. Available from author on request.

———. 1993. The Political Economy of the Federal Employees Health Benefits Program. In *Health Policy Reform: Competition and Controls*, ed. Robert B. Helms, 269–307. Washington, D.C.: AEI Press.

———. 2003a. *The FEHBP as a Model for Medicare Reform: Separating Fact from Fiction*. Heritage Foundation. Backgrounder No. 1674. http://www.heritage.org/ Research/HealthCare/bg1674.cfm (accessed June 30, 2009).

———. 2003b. *Using the Federal Employees' Model: Nine Tests for Rational Medicare Reform*. Heritage Foundation. Backgrounder No. 1675. http://www.heritage.org/ Research/HealthCare/bg1675.cfm (accessed June 30, 2009).

———, and the Editors of Washington Consumers' *CHECKBOOK*. 2008 and prior years. *CHECKBOOK's Guide to Health Plans for Federal Employees*. Washington, D.C.: Center for the Study of Services. Also available online at www.guidetohealthplans.org (accessed June 30, 2009).

———. 2009. *Why a New Public Plan Will Not Improve American Health Care*. Heritage Foundation Backgrounder No. 2267. http://www.heritage.org/Research/ HealthCare/bg2267.cfm (accessed June 30, 2009).

Freudenheim, Milt. 2007. To Save Later, Some Employers Are Offering Free Drugs Now. *New York Times*. February 21.

Fuchs, Beth. 2001. Increasing Health Insurance Coverage through an Extended Federal Employees Health Benefits Program. *Inquiry* 38 (Summer): 177–92.

———, and Lisa Potetz. 2007. *Medicare Consumer-Directed Health Plans: Medicare MSAs and HSA-Like Plans in 2007*. Henry J. Kaiser Family Foundation. http://www. kff.org/medicare/7623.cfm (accessed June 30, 2009).

Furman, Jason. 2008. Health Reform through Tax Reform: A Primer. *Health Affairs* 27 (3): 622–32.

Gawande, Atul. 2009. The Cost Conumdrum: What a Texas Town Can Teach Us about Health Care. *New Yorker*. June 1.

Ginsburg, Paul B. 2003. Can Hospitals and Physicians Shift the Effects of Cuts in Medicare Reimbursement to Private Payers? *Health Affairs* Web Exclusive. October 8. http://content.healthaffairs.org/cgi/reprint/hlthaff.w3.472v1 (accessed June 30, 2009).

Glied, Sherry, and Mark Stabile. 2001. Avoiding Health Insurance Crowd-Out: Evidence from the Medicare as Secondary Payer Legislation. *Journal of Health Economics* 20 (2): 239–60.

Goda, Gospi Shah, John B. Shoven, and Sita Nataraj Slavov. 2007. A Tax on Work for the Elderly: Medicare as a Secondary Payer. August. National Bureau of Economic

Research Working Paper. https://www.nber.org/programs/ag/rrc/NB07-11%20Goda,%20Shoven,%20Slavov%20FINAL.pdf (accessed June 30, 2009).

Gold, Marsha. 2001. Medicare+Choice: An Interim Report Card. *Health Affairs* 20 (4): 120–38.

———. 2003. Can Managed Care and Competition Control Medicare Costs? *Health Affairs* Web Exclusive. April 2. http://content.healthaffairs.org/cgi/reprint/hlthaff.w3.176v1 (accessed June 30, 2009).

———. 2007. *Private Plans in Medicare: A 2007 Update*. Henry J. Kaiser Family Foundation. www.kff.org/medicare/upload/7622.pdf (accessed June 30, 2009).

———. 2008. Medicare Private Plans: A Report Card on Medicare Advantage. *Health Affairs* Web Exclusive. November 24. http://content.healthaffairs.org/webexclusives/index.dtl?year=2008 (accessed June 30, 2009).

Gottlieb, Scott. 2008. What's at Stake in the Medicare Showdown. *Wall Street Journal*. June 24.

Gray, Bradley M., and Thomas M. Selden. 2002. Adverse Selection and the Capped Premium Subsidy in the Federal Employees Health Benefits Program. *Journal of Risk and Insurance* 69 (2): 209–24.

Grayson, C. Jackson, with Louis Neeb. 1974. *Confessions of a Price Controller*. Homewood, Ill.: Dow Jones-Irwin.

Gruber, Jonathan. 2006. *The Role of Consumer Copayments for Health Care: Lessons from the RAND Health Insurance Experiment and Beyond*. Henry J. Kaiser Family Foundation. October. http://www.kff.org/insurance/upload/7566.pdf (accessed June 30, 2009).

———. 2009. Choosing a Medicare Part D Plan: Are Medicare Beneficiaries Choosing Low-Cost Plans? Henry J. Kaiser Family Foundation. March. http://www.kff.org/medicare/upload/7864.pdf (accessed June 30, 2009).

———, and Kosali Simon. 2008. Crowd-Out 10 Years Later: Have Recent Public Insurance Expansions Crowded Out Private Health Insurance? *Journal of Health Economics* 27 (2): 201–17.

Hacker, Jacob S., and Theodore R. Marmor. 2004. Medicare Reform: Fact, Fiction and Foolishness. *Public Policy and Aging Report* 13 (4). http://mba.yale.edu/faculty/PDF/hudson.pdf (accessed June 30, 2009).

Helms, Robert B., ed. 1993. *Health Policy Reform: Competition and Controls*. Washington, D.C.: AEI Press.

———. 1999. The Tax Treatment of Health Insurance: Early History and Evidence, 1940–1970. In *Empowering Health Care Consumers Through Tax Reform*, ed. Grace-Marie Arnett, 1–25. Ann Arbor, Mich.: University of Michigan Press.

———. 2007. *The Medicaid Commission Report: A Dissent*. American Enterprise Institute. January. http://www.aei.org/docLib/20070111_200701AHPOg.pdf (accessed June 30, 2009).

————. 2008. Tax Policy and the History of the Health Insurance Industry. In *Using Taxes to Reform Health Insurance*, ed. Henry J. Aaron and Leonard E. Burman, 13–35. Washington, D.C.: Brookings Institution Press.

————. 2009. Taxing Health Insurance: A Tax Designed to Be Avoided. *AEI Health Policy Outlook*. June. http://www.aei.org/docLib/07%20HPO%20Helms%20June-g.pdf (accessed June 30, 2009).

Henderson, Karen LeCraft. 2009. *Consumers' Checkbook, Center for the Study of Services v. United States Department of Health and Human Services*. United States Court of Appeals for the District of Columbia Circuit. January 30. http://pacer.cadc.uscourts.gov/docs/common/opinions/200901/07-5343-1162054.pdf (accessed June 30, 2009).

Hernandez, Raymond. 2008. What Would You Drive, If the Taxpayers Paid? *New York Times*. May 1.

Hoadley, Jack, Jennifer Thompson, Elizabeth Hargrave, Juliette Cubanski, and Tricia Neuman. 2008. Medicare Part D 2009 Data Spotlight: Premiums. Henry J. Kaiser Family Foundation. November. http://www.kff.org/medicare/upload/7835.pdf (accessed June 30, 2009).

Hsu, John, et al. 2006. Unintended Consequences of Caps on Medicare Drug Benefits. *New England Journal of Medicine* 354 (June 1): 2349–59.

Hyman, David A. 2006. *Medicare Meets Mephistopheles*. Washington, D.C.: Cato Institute.

Iglehart, John K. 1981. Drawing the Lines for the Debate on Competition. *New England Journal of Medicine* 305 (5): 291–96.

Jaffe, Susan. 2009a. Medicare Advantage Plans. Health Affairs Health Policy Brief. April 29. http://www.healthaffairs.org/healthpolicybriefs/brief_pdfs/healthpolicybrief_1.pdf (accessed June 30, 2009).

————. 2009b. Competitive Bidding in Medicare Advantage. Health Affairs Health Policy Brief. June 5. http://www.healthaffairs.org/healthpolicybriefs/brief_pdfs/healthpolicybrief_3.pdf (accessed June 30, 2009).

Jencks, Stephen F., Mark V. Williams, and Eric A. Coleman. 2009. Rehospitalizations among Patients in the Medicare Fee-for-Service Program. *New England Journal of Medicine* 360 (14): 1418–28.

Johnson, Carrie. 2008. Medicare Fraud a Growing Problem: Medicare Pays Most Claims Without Review. *Washington Post*. June 13.

Jones, Stanley B. 1989. Can Multiple Choice Be Managed to Constrain Health Care Costs? *Health Affairs* 8 (3): 51–59.

————, and Marion Ein Lewin, eds. 1996. *Improving the Medicare Market: Adding Choice and Protections*. Washington, D.C.: National Academies Press.

Joyce, Geoffrey, Jose J. Escarce, Matthew D. Solomon, and Dana P. Goldman. 2002. Employer Drug Benefit Plans and Spending on Prescription Drugs. *JAMA* 288 (14): 1733–39. http://jama.ama-assn.org/cgi/reprint/288/14/1733.pdf (accessed June 30, 2009).

Kaiser Family Foundation. 2009. Medicare: A Timeline of Key Developments. http://www.kff.org/medicare/timeline/pf_entire.htm (accessed June 30, 2009).

———. n.d. Medicare Health and Prescription Drug Plan Tracker. http://healthplantracker.kff.org (accessed June 30, 2009).

Kennedy, Henry H. 2008. *Memorandum Opinion: Ilene Hays and L. P. Dey v. Michael Leavitt, Secretary of the Department of Health and Human Services.* United States District Court for the District of Columbia. https://ecf.dcd.uscourts.gov/cgi-bin/show_public_doc?2008cv1032-22 (accessed June 30, 2009).

Kennedy, John F. 1962. Quotations of John F. Kennedy. March 21. http://www.jfklibrary.org/Historical+Resources/Archives/Reference+Desk/Quotations+of+John+F+Kennedy.htm (accessed June 30, 2009).

Kesselheim, Aaron S., and David M. Studdert. 2008. Whistleblower-Initiated Enforcement Actions against Health Care Fraud and Abuse in the United States, 1996 to 2005. *Annals of Internal Medicine* 149 (5): 342–49.

Kessler, Daniel P. 2007. Cost Shifting in California Hospitals: What Is the Effect on Private Payers? California Foundation for Commerce and Education. June 6. http://www.cfcepolicy.org/Reports/ (accessed June 30, 2009).

King, Kathleen M., and Mark Schlesinger, eds. 2003. *Final Report of the Study Panel on Medicare and Markets—The Role of Private Health Plans in Medicare: Lessons from the Past, Looking to the Future.* Washington, D.C.: National Academy of Social Insurance. http://www.nasi.org/publications2763/publications_show.htm?doc_id=197700 (accessed June 30, 2009).

Kling, Jeffrey R., Sendhil Mullainathan, Eldar Shafir, Lee Vermeulen, and Marian V. Wrobel. 2009. Misperception in Choosing Medicare Drug Plans. November. http://www.gsb.stanford.edu/facseminars/events/political_economy/documents/pe_02_09_mullainathan.pdf (accessed June 30, 2009).

Kolata, Gina. 2003. Patients in Florida Lining Up for All that Medicare Covers. *New York Times.* September 13.

Kyl, Jon. 2003. What Is True Medicare Reform? Heritage Foundation Lecture No. 805. October 23 (shortly before enactment of the Medicare Modernization Act). http://www.heritage.org/Research/HealthCare/HL805.cfm (accessed June 30, 2009).

Lachance, Janice. 2000. Opening remarks. Strategic Compensation Conference. August 28. www.opm.gov/speeches/2000/Lachance08-28-00.htm (accessed June 30, 2009).

Lee, Jason S., Robert A. Berenson, Rick Mayes, and Anne K. Gauthier. 2003. Medicare Payment Policy: Does Cost Shifting Matter? *Health Affairs* Web Exclusive. October 8. http://content.healthaffairs.org/cgi/reprint/hlthaff.w3.480v1 (accessed June 30, 2009).

Lemieux, Jeff. 2003. Medicare vs. FEHB Spending: A Rare, Reasonable Analysis. Centrists.Org. June 23. http://www.centrists.org/pages/2003/06/23_lemieux_health.html (accessed June 30, 2009).

————, Teresa Chovan, and Karen Heath. 2008. Medigap Coverage and Medicare Spending: A Second Look. *Health Affairs* 27 (2): 469–77.

Leonhardt, David. 2008. High Costs Courtesy of Congress. *New York Times.* June 25.

Levit, Katharine, Cynthia Smith, Cathy Cowan, Art Sensenig, Aaron Catlin, and the Health Accounts Team. 2004. Health Spending Rebound Continues in 2002. *Health Affairs* 23 (1): 147–59.

Lichtenberg, Frank R., and Shawn X. Sun. 2007. The Impact of Medicare Part D on Prescription Drug Use by the Elderly. *Health Affairs* 26 (6): 1735–44.

Lichtenstein, Carolyn et al. 2004. *Evaluation of Parity in the Federal Employees Health Benefits (FEHB) Program: Final Report.* Northrop Grumman Information Technology Inc. December. http://aspe.hhs.gov/daltcp/reports/parity.htm (accessed September 20, 2008).

Manning, Willard, Joseph P. Newhouse, Naihua Duan, Emmett B. Keeler, Arleen Leibowitz, and M. Susan Marquis. 1987. Health Insurance and the Demand for Medical Care: Evidence from a Randomized Experiment. *American Economic Review* 77 (3) 251–77.

Marmor, Theodore. 2000. *The Politics of Medicare.* 2d ed. Hawthorne, NY: Aldine.

McArdle, Frank B. 1995. Opening Up the Federal Employees Health Benefits Program. *Health Affairs* 14 (2): 40–50.

Meckler, Laura. 2009. Obama's Health Expert Gets Political. *Wall Street Journal.* July 22.

Merlis, Mark. 1999. *Medicare Restructuring: The FEHBP Model.* Henry J. Kaiser Family Foundation. http://www.kff.org/medicare/1461-index.cfm (accessed September 30, 2008).

————. 2003. *The Federal Employees Health Benefits Program: Program Design, Recent Performance and Implications for Medicare Reform.* Henry J. Kaiser Family Foundation. http://www.kff.org/medicare/6081-index.cfm (accessed June 30, 2009).

————. 2007. *Medicare Advantage Payment Policy.* National Health Policy Forum. http://www.nhpf.org/library/background-papers/BP_MAPaymentPolicy_09-24-07.pdf (accessed June 30, 2009).

Moffit, Robert E. 1992. *Consumer Choice in Health: Learning from the Federal Employees Health Benefit Program.* Heritage Foundation. Backgrounder No. 878. http://www.heritage.org/Research/SocialSecurity/bg878.cfm?renderforprint=1 (accessed June 30, 2009).

————. 2008. *The Success of Medicare Advantage Plans: What Seniors Should Know.* Heritage Foundation. Executive Summary No. 2142. http://www.heritage.org/Research/HealthCare/bg2142es.cfm (accessed June 30, 2009).

Morrisey, Michael A. 1994. *Cost Shifting in Health Care.* Washington, D.C.: AEI Press.

————. 2003. Cost Shifting: New Myths, Old Confusion, and Enduring Reality. *Health Affairs* Web Exclusive. October 8. http://content.healthaffairs.org/cgi/reprint/hlthaff.w3.489v1 (accessed June 30, 2009).

———. 2005. *Price Sensitivity in Health Care: Implications for Health Care Policy*. Washington, D.C.: National Federation of Independent Business. http://www.nfib.com/page/researchFoundation (accessed June 30, 2009).

Murray, Shailagh. 2009. Obama Eyes the Purse Strings for Medicare. *Washington Post*. July 16.

Neuman, Patricia, Ed Maibach, Katharine Dusenbury, Michelle Kitchman, and Pam Zupp. 1998. Marketing HMOs to Medicare Beneficiaries. *Health Affairs* 17 (4): 132–39.

Newhouse, Joseph P. 2001. *Medicare*. Paper prepared for the Conference on Economic Policy During the 1990s, Kennedy School of Government, June 27–30. http://www.ksg.harvard.edu/m-rcbg/Conferences/economic_policy/Medicare_Newhouse.pdf (accessed June 30, 2009).

———. 2002. *Pricing the Priceless: A Health Care Conundrum*. Cambridge, MA: MIT Press.

———. 2004. Consumer-Directed Health Plans and the RAND Health Insurance Experiment. *Health Affairs* 23 (6): 107–13.

———. 2006. Reconsidering the Moral Hazard-Risk Avoidance Tradeoff. *Journal of Health Economics* 25 (5): 1005–14.

Oberlander, Jonathan. 2003. *The Political Life of Medicare*. Chicago: University of Chicago Press.

O'Rourke, P.J. 1993. The Liberty Manifesto. The Cato Institute. May 6. http://www.cato.org/pub_display.php?pub_id=6857 (accessed June 30, 2009).

Pauly, Mark V. 1999. Medical Care Costs, Benefits, and Effects: Conceptual Issues for Measuring Price Change. In *Measuring the Prices of Medical Treatments*, ed. Jack E. Triplett. Washington, D.C.: Brookings Institution Press.

———. 2004. Means-Testing in Medicare. 2004. *Health Affairs* Web Exclusive. December 8. http://content.healthaffairs.org/cgi/reprint/hlthaff.w4.546v1 (accessed June 30, 2009).

———. 2007. The Truth about Moral Hazard and Adverse Selection. Herbert Lourie Memorial Lecture on Health Policy. Center for Policy Research, Maxwell School, Syracuse University. http://www-cpr.maxwell.syr.edu/lourie_lecture/lourie.htm (accessed June 30, 2009).

———. 2008. *Markets Without Magic: How Competition Might Save Medicare*. Washington, D.C.: AEI Press.

Pear, Robert. 2006. Last-Minute Inserts Offer Benefits in Medicare Bill. *New York Times*. December 15, A16.

———. 2007. Select Hospitals Reap a Windfall Under Child Health Bill. *New York Times*. August 12.

———. 2008a. Bailout Provides More Mental Health Coverage. *New York Times*. October 6.

———. 2008b. Concerned about Costs, Congress Pushes Curbs on Doctor-Owned Hospitals. *New York Times*. June 8.

Peppe, Elizabeth, Jim Mays, Sarah Beavers, Holen Chang, and Monica Brenner. 2005. Medicare Financing Issues Draft Final Report. Unpublished manuscript. Actuarial Research Corporation. September 15.

Pollack, Andrew. 2009. Medicare Blow to Virtual Colonoscopies. *New York Times*. February 13.

Pope, Gregory C., Leslie Greenwald, John Kautter, Brian Dulisse, and Nathan West. 2007. *Medicare Advantage Plan Availability, Premiums and Benefits, and Beneficiary Enrollment in 2006*. Final Report for CMS Office of Research, Development, and Information. RTI International. November. http://www.allhealth.org/BriefingMaterials/RTIMedicareadvantageplan-1449.pdf (accessed June 30, 2009).

Price, J. R., and J. W. Mays. 1985. Biased Selection in the Federal Employees Health Benefits Program. *Inquiry* 22 (1): 67–77.

Reed, Thomas B. 1884. As quoted in Samuel W. McCall. 1914. *The Life of Thomas B. Reed*. Boston and New York: Houghton Mifflin Company.

Rettenmaier, Andrew J., and Thomas R. Saving. 2007. *The Diagnosis and Treatment of Medicare*. Washington, D.C.: AEI Press.

Rettig, Richard, Peter D. Jacobson, Cynthia M. Farquhar, and Wade M. Aubry. 2007. *False Hope: Bone Marrow Transplantation for Breast Cancer*. New York: Oxford University Press.

Rice, Thomas, and Katherine A. Desmond. 2002. An Analysis of Reforming Medicare through a "Premium Support" Program. Henry J. Kaiser Family Foundation. February. http://www.kff.org/uninsured/upload/An-Analysis-of-Reforming-Medicare-Through-a-Premium-Support-Program-Report.pdf (accessed June 30, 2009).

———, Katherine Desmond, and Jon Gabel. 1990. The Medicare Catastrophic Coverage Act: A Post-mortem. *Health Affairs* 9 (3): 75–87. http://content.healthaffairs.org/cgi/reprint/9/3/75? (accessed June 30, 2009).

Rivlin, Alice, and Joseph R. Antos, eds. 2007. *Restoring Fiscal Sanity 2007: The Health Spending Challenge*. Washington, D.C.: Brookings Institution Press.

Schmid, Stuart G. 1995. Geographic Variation in Medical Costs: Evidence from HMOs. *Health Affairs* 14 (1): 271–75.

Schultze, Charles L. 1977. *The Public Use of Private Interest*. Washington, D.C.: Brookings Institution.

Schuster, Mark A., Elizabeth A. McGlynn, and Robert H. Brook. 2002. *How Good Is the Quality of Health Care in the United States?* Santa Monica, Calif.: RAND.

Sheils, John, and Randal Haught. 2008. Comprehensive Health Reform Costs Less: A Comparison of Four Proposals. The Lewin Group Staff Working Paper. December 17. http://wyden.senate.gov/issues/Healthy%20Americans%20Act/122008lewin_report.pdf (accessed June 30, 2009).

Sparrow, Malcolm K. 2000. *License to Steal*. Boulder, Colo.: Westview Press.

Thaler, Richard H., and Cass R. Sunstein. 2009. *Nudge: Improving Decisions About Health, Wealth, and Happiness*. New York, N.Y.: Penguin Books.

Triplett, Jack E., ed. 1999. *Measuring the Prices of Medical Treatments.* Washington, D.C.: Brookings Institution.

U.S. Boards of Trustees of the Federal Hospital Insurance and Federal Supplementary Medical Insurance Trust Funds. 2009 and prior years. *Annual Report of the Boards of Trustees of the Federal Hospital Insurance and Federal Supplementary Medical Insurance Trust Funds.* Washington, D.C.: Boards of Trustees. http://www.ssa.gov/OACT/TR/TR08/index.html (accessed June 30, 2009).

U.S. Congress, Joint Economic Committee. 2006. *Hearing on The Next Generation of Health Information Tools for Consumers.* 109th Cong., 2nd sess. May 10. http://ftp.resource.org/gpo.gov/hearings/109s/29936.pdf (accessed June 30, 2009)

U.S. Congressional Budget Office. 2004. An Analysis of the Literature on Disease Management Programs: Letter to the Honorable Don Nickles from Douglas Holtz-Eakin, CBO director. http://www.cbo.gov/ftpdocs/59xx/doc5909/10-13-DiseaseMngmnt.pdf (accessed June 30, 2009).

———. 2005. *Geographic Variation in Health Care Spending.* http://www.cbo.gov/doc.cfm?index=8972 (accessed June 30, 2009).

———. 2006a. *Consumer-Directed Health Plans: Potential Effects on Health Care Spending and Outcomes.* December. http://www.cbo.gov/ftpdocs/77xx/doc7700/12-21-HealthPlans.pdf (accessed June 30, 2009).

———. 2006b. *Designing a Premium Support System for Medicare.* December. http://www.cbo.gov/ftpdocs/76xx/doc7697/12-08-Medicare.pdf (accessed June 30, 2009).

———. 2007a. *Budget Options February 2007.* http://www.cbo.gov/ftpdocs/78xx/doc7821/02-23-BudgetOptions.pdf (accessed June 30, 2009).

———. 2007b. *The Long-Term Outlook for Health Care Spending.* November. http://www.cbo.gov/ftpdocs/87xx/doc8758/11-13-LT-Health.pdf (accessed June 30, 2009).

———. 2008a. *Budget Options: Volume 1 Health Care.* December. http://www.cbo.gov/ftpdocs/99xx/doc9925/12-18-HealthOptions.pdf (accessed June 30, 2009).

———. 2008b. *H.R. 6331 Medicare Improvements for Patients and Providers Act of 2008.* Congressional Budget Office cost estimate. July 23. http://www.cbo.gov/ftpdocs/95xx/doc9595/hr6331pgo.pdf (accessed June 30, 2009).

———. 2009a. The Effects of Proposals to Increase Cost Sharing in TRICARE. June. http://www.cbo.gov/ftpdocs/102xx/doc10261/toc.html (accessed June 30, 2009).

———. 2009b. Letter to Senator Mike Crapo concerning options to change MA benchmarks, May 18. http://www.cbo.gov/ftpdocs/102xx/doc10233/05-18-Letter_Hon_Crapo_on_4_MA_options.pdf (accessed June 30, 2009).

U.S. Congressional Research Service. 1989. *The Federal Employees Health Benefits Program: Possible Strategies for Reform.* Washington, D.C.: Government Printing Office.

———. 2008. Medicare Part D Prescription Drug Benefit: A Primer, by Jennifer O'Sullivan. Order Code RL34280. August 20. https://wikileaks.org/leak/crs/RL34280.pdf (accessed June 30, 2009).

———. 2009a. Federal Employees: Pay and Pension Increases since 1969, by Patrick Purcell. Order Code 94-971. January 8. http://digitalcommons.ilr.cornell.edu/cgi/viewcontent.cgi?article=1602&context=key_workplace (accessed June 30, 2009).

———. 2009b. Setting and Valuing Health Insurance Benefits, by Chris L. Peterson. Order Code R40491. April 6. http://assets.opencrs.com/rpts/R40491_20090406.pdf. (accessed June 30, 2009).

———. 2009c. Medicare Secondary Payer: Coordination of Benefits, by Hinda Chaikind. Order Code RL33587. July 10. http://assets.opencrs.com/rpts/RL33587_20080710.pdf (accessed June 30, 2009).

U.S. Department of Health and Human Services. 2007. Agency Financial Report: FY 2007. http://www.hhs.gov/afr/fullafrreport2007.pdf (accessed June 30, 2009).

———. 2007. Medicare Program; Revisions to the Medicare Advantage and Part D Prescription Drug Contract Determinations, Appeals, and Intermediate Sanctions Processes; Final Rule with Comment Period. December 5. 72 FR 68700, at pages 68707-8. http://frwebgate5.access.gpo.gov/cgi-bin/PDFgate.cgi?WAISdocID=172002379918+9+2+0&WAISaction=retrieve (accessed June 30, 2009).

U.S. Department of Health and Human Services. Centers for Medicare and Medicaid Services. 2006a. Medicare and Medicaid Statistical Supplement for 2005. Health Care Financing Review. http://www.cms.hhs.gov/MedicareMedicaidStatSupp/LT/list.asp#TopOfPage (accessed July 27, 2009).

———. 2006b. National Benchmark Shows Impact of Strong Competitive Bidding and Smart Beneficiary Choices. Press release. August 15. http://www.cms.hhs.gov/apps/media/press_releases.asp (accessed June 30, 2009).

———. 2007. Medicare Part D Plan Premiums for 2008 Show Continued Impact of Strong Competition. Press release. August 13. http://www.cms.hhs.gov/apps/media/press_releases.asp (accessed June 30, 2009).

———. 2008a. Fact Sheet: Suppliers Selected for New Program that Reduces Costs for Certain Durable Medical Equipment. Press release. May 19. http://www.cms.hhs.gov/apps/media/fact_sheets.asp (accessed June 30, 2009).

———. 2008b. Lower Medicare Part D Costs than Expected in 2009: Beneficiary Satisfaction Remains High. Press release. August 14. http://www.cms.hhs.gov/apps/media/press_releases.asp (accessed June 30, 2009).

———. 2008c. Medicare & You 2009. http://www.medicare.gov/Publications/Pubs/pdf/10050.pdf (accessed June 30, 2009).

———. 2008d. Medicare Physician Guide: A Resource for Residents, Practicing Physicians, and Other Health Care Professionals. http://www.cms.hhs.gov/MLNProducts/downloads/physicianguide.pdf (accessed June 30, 2009).

———. 2009a. 2010 Call Letter. March 30. http://www.cms.hhs.gov/PrescriptionDrugCovContra/Downloads/2010CallLetter.pdf (accessed June 30, 2009).

————. 2009b. Coverage Decision Memorandum for Screening Computed Tomographic (CT) Colonography for Colorectal Cancer. May 12. http://www.cms.hhs.gov/mcd/viewdecisionmemo.asp?from2=viewdecisio%20nmemo.asp&id=220& (accessed June 30, 2009).

————. 2009c. Fact Sheet: Changes to the Competitive Bidding Program for Certain Durable Medical Equipment, Prosthetics, Orthotics, and Supplies. Press release. January 15. http://www.cms.hhs.gov/apps/media/fact_sheets.asp (accessed June 30, 2009).

————. 2009 and prior years. Ratebooks and Supporting Data. In Medicaid Advantage Rates and Statistics. http://www.cms.hhs.gov/MedicareAdvtgSpecRateStats/RSD/itemdetail.asp?filterType=none (accessed July 31, 2009).

U.S. Department of Health and Human Services. Office of the Inspector General. 1991. *Marketing Practices of South Florida HMOs Serving Medicare Beneficiaries.* OEI-04-91-00630, November 1991. http://oig.hhs.gov/oei/reports/oei-04-91-00630.pdf (accessed June 30, 2009).

————. 2005. Medicare and FEHBP Payment Rates for Home Oxygen Equipment. OEI-09-03-00160, March (revised). http://oig.hhs.gov/oei/reports/oei-09-03-00160.pdf (accessed June 30, 2009).

————. 2007a. *Aberrant Billing in South Florida for Beneficiaries with HIV/AIDS.* September. http://www.oig.hhs.gov/oei/reports/oei-09-07-00030.pdf (accessed June 30, 2009).

————. 2007b. *The Department of Health and Human Services and the Department of Justice Health Care Fraud and Abuse Control Program Annual Report for FY 2006.* November. http://www.oig.hhs.gov/publications/docs/hcfac/hcfacreport2006.pdf (accessed June 30, 2009).

————. 2008. *South Florida Durable Medical Equipment Suppliers: Results of Appeals.* October. http://www.oig.hhs.gov/oei/reports/oei-03-07-00540. (accessed June 30, 2009).

————. 2009a. *Comparing Pharmacy Reimbursement: Medicare Part D to Medicaid.* October. http://www.oig.hhs.gov/oei/reports/oei-03-07-00350.pdf (accessed June 30, 2009).

————. 2009b. *Semiannual Report to Congress: October 1, 2008—March 31, 2009.* http://oig.hhs.gov/publications/docs/semiannual/2009/semiannual_spring2009.pdf (accessed June 30, 2009).

U.S. Department of Justice. 2002. PacifiCare Health Systems to Pay U.S. More than $87 Million to Resolve False Claims Act Allegations. Press release. April 2. http://www.usdoj.gov/opa/pr/2002/April/02_civ_217.htm (accessed June 30, 2009).

————. 2009. Eli Lilly and Company Agrees to Pay $1.415 Billion to Resolve Allegations of Off-Label Promotion of Zyprexa. Press release. January 15. http://www.usdoj.gov/opa/pr/2009/January/09-civ-038.html (accessed July 16, 2009).

U.S. General Accounting Office. 1992. *Federal Health Benefits Program: Stronger Controls Needed to Reduce Administrative Costs.* GAO/GGD-92-37. February. http://archive.gao.gov/t2pbat7/145858.pdf (accessed June 30, 2009).

———. 1995. Medicare Secondary Payer Program: Actions Needed to Realize Savings. Testimony of Sarah F. Jaggar. GAO/T-HEH-95-92. February 23. http://archive.gao.gov/t2pbat2/153561.pdf (accessed June 30, 2009).

———. 1999. *Medicare+Choice: New Standards Could Improve Accuracy and Usefulness of Plan Literature.* April. http://www.gao.gov/archive/1999/he99092.pdf (accessed June 30, 2009).

———. 2002. *Federal Employees' Health Plans: Premium Growth and OPM's Role in Negotiating Benefits.* GAO-03-236. December. http://www.gao.gov/new.items/d03236.pdf (accessed June 30, 2009).

U.S. Government Accountability Office. 2005. *Federal Employees' Health Plans: Competition and Other Factors Linked to Wide Variation in Health Care Prices.* GAO-05-856. August. http://www.gao.gov/new.items/d05856.pdf (accessed June 30, 2009).

———. 2008a. *Medicare Advantage: Characteristics, Financial Risks, and Disenrollment Rates of Beneficiaries in Private Fee-for-Service Plans.* Washington, D.C.: GAO-09-25. December. http://www.gao.gov/new.items/d0925.pdf (accessed June 30, 2009).

———. 2008b. *Some Plan Sponsors Have Not Completely Implemented Fraud and Abuse Programs, and CMS Oversight Has Been Limited.* GAO-08-760. July. http://www.gao.gov/new.items/d08760.pdf (June 30, 2009).

U.S. House of Representatives. Committee on Energy and Commerce. 2008. GAO Report: PFFS Plans Expose Beneficiaries to Serious Financial Risk; Are Unpopular with Beneficiaries. Press release. http://energycommerce.house.gov/index.php?option=com_content&view=article&id=1460&catid=17:benefits&Itemid=58 (accessed June 30, 2009).

———. Committee on Government Reform. Subcommittee on the Civil Service, Census and Agency Organization. 2002. *Recent Developments in the Federal Employees Health Benefits Program: Hearing before the Subcommittee on the Civil Service, Census and Agency Organization of the Committee on Government Reform.* 107th Cong., 2d sess. Testimony of Walton Francis. December 11. http://frwebgate.access.gpo.gov/cgi-bin/useftp.cgi?IPaddress=162.140.64.21&filename=87416.pdf&directory=/diskc/wais/data/107_house_hearings (accessed June 30, 2009).

———. Committee on Oversight and Government Reform. Subcommittee on Civil Service. 1997. *Premium Increases in the Federal Employees Health Benefits Program.* Statement of Joseph R. Antos, assistant director for health and human resources, Congressional Budget Office, before the Subcommittee on Civil Service of the Committee on Government Reform and Oversight. 105th Cong., sess. 1. October 8. http://www.cbo.gov/doc.cfm?index=133&type=0 (accessed June 30, 2009).

———. Subcommittee on Federal Workforce, Postal Service, and the District of Columbia. 2008. *FEHBP Financial Problems and Blue Cross Benefit Reductions and*

Premium Increases: Hearing before the Subcommittee on Federal Workforce, Postal Service, and the District of Columbia, Committee on Oversight and Government Reform. 110th Cong., 2d sess. Testimony of Walton Francis. December 3. http://federalworkforce.oversight.house.gov/documents/20081203144040.pdf (accessed June 30, 2009).

————. Committee on the Budget. 2007. *The Medicare Advantage Program.* Testimony of Peter R. Orszag, director, Congressional Budget Office. June 28. http://www.cbo.gov/ftpdocs/82xx/doc8265/06-28-MedicareAdvantage.pdf (accessed June 30, 2009).

————. Committee on Ways and Means. 2004 and prior years. *2004 Green Book: Background Material and Data on the Programs within the Jurisdiction of the Committee on Ways and Means.* http://www.gpoaccess.gov/wmprints/green/index.html (accessed June 30, 2009).

————. Committee on Ways and Means. Subcommittee on Health. 2007a. *The Medicare Advantage Program: Hearing before the Subcommittee on Health of the Committee on Ways and Means.* 110th Cong., 1st sess. Testimony of Mark E. Miller, executive director of the U.S. Medicare Payment Advisory Commission. March 21. http://waysandmeans.house.gov/hearings.asp?formmode=detail&hearing=543 (accessed June 30, 2009).

————. 2007b. *The Medicare Advantage Program: Hearing before the Subcommittee on Health of the Committee on Ways and Means.* 110th Cong., 1st sess. March 21. Testimony of Leslie A. Norfolk, acting administrator, Centers for Medicare and Medicaid Services. http://waysandmeans.house.gov/hearings.asp?formmode=view& id=6551 (accessed June 30, 2009).

————. 2007c. *The Medicare Advantage Program: Hearing before the Subcommittee on Health of the Committee on Ways and Means.* 110th Cong., 1st sess. March 21. Testimony of Peter R. Orszag, director, Congressional Budget Office. http://www. cbo.gov/ftpdocs/78xx/doc7879/03-21-Medicare.pdf (accessed June 30, 2009).

U.S. Medicare Payment Advisory Commission. 2006. Medicare Advantage Benchmarks and Payments Compared with Average Medicare Fee-for-Service Spending. *Medicare Briefs.* http://www.medpac.gov/publications/other_reports/MedPAC_ briefs_MA_relative_payment.pdf (accessed June 30, 2009).

————. 2007. *Report to the Congress: Medicare Payment Policy (March 2007).* http://www.medpac.gov/documents/Mar07_EntireReport.pdf (accessed June 30, 2009).

————. 2008a. *A Data Book: Healthcare Spending and the Medicare Program (June 2008).* http://www.medpac.gov/documents/Jun08DataBook_Entire_report.pdf (accessed June 30, 2009).

————. 2008b. Durable Medical Equipment Payment System. *Payment Basics.* October. http://www.medpac.gov/documents/MedPAC_Payment_Basics_08_DME.pdf (accessed June 30, 2009).

———. 2008c. Medicare Advantage Program Payment System. *Payment Basics.* October. http://www.medpac.gov/documents/MedPAC_Payment_Basics_08_MA. pdf (accessed June 30, 2009).

———. 2008d. Part D Payment System. *Payment Basics.* October. http://www. medpac.gov/documents/MedPAC_Payment_Basics_08_PartD.pdf (accessed June 30, 2009).

———. 2009. *Report to the Congress: Medicare Payment Policy (March 2009).* http:// www.medpac.gov/documents/Mar09_March%20report%20testimony_ WM%20FINAL.pdf (accessed June 30, 2009).

U.S. National Center for Educational Statistics. 2003. National Assessment of Adult Literacy. http://nces.ed.gov/naal/index.asp (accessed June 30, 2009).

U.S. Office of Management and Budget. 2008. Program Assessment: Federal Employees Group Life Insurance. ExpectMore.gov. http://www.whitehouse.gov/omb/ expectmore/summary/10000360.2004.html (accessed June 30, 2009).

———. 2009 and prior years. Budget of the United States Government for Fiscal Year 2010 (and prior years). Appendix: Department of Health and Human Services and Office of Personnel Management. www.whitehouse.gov/omb/budget/ appendix/ (accessed June 30, 2009).

U.S. Office of Personnel Management. 1982 and prior years. Insurance Report. Washington, D.C.: Government Printing Office.

———. 2000. OPM Announces 2001 FEHB Premium Rates. Press release. September 15. www.opm.gov/pressrel/2000/fehb%20open%20season%202000.htm (accessed June 30, 2009).

———. 2008a and prior years. *Guide to Federal Benefits for Federal Retirees and Their Survivors* (formerly titled *Guide to Federal Employees Health Benefits Plans for Federal Retirees and Their Survivors*). http://www.opm.gov/insure/health/planinfo/ 2009/guides/70-09.pdf (accessed June 30, 2009).

———. 2008b and prior years. *Guide to Federal Benefits for Federal Civilian Employees* (formerly titled *Guide to Federal Employees Health Benefits Plans for Federal Civilian Employees*). http://www.opm.gov/insure/health/planinfo/2009/guides/70-01. pdf (accessed June 30, 2009).

———. 2008c and prior years. *Open Season Health Benefits Guide [for Retirees].* Office of Personnel Management mailing to all federal civilian retirees. Washington, D.C.

———. 2008d and prior years. *Guide to Federal Benefits for Federal Retirees and Their Survivors* (formerly titled *Guide to Federal Employees Health Benefits Plans for Federal Retirees and Their Survivors*). http://www.opm.gov/insure/health/planinfo/ 2009/guides/70-09.pdf (accessed June 30, 2009).

———. n.d. *Federal Employees Health Benefits Program Handbook.* http://www. opm.gov/insure/health/reference/handbook/fehb00.asp (accessed June 30, 2009).

U.S. Office of Personnel Management. Office of the Inspector General. 2007. *Semiannual Report to the Congress: April 1, 2007–September 30, 2007.* http://www. opm.gov/about_opm/reports/InspectorGeneral/pdf/SAR37.pdf (accessed June 30, 2009).

———. 2008. *Semiannual Report to the Congress: October 1, 2007–March 31, 2008.* http://www.opm.gov/about_opm/reports/InspectorGeneral/pdf/SAR38.pdf (accessed June 30, 2009).

U.S. Office of Personnel Management. Office of Workforce Information. n.d. "Federal Employment Statistics." Central Personnel Data File (CPDF). http://www.opm. gov/feddata/html/Age_Dist.asp (accessed June 30, 2009).

U.S. Senate. Committee on Finance. 1997. *Medicare Reform and the Federal Employees Health Benefits Program.* 105th Cong., sess. 1. Testimony by Robert D. Reischauer. May 21. Washington, D.C.: Government Printing Office.

———. 2000. *Medicare Reform: Leading Proposals Lay Groundwork, While Design Decisions Lie Ahead.* 106th Cong., sess. 2. Testimony by Daniel Walker before the Committee on Finance, as reported by the General Accounting Office in GAO/ T-HEHS/AIMD-00-103. February 24. http://www.gao.gov/archive/2000/ h100103t.pdf (accessed June 30, 2009).

———. 2007. *The Medicare Prescription Drug Benefit: Review and Oversight.* 110th Cong., sess. 1. Statement by Abby L. Block. May 8. http://finance.senate.gov/ hearings/testimony/2007test/050807testab.pdf (accessed June 30, 2009)

———. 2008a. *The Long-Term Budget Outlook and Options for Slowing the Growth of Health Care Costs: Hearing before the Committee on Finance.* 110th Cong., sess. 2. Testimony of Peter R. Orszag, director, Congressional Budget Office. June 17. http://www.cbo.gov/ftpdocs/93xx/doc9385/06-17-LTBO_Testimony.pdf (accessed June 30, 2009).

———. 2008b. *Private Fee-for-Service Plans in Medicare Advantage: A Closer Look: A Hearing before the Committee on Finance.* 110th Cong., sess. 2. Testimony of Mark E. Miller, executive director of the U.S. Medicare Payment Advisory Commission. January 30. http://finance.senate.gov/hearings/testimony/2008test/ 013008mmtest.pdf (accessed June 30, 2009).

———. 2009. *Financing Comprehensive Health Care Reform: Proposed Health System Savings and Revenue Options.* Description report of the Senate Finance Committee to the U.S. Congress. May 20. http://finance.senate.gov/sitepages/leg/LEG% 202009/051809%20Health%20Care%20Description%20of%20Policy%20 Options.pdf (accessed June 30, 2009).

U.S. Senate. Committee on Homeland Security and Government Affairs. Subcommittee on Government Management, the Federal Workforce, and the District of Columbia. 2007. *Up, Up, and Away! Growth Trends in Health Care Premiums for Active and Retired Federal Employees: Hearing before the Subcommittee on Oversight of Government Management, the Federal Workforce, and the District of Columbia of the Committee on Homeland Security and Government Affairs.* 110th Cong., sess. 1. Testimony of John E. Dicken. May 18. http://hsgac.senate.gov/public/_files/testimonydicken.pdf (accessed June 30, 2009).

U.S. Senate. Committee on the Judiciary. Subcommittee on Crime and Drugs. 2009. *Criminal Prosecution as a Deterrent to Health Care Fraud.* 111th Cong., sess. 1. Testimony of Malcolm K. Sparrow. May 20. http://judiciary.senate.gov/hearings/testimony.cfm?id=3860&wit_id=7953 (accessed June 30, 2009).

U.S. Senate. Joint Economic Committee. 2003. *Health Insurance Spending Growth—How Does Medicare Compare?* Description report by Michael J. O'Grady, on behalf of the Joint Economic Committee, to the U.S. Congress. June 10. Washington, D.C.: Government Printing Office.

———. 2004. *Expanding Consumer Choice and Addressing "Adverse Selection" Concerns in Health Insurance: Hearing before the Joint Economic Committee.* 108th Cong., sess. 2. Testimony of James H. Cardon. September 24. http://jec.senate.gov/archive/Documents/Hearings/cardontestimony22sep2004.pdf (accessed June 30, 2009).

U.S. Senate. Special Committee on Aging. 1987. *Prescription Drugs and the Elderly: The High Cost of Growing Old: Hearing before the Special Committee on Aging.* 100th Cong., 1st sess. July 20. Washington, D.C.: Government Printing Office.

———. 2003. *The Role of Market Competition in Strengthening Medicare.* Testimony of Joseph R. Antos. May 6. http://aging.senate.gov/events/hr99ja.pdf (accessed June 30, 2009).

Van de Ven, Wynand P. M. M., and Frederik T. Schut. 2008. Universal Mandatory Health Insurance in the Netherlands: A Model for the United States? *Health Affairs* 27 (3): 771–81. http://content.healthaffairs.org/cgi/reprint/27/3/771?maxtoshow=&HITS=10&hits=10&RESULTFORMAT=&author1=van+de+ven&andorexact fulltext=and&searchid=1&FIRSTINDEX=0&resourcetype=HWCIT (accessed June 30, 2009).

Vladeck, Bruce C. 1999. The Political Economy of Medicare. *Health Affairs* 18 (1): 22–36. http://content.healthaffairs.org/cgi/reprint/18/1/22?maxtoshow=&HITS=25&hits=25&RESULTFORMAT=&author1=vladeck&andorexact fulltext=and&searchid=1&FIRSTINDEX=0&resourcetype=HWCIT (accessed June 30, 2009).

Weems, Kerry N., and Benjamin E. Sasse. 2009. Is Government Health Insurance Cheap? The False Comparison between the Costs of Public and Private Medical Plans. *Wall Street Journal.* April 14. http://online.wsj.com/article/SB123966918025015509.html (accessed June 30, 2009).

Wennberg, John E., Elliot S. Fisher, and Jonathan S. Skinner. 2002. Geography and the Debate over Medicare Reform. *Health Affairs* Web Exclusive. February 13. http://content.healthaffairs.org/cgi/reprint/hlthaff.w2.96v1 (accessed June 30, 2009).

———, Elliot S. Fisher, Jonathan S. Skinner, and Kristen K. Bronner. 2007. Extending the P4P Agenda, Part 2: How Medicare Can Reduce Waste and Improve the

Care of the Chronically Ill. *Health Affairs* 26 (6): 1575–85.

———, Annette M. O'Connor, E. Dale Collins, and James N. Weinstein. 2007. Extending the P4P Agenda, Part 1: How Medicare Can Improve Patient Decision Making and Reduce Unnecessary Care. *Health Affairs* 26 (6): 1564–74.

White, Joseph. 2009. Dangerous Confusion on Medicare Cost Control. June 5. Health Affairs Blog Archives. http://healthaffairs.org/blog/2009/06/05/dangerous-confusion-on-medicare-cost-control/ (accessed June 30, 2009).

Wilensky, Gail R., and Joseph P. Newhouse. 1999. Medicare: What's Right? What's Wrong? What's Next? *Health Affairs* 18 (1): 92–106.

Yamamoto, Dale, Tricia Neuman, and Michelle Kitchman Strollo. 2008. *How Does the Benefit Value of Medicare Compare to the Benefit Value of Typical Large Employer Plans?* Kaiser Family Foundation. September. www.kff.org/medicare/upload/7768.pdf (accessed June 30, 2009).

Yoder, Eric. 2000. Insurance Gap. *Government Executive*. November 1. http://www.govexec.com/features/1100/1100s7.htm (accessed June 30, 2009).

Zaraboza, Carlos, and Scott Harrison. 2008. Payment Policy and the Growth of Medicare Advantage. *Health Affairs* Web Exclusive. November. http://content.healthaffairs.org/cgi/content/abstract/hlthaff.28.1.w55v1 (accessed June 30, 2009).

Zhang, Yuting, Julie M. Donohue, Judith R. Lave, Gerald O'Donnell, and Joseph P. Newhouse. 2009. The Effect of Medicare Part D on Drug and Medical Spending. *New England Journal of Medicine* 361 (1): 52–61.

Index

About the Author

Walton Francis is a self-employed policy analyst, expert in the analysis and evaluation of public programs. His education includes a BA with Honors and Highest Distinction (Indiana University), and master's degrees from Yale (MA Political Science) and Harvard (MPP Public Policy, MA Public Administration) universities.

Francis developed regulatory, budgetary, and legislative reforms for many policies and programs while working at the U.S. Office of Management and Budget and in the Office of the Assistant Secretary for Planning and Evaluation at the U.S. Department of Health and Human Services. At HHS he won awards for eliminating unnecessary burdens from regulations and for making regulation of health services more cost-effective. He has written extensively on regulatory reform and review, and prepared or directed the preparation of dozens of regulatory impact analyses comparing the costs and benefits of policy alternatives. Regulatory initiatives in which he played a major policy and analytic role include organ transplantation reform, establishment of state-run programs to reduce teenage smoking, performance standards for clinical laboratories, establishment of block grants, and banning discrimination against persons with handicaps. He has identified hundreds of unreasonably burdensome and ineffective regulatory provisions in draft HHS rules and usually (but not always) succeeded in eliminating them.

In addition, he pioneered the systematic comparison of health insurance plans from a consumer perspective. Francis has for thirty years authored the annual *CHECKBOOK's Guide to Health Plans for Federal Employees*. He has testified before Congress on reforming the Federal Employees Health Benefits Program and on reforming Medicare.

Jeremy Rabkin
Professor of Law
George Mason University
School of Law

Richard J. Zeckhauser
Frank Plumpton Ramsey Professor
of Political Economy
Kennedy School of Government
Harvard University

Research Staff

Gerard Alexander
Visiting Scholar

Ali Alfoneh
Visiting Research Fellow

Joseph Antos
Wilson H. Taylor Scholar in Health
Care and Retirement Policy

Leon Aron
Resident Scholar; Director of
Russian Studies

Michael Auslin
Resident Scholar

Claude Barfield
Resident Scholar

Michael Barone
Resident Fellow

Roger Bate
Legatum Fellow in Global Prosperity

Walter Berns
Resident Scholar

Andrew G. Biggs
Resident Scholar

Edward Blum
Visiting Fellow

Dan Blumenthal
Resident Fellow

John R. Bolton
Senior Fellow

Karlyn Bowman
Senior Fellow

Alex Brill
Research Fellow

John E. Calfee
Resident Scholar

Charles W. Calomiris
Visiting Scholar

Lynne V. Cheney
Senior Fellow

Steven J. Davis
Visiting Scholar

Mauro De Lorenzo
Resident Fellow

Christopher DeMuth
D. C. Searle Senior Fellow

Thomas Donnelly
Resident Fellow

Nicholas Eberstadt
Henry Wendt Scholar in Political
Economy

Jon Entine
Visiting Fellow

John C. Fortier
Research Fellow

David Frum
Resident Fellow

Newt Gingrich
Senior Fellow

Scott Gottlieb, M.D.
Resident Fellow

Kenneth P. Green
Resident Scholar

Michael S. Greve
John G. Searle Scholar

Kevin A. Hassett
Senior Fellow; Director,
Economic Policy Studies

Steven F. Hayward
F. K. Weyerhaeuser Fellow

Robert B. Helms
Resident Scholar

Frederick M. Hess
Resident Scholar; Director,
Education Policy Studies

Ayaan Hirsi Ali
Visiting Fellow

R. Glenn Hubbard
Visiting Scholar

Frederick W. Kagan
Resident Scholar

Leon R. Kass, M.D.
Hertog Fellow

Andrew Kelly
Research Fellow

Irving Kristol
Senior Fellow Emeritus

Desmond Lachman
Resident Fellow

Lee Lane
Resident Fellow; Codirector of the
AEI Geoengineering Project

Adam Lerrick
Visiting Scholar

Philip I. Levy
Resident Scholar

Lawrence B. Lindsey
Visiting Scholar

John H. Makin
Visiting Scholar

Aparna Mathur
Research Fellow

Lawrence M. Mead
Visiting Scholar

Allan H. Meltzer
Visiting Scholar

Thomas P. Miller
Resident Fellow

Hassan Mneimneh
Visiting Fellow

Charles Murray
W. H. Brady Scholar

Roger F. Noriega
Visiting Fellow

Michael Novak
George Frederick Jewett Scholar
in Religion, Philosophy, and
Public Policy

Norman J. Ornstein
Resident Scholar

Richard Perle
Resident Fellow

Tomas J. Philipson
Visiting Scholar

Alex J. Pollock
Resident Fellow

Vincent R. Reinhart
Resident Scholar

Michael Rubin
Resident Scholar

Sally Satel, M.D.
Resident Scholar

Gary J. Schmitt
Resident Scholar; Director of
Advanced Strategic Studies

Mark Schneider
Visiting Scholar

David Schoenbrod
Visiting Scholar

Nick Schulz
DeWitt Wallace Fellow; Editor-in-Chief,
American.com

Roger Scruton
Resident Scholar

Kent Smetters
Visiting Scholar

Christina Hoff Sommers
Resident Scholar; Director,
W. H. Brady Program

Phillip Swagel
Visiting Scholar

Samuel Thernstrom
Resident Fellow; Director, AEI Press;
Codirector of the AEI
Geoengineering Project

Bill Thomas
Visiting Fellow

Alan D. Viard
Resident Scholar

Peter J. Wallison
Arthur F. Burns Fellow in
Financial Policy Studies

David A. Weisbach
Visiting Scholar

Paul Wolfowitz
Visiting Scholar

John Yoo
Visiting Scholar